A-level Study Guide

Economics

Ian Etherington

Charles Smith

Matthew Smith

Revision Express

Acknowledgements

Crown copyright material is reproduced with the permission of the Controller of HMSO and the Queen's Printer for Scotland.

Series Consultants: Geoff Black and Stuart Wall

Pearson Education Limited

Edinburgh Gate, Harlow

Essex, CM20 2JE, England

and Associated Companies throughout the world

www.pearsoned.co.uk

© Pearson Education Limited 2006

The rights of Ian Etherington, Charles Smith and Matthew Smith to be identified as authors of this work have been asserted by them in accordance with the Copyright, Designs and Patents Act 1988.

British Library Cataloguing-in-Publication Data

A catalogue record for this book is available from the British Library

ISBN-13: 978-1-4058-0745-6

ISBN-10: 1-4058-0745-8

10 9 8 7 6 5 4 3 2 1

10 09 08 07 06

Set by 35 in Univers, Cheltenham

Printed by Ashford Colour Press, Gosport, Hants

Market theory and applications

People often say that economists can never agree. This is not true. For example, around the world there is a high level of agreement among economists on how markets work and on what markets can and cannot achieve. As we note throughout this chapter, **prices** act as signals in a market to both producers and consumers, helping to guide their decision-making. Sometimes these price signals will help to bring about an **equilibrium**, or balance, between production and consumption. At other times they may fail in this role, leaving a disequilibrium, or imbalance, between production and consumption.

Exam themes

→ Scarcity, choice, opportunity cost

→ Demand, supply, market price

→ Elasticity

→ Price controls

→ Labour markets, minimum wage

Topic checklist

AS ○ A2 ●	Edexcel	AQA	OCR	WJEC	CCEA
Production possibilities (1)	○●	○●	○●	○●	○
Production possibilities (2)	○●	○●	○●	○●	○
Demand and supply	○	○●	○●	○	○
How prices change	○	○●	○	○	○
Price elasticity of demand (1)	○	○	○	○	○
Price elasticity of demand (2)	○	○●	○	○	○
Other elasticities	○	○	○●	○	○
Minimum price controls	○	○●	○●	○	○
Maximum price controls	○	○	○	○	○
Parallel markets		○			
Labour markets	●	●	●	○	○
The minimum wage	○●	○●	○●	○●	○

Production possibilities (1)

The production possibility frontier (PPF), also known as the production possibility curve (PPC), is useful for illustrating ideas that are central to the basic economic problem.

The basic problems of production

Every society has to make basic choices:

→ What to produce: the problem of product mix.
→ How to produce it: the problem of factor combination.
→ For whom to produce: the problem of income distribution.

The production possibility frontier

Different types of PPF diagram can be used to tell us some important things about economic principles, such as choices, opportunity costs, efficiency and equity.

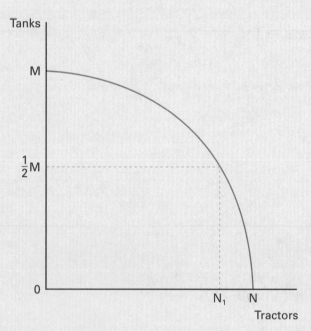

Production possibility curve

Choices

Suppose a country is making a very stark choice: war or peace. It can use its factors of production to produce either tanks (for warlike purposes) or tractors (for peaceful purposes). The diagram above shows how different resources, or inputs, can be used to produce an output. If all resources are devoted to tractors, then the distance ON along the horizontal axis measures the maximum output of tractors. At the other extreme, the country could produce no tractors and devote itself entirely to producing OM units of tanks, measured along the vertical axis.

Diminishing returns

If we join points M and N, we have a line that shows the different combinations of tanks and tractors that are possible if the country is maximising its output. Note the shape of this line: it is convex to the origin (viewed from the origin, it bends away). This shape gives us the following pattern. If we start at any point on the curve, with a given number of tanks and tractors and then, say, halve the number of tanks, we can produce more tractors, but less than twice as many. Similarly, if we reduce the number of tanks by a factor of three, we increase the output of tractors, but by less than three times as much. Or to look at this another way, as we reduce the number of tanks, we get fewer and fewer extra tractors. This is known as **diminishing returns** and it happens because the resources that can be used to make tanks are not instantly 'switchable': in order to make a different product, machines need to be adapted, people need to be retrained, and computers need to be reprogrammed. In the language of economics, we say that factors of production are not perfectly mobile.

Link

See the **law of diminishing returns**, page 34.

Check the net

For more on the basic economic problem, visit www.tt100.biz.

Exam question (20 minutes)   answer: page 28

Five people on a reality TV show are stranded in a part of the jungle where there are only two natural sources of food: coconuts and fish. With the equipment they are given, they find that each person can collect four coconuts or catch two fish in an hour. They decide that they will all work for three hours a day.

(a) Draw the daily production possibility curve for this economy.

(b) Explain the shape of this PPC.

(c) At the end of the first working day, the group has collected 30 coconuts and 10 fish. Is the group working efficiently?

(d) Suppose three of the group decide that they are too afraid of heights to be able to climb coconut trees, while the other two are afraid of water and therefore unable to go fishing. What would the PPC look like in this case, and what are the implications?

Production possibilities (2)

Choices are necessary because of 'scarcity'. The fact that resources are finite, or limited, creates an **opportunity cost**. As economists, we are very interested in ways of maximising choices and minimising costs. The idea of 'efficiency' is crucial to this maximising and minimising behaviour.

Checkpoint 1

Explain the difference between scarcity in an everyday sense and scarcity in an economic sense.

Opportunity cost

If we produce extra tanks, then we have to sacrifice tractors. This is because of limited resources and is known as 'opportunity cost'.

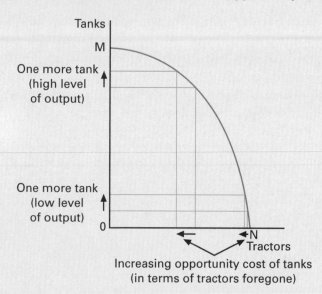

Opportunity costs on the production possibility frontier

The convex shape of the PPF shows us that opportunity cost increases as output increases. For example, as we produce more tanks, each extra tank produced means more tractors sacrificed (foregone), since the resources switched are progressively less suited to producing tanks and more suited to producing tractors.

Since economics is about making the best use of resources, it is important that inputs are used as effectively as possible in order to create output. As economists, we use two main measures of efficiency.

The jargon

Opportunity cost. A measure of the cost of using scarce resources to produce one particular good or service in terms of the alternatives foregone. For example, if more resources are used to produce apples, then fewer resources are available to produce oranges.

Checkpoint 2

Explain how a consumer, as opposed to a producer, can face an opportunity cost.

Economic efficiency

→ **Productive efficiency**, also known as **technical efficiency**, is the maximising of the output of goods and services demanded by consumers at minimum resource cost.

→ **Allocative efficiency**, also known as **Pareto efficiency**, occurs when it is not possible to produce more of one good without producing less of another, or, to put it another way, when it is impossible to make one group of producers or consumers better off without making another group worse off.

In the diagram below, point A is productively inefficient because it is within the PPF, and the economy is capable of using its resources to produce higher levels of output. Point A is also allocatively inefficient because it is possible to produce more tractors without sacrificing tanks.

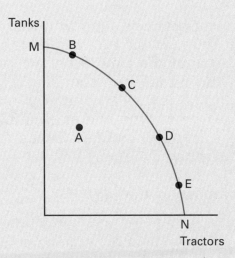

Efficiency and equity

Point B is productively efficient; it is also allocatively efficient. Productive and allocative efficiency therefore occur together along the PPF.

However, points C, D and E are equally efficient to point B (there is an infinite number of equally efficient points along the PPF). Which point should a country choose? This will depend on people's ideas of **equity** rather than efficiency, and this is not a purely economic problem. It depends on the type of society in which people live: Do they wish to leave all decisions to market forces or to politicians? Do they want rich people to have more power than poor people over economic choices? In the case of tanks versus tractors, do they want to devote resources to warlike uses or peaceful uses?

Value judgements, positive and normative questions ●●●

The ultimate choice between tanks and tractors is made partly on the basis of economics but also on the basis of political decisions and people's concepts of justice, fairness and society in the broadest sense. Many economists believe that they should try to restrict their studies to objective reality and that they should attempt to answer only positive questions (these are questions about objective reality). However, it is inevitable that value judgements (people's views of what ought to be) will affect economic decision-making and policy.

Check the net

www.tt100.biz.

Exam questions (10 minutes)   answers: page 28

Choose the best answer in each case. Then explain why you chose this answer and why you rejected each of the others.

1. Which one of the following is a normative statement?
    (a) Economic resources are classified as land, labour, capital and enterprise.
    (b) Oil is a scarce resource.
    (c) Resources are distributed unfairly.
    (d) Gold is distributed unequally.

2. An economy is productively efficient if it maximises:
    (a) Average living standards.   (c) Investment.
    (b) Output per unit of input.   (d) Employment.

Demand and supply

You need a ball-point pen. You find that in your local newsagent's shop, pens are available at 37 pence each. How is it that the raw materials to make these pens were brought together from all over the world to produce a pen that is available to you in a convenient place at a convenient time and at an affordable price? The answer is through **market forces**, the magic of demand and supply.

The determinants of demand

Price

Demand is affected by price. According to the law of demand, the higher the price, the lower the quantity demanded. This law operates because consumers wish to obtain maximum benefit from their hard-earned income. Lower prices mean that their budget goes further and, therefore, gives them more benefit. So consumers generally prefer lower prices to higher prices. This can be illustrated using a demand curve.

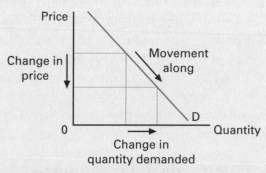

The law of demand

A change in price will cause a **movement along** the demand curve.

The conditions of demand

Anything other than price that affects demand is known as a **condition of demand**. These conditions are:

→ Incomes.
→ The price of related goods (substitutes and complements).
→ Tastes (including influences such as advertising, fashions and trends).
→ Other factors, such as population changes and changes in the weather.

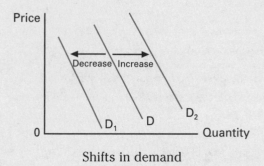

Shifts in demand

When one of these underlying conditions changes, we **shift** the demand curve: to the right for a general increase in demand or to the left for a general decrease in demand.

The jargon

Market. A network bringing together consumers and producers, enabling them to make deals about the prices of goods and services and the quantities bought and sold.

The jargon

Substitutes are products bought in place of each other, e.g. tea and coffee. **Complements** are products bought with each other, e.g. cups and saucers. **Derived demand** is a special case of complementary demand and occurs when the demand for one product follows automatically from the demand for another, e.g. the demand for petrol is derived from the demand for car travel.

Checkpoint 1

Explain how an increase in people's incomes can be expected to shift the demand curve for new cars.

The determinants of supply

Price

Like demand, supply is affected by price. According to the law of supply, the higher the price, the greater the quantity supplied. This law operates because producers wish to obtain maximum profit from business activities. Higher prices make it easier to cover costs and make profits. So producers generally prefer higher prices to lower prices. This can be illustrated using a supply curve.

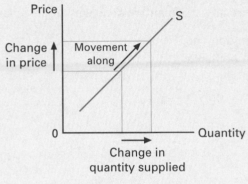

The law of supply

A change in price will cause a **movement along** the supply curve.

The conditions of supply

Anything other than price that affects demand is known as a **condition of supply**. These conditions are:

→ Costs of production.
→ The output of related goods (joint supply, by-products, competitive supply).
→ Events beyond human control, such as climatic conditions creating unpredictably good or bad harvests for agricultural products.
→ Other factors, such as taxes or subsidies.

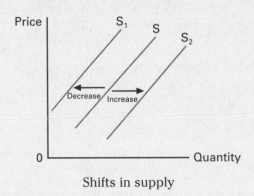

Shifts in supply

When one of these underlying conditions of supply changes, we **shift** the supply curve: to the right for a general increase in supply or to the left for a general decrease in supply.

Exam question (15 minutes)   answer: page 28

Using the concept of derived demand, explain why oil is important not only for the transport industry but also for the economy as a whole.

The jargon

Joint supply is when the supply of one product increases the supply of another, e.g. petrol and petroleum by-products, beef and leather. **Competitive supply** is when the supply of one product reduces the supply of another, e.g. if sheep are kept alive for their wool, then the supply of lamb meat is reduced, at least in the short run.

Checkpoint 2

Explain how an increase in transport costs can be expected to shift the supply curve for bananas.

Watch out!

Be careful to distinguish between a shift of a demand or supply curve (caused by a change in one of the underlying conditions) and a movement along a curve (caused by a change in price). A shift of demand or supply will happen first; it will then be followed by a movement along the curve which has not shifted.

Check the net

For interactive demand and supply curves, check www.bized.ac.uk.

How prices change

Why do house prices often rise quickly? Why have the prices of computers and mobile phones fallen over the years? We use supply and demand analysis to help answer such questions.

Changes in demand and supply conditions

As economists, we explain price changes by considering market equilibrium and by analysing what happens when markets move from one equilibrium point to another.

Basically, there are four main reasons why prices change.

1   An increase in demand.
2   A decrease in demand.
3   An increase in supply.
4   A decrease in supply.

These four cases are shown in the diagrams below.

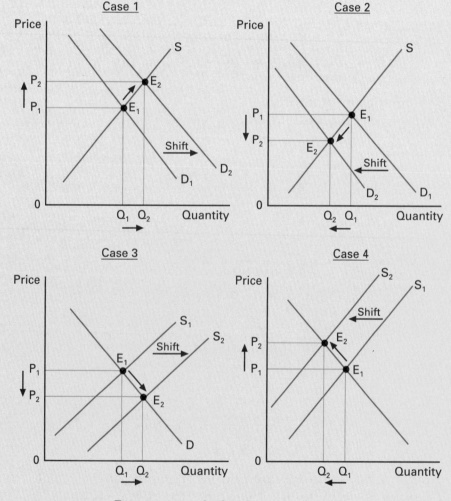

Four ways in which prices can change

10

In each of these diagrams, there is a sequence of events.

1 Something happens to create a **disturbance of market equilibrium**: there is change in either one of the underlying conditions of demand or the underlying conditions of supply. This leads to . . .
2 A **shift**, either in the demand curve or in the supply curve. This leads to . . .
3 Either a **surplus** if the current market price is held (which tends to reduce price), or a **shortage** (which tends to increase price). This leads to . . .
4 A **price change**. This leads to . . .
5 A **movement along**. (If demand shifted at stage 2, then there is a movement along the supply curve; if it was demand that shifted, then there is a movement along the supply curve.) This leads to . . .
6 A change in the **size of the market**, measured along the quantity axis in the graph. The market either expands, with a greater quantity being bought and sold than before, or shrinks, with a smaller quantity being bought and sold.

Checkpoint 1

Explain why a surplus tends to reduce price, while a shortage tends to increase price.

Example ●●●

Consider the case of the housing market in the UK. In recent decades, prices have risen continuously. Why is this? Basically, it is because of higher incomes and higher demand. We live in a country with a housebuying culture – just look at all the TV programmes about trading in property. Successive governments have encouraged British citizens to buy rather than rent. The result is that as our incomes rise, we tend to put a large proportion of income into housing (housing has a high income elasticity of demand – see page 16). The diagram for Case 1 illustrates what has happened; the sequence of events can be described as follows:

1 Higher incomes, together with surrounding cultural factors led to . . .
2 A shift in demand to the right. This led to . . .
3 A shortage at current prices. This led to . . .
4 Higher prices (an increase from P_1 to P_2). This led to . . .
5 A movement along the supply curve (housebuilding became a more profitable activity). This led to . . .
6 An expansion of the market, with a greater quantity of houses being bought and sold at the higher prices.

Checkpoint 2

Which of the four cases would describe the effects on the market for milk of a disease that kills dairy cows? Describe the sequence of events.

Exam question (20 minutes)   answer: page 29

> Next month (January) a budget hotel chain, is offering 'on-line' rooms for certain Friday and Saturday dates along parts of the M4 and some other locations for as little as £5 per night. This is cheaper even than the youth hostel.
>
> Source: A national newspaper, travel section.

With the help of a supply and demand diagram, explain why this hotel chain reduces its prices at some locations on certain days of the week or times of the year.

Price elasticity of demand (1)

Price elasticity of demand (PED) attempts to measure how consumers react to a change in price. Knowledge of consumer responsiveness to price (and other determinants of demand) is important intelligence for producers, sellers and government planners.

Definition and measurement of price elasticity of demand

In general terms, PED refers to the degree of responsiveness of consumers to a change in price. In order to measure PED, we usually use the formula

$$PED = \frac{\text{percentage change in quantity demanded}}{\text{percentage change in price}}$$

For example, if price changes by 10% and quantity demanded changes by 5%, then PED is 5/10 = 0.5. This shows that consumers are relatively unresponsive to price (demand is price-inelastic). An elasticity coefficient greater than 1 indicates that demand is price-elastic – consumers are responsive to price changes (quantity demanded changes by a greater percentage than price). If price changes by 10% and consumers react with a 10% change in quantity demanded, then the elasticity formula gives a coefficient of 10/10 = 1 (we refer to this as unit elasticity) and demand is neither price-elastic nor price-inelastic but is on the border between the two.

Price elasticities along a straight-line demand curve

The elasticity formula that we usually use depends on percentage changes. Because percentage changes depend on a starting point (10% of £2 is different from 10% of £200), elasticity has a different value at every point on a straight-line demand curve.

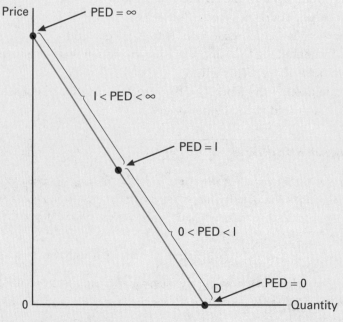

Price elasticity of demand (PED) along a straight-line demand curve

The main things to remember are:

→ At the top of the demand curve, PED = infinity.
→ Halfway down the demand curve, PED = 1.
→ At the bottom of the demand curve, PED = 0.
→ PED falls as we move down the demand curve.
→ Demand is price-elastic in the top half and price-inelastic in the bottom half of the demand curve.

Factors affecting the size of price elasticity of demand

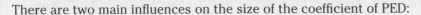

There are two main influences on the size of the coefficient of PED:

→ **The substitution effect:** products without many substitutes are likely to have lower PED than those with many substitutes or with closer substitutes. Oil and petrol tend to have low PED, because we have yet to properly develop alternatives to fuel our transport needs or for use as raw materials for industry.
→ **The income effect:** a family holiday takes up a larger fraction of family income than, say, a daily newspaper. If the price of a £3000 holiday changes by 10%, then there is likely to be a greater response by consumers than when the price of a 50p newspaper changes by the same percentage.

Other possible influences include:

→ **The durability of a good:** a car wears out gradually; thus, the owner usually has some time in which to consider replacing it and so can react to higher prices by postponing replacement or to any special offers by bringing replacement forward. If, say, a lightbulb suddenly pops, then a replacement needs to be bought immediately, without much reference to how prices have changed. So, the greater the possibility of postponement, the larger the PED.
→ **Addictiveness:** this is a special case of the substitution effect, because people who are addicted to, say, cigarettes believe that they cannot manage without them; in other words, there is no substitute, which lowers their PED.

The jargon

When PED = 1, we often refer to this as 'unit elasticity'.

Examiner's secrets

Candidates often talk about goods being 'luxuries' or 'necessities' and claim that luxuries have high PED while necessities have low PED. This causes all sorts of problems, because it can lead to the conclusion, for example, that cigarettes are a necessity. It is far better to talk about products that, in the opinion of consumers, have many substitutes, and those that do not have substitutes. When you think about it, this is what we really mean when we talk about 'luxuries' and 'necessities'.

Checkpoint 2

Which of these items would you expect to be price-elastic and which price-inelastic? Justify your answer. Foreign holidays, new cars, houses, bread.

Examiner's secrets

In examinations, candidates nearly always highlight 'addictive goods' when discussing factors influencing PED. It is far better to discuss the substitution effects and income effects of a price change before considering any other possible factors influencing PED.

Check the net

For an interactive look at PED, check out the interactive demand and supply curves on www.bized.ac.uk.

Exam question (30 minutes)   answer: page 29

Explain the importance of PED to each of the following government policies:

(a) Discouraging the use of cars through fuel taxes.

(b) Free or subsidised eye tests and dental checks.

(c) Tuition fees in higher education.

Price elasticity of demand (2)

Why is PED important? To answer this question, we need to examine how changes in price affect total revenue (TR). A knowledge of PED enables us to do this.

Total revenue and price elasticity of demand ●●●

Many firms pay a great deal of attention to something called **yield management**. This activity attempts to maximise total revenue. A budget airline, for example, makes a profit by reducing its costs to the lowest possible level. It does this by cutting out frills such as in-flight meals. It then tries to ensure that each airline seat is sold at a price that brings in the largest possible amount of revenue. It relies on a knowledge of PED to do this. Generally speaking, as the date and time of an airline flight get closer, so the PED falls. This means that you can usually buy a cheaper ticket by booking well in advance.

The relationship between PED and TR is as follows:

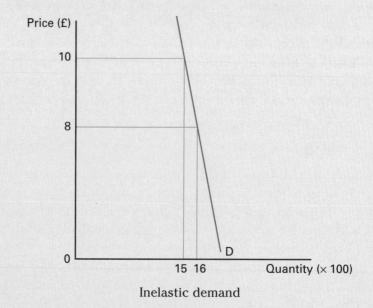

Inelastic demand

➡ PED < 1: if price rises, TR rises; if price falls, TR falls.

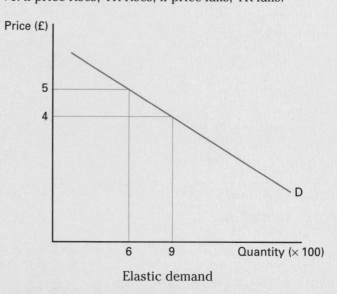

Elastic demand

➡ PED > 1: if price rises, TR falls; if price falls, TR rises.

The jargon

Total revenue = price × quantity sold.

Checkpoint 1

Why is it that the PED for an airline ticket generally gets lower as we approach the date and time of travel?

Checkpoint 2

The train fare from Fulchester to London is £120 before 9 a.m., but then it falls to £35. Use PED to explain why this is so.

Take note

For a price increase, TR increases from £12,800 to £15,000 in the first diagram, falls from £3,600 to £3,000 in the second, and stays at £2,000 in the third (see opposite).

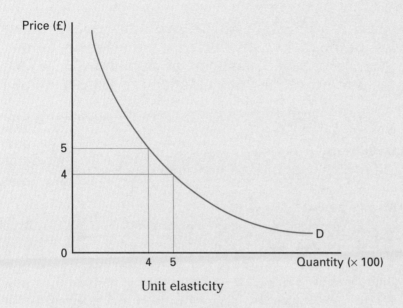

Price (£)

Unit elasticity

Quantity (× 100)

→ PED = 1; if price rises or falls, TR remains constant.

Check the net

For a quiz on elasticity, visit www.tutor2u.com.

Exam question (30 minutes)   answer: page 29

The figures below show the price of a single fare from South Midlands Airport to Barcelona if booked by Internet on the Quick-Jet website on Monday 5 January (all dates in January, tax not included).

Date of travel	Price (£)	Date of travel	Price (£)
Tues 6	71.49	Tues 13	16.49
Wed 7	51.49	Wed 14	21.49
Thur 8	41.49	Thur 15	26.49
Fri 9	41.49	Fri 16	41.49
Sat 10	31.49	Sat 17	26.49
Sun 11	31.49	Sun 18	26.49
Mon 12	26.49	Mon 19	16.49
		Mon 26	11.49

Explain possible ways in which price elasticity of demand can help to account for patterns in the prices quoted.

Other elasticities

Apart from PED, there are two other demand elasticities we need to consider: income elasticity of demand (YED) and cross-elasticity of demand (CED). We also need to consider price elasticity of supply (PES).

Income elasticity of demand

Definition
The responsiveness of consumers to changes in income.

Measurement

$$\frac{\text{Percentage change in quantity demanded}}{\text{percentage change in income}}$$

Significance
YED helps to explain several important economic phenomena. For example, it is known that as a country's living standards rise and incomes increase, so the percentage of the population employed in agriculture falls and the percentage employed in manufacturing increases. This is because food has a relatively low YED compared with manufactured products. Then, as incomes rise still further, the demand for services rises very quickly (services such as transport, health, education, leisure and tourism have high income elasticities) and the majority of the working population is employed in the service sector.

Cross-elasticity of demand

Definition
The responsiveness of consumers of one product to changes in the price of another product.

Measurement

$$\frac{\text{Percentage change in quantity demanded of product } x}{\text{percentage change in price of product } y}$$
$$= \text{CED of } x \text{ with respect to } y$$

Significance
If the CED between two goods is zero, then the products are bought independently of each other. If the CED is positive, then they are bought as substitutes; the greater the coefficient, the closer the substitutes. If the CED is negative, then the products are bought as complements; the greater the coefficient, the closer are the complements.

Price elasticity of supply

Definition
The responsiveness of producers to changes in the price of their product.

Measurement

$$\frac{\text{Percentage change in quantity supplied}}{\text{percentage change in price}}$$

Significance

Supply elasticity depends on the ability of producers to mobilise the factors of production. The longer the time period, the greater the ability to put together factors of production. For example, the supply of houses is very inelastic in the short run but more elastic in the long run. In the very long run, supply curves can actually slope downwards, so that a greater quantity is supplied as prices fall (this has happened with, for example, personal computers, satellite dishes, digital radios and mobile phones).

Link

See **mobility** of factors, page 5.

Link

See **economies of scale**, page 36.

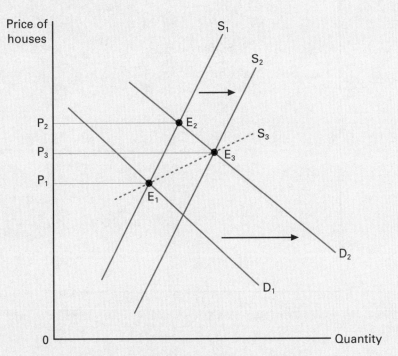

Price elasticity of supply (PES) in the short and long run

→ The demand for houses increases from D_1 to D_2.
→ In the short run, supply is inelastic and price rises from P_1 to P_2.
→ In the long run, housebuilders can shift supply from S_1 to S_2, and price falls to P_3.
→ The long-run supply curve, S_3, is more elastic than the two short-run curves, S_1 and S_2.

Exam question (20 minutes)   answer: page 30

Product *z* has a high income elasticity of demand and a high cross-elasticity of demand with its closest substitute. Is it likely to have a low or high coefficient of price elasticity of demand? Explain your answer.

Minimum price controls

What is likely to happen when prices are set at a level that is not the free market equilibrium price? Sometimes, a decision to prevent equilibrium price can be made by some sort of pricing authority; that is, a body that is in a position to influence price. Examples could include a government department or agency, an international body such as the European Commission, or a company willing to sell at less than maximum profit

The jargon

P_{min} = minimum price level; this is often known as a **floor price**.

Equilibrium prevented: 'price too low'

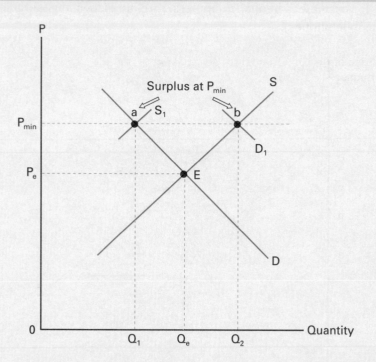

Examiner's secrets

In examinations, a surplus, as in this diagram (or a shortage, as in the diagram on page 20) should always be associated with a price. It is wrong to refer in an exam answer to *the* surplus, as if there were only one, because if you inspect the diagram carefully you will realise that there is a different surplus (or shortage) at each and every price – and no surplus or shortage at all at the equilibrium price.

Floor prices

A minimum price such as P_{min} in the diagram sets a **floor price** below which prices are not allowed to fall. It is higher than equilibrium and it encourages producers to produce. It also discourages consumers from consuming. It therefore creates a **surplus** at that price, as shown in the diagram. This surplus needs to be managed by either reducing supply or increasing demand.

Demerit goods

Point a in the diagram can be applied to the case of cigarettes. They are taxed because they are bad for you. They are also bad for the non-smoker, and economists regard them as **demerit goods**.

Checkpoint 1

Whatever form the pricing authority takes, there is one crucial point to be made: unless the authority can control either supply or demand, then it cannot control prices. Explain carefully why this is so.

The tax, in effect, increases production costs and shifts the supply curve for cigarettes to the left (to S_1) and achieves a new equilibrium point, a. The higher price discourages consumption and production.

Agricultural support policies

One way of protecting farmers from unpredictable prices, and so keeping them in business and safeguarding our food supplies, is to offer them a minimum guaranteed price. What happens under an intervention buying scheme, such as the Common Agricultural Policy (CAP) of the European Union?

→ The surplus created by the floor price is bought up by the EU's authorities and put into storage.
→ Intervention buying in effect shifts the demand curve rightwards to D_1, and aims at equilibrium point b. The idea is that in a following year, when there is a bad harvest and prices are soaring, these stocks can be released in order to maintain supplies and stabilise prices downwards.
→ However, in practice, the CAP has encouraged overproduction year after year, so that butter mountains, grain mountains and wine lakes build up, with the result that as well as paying high prices, consumers as taxpayers are covering the cost of maintaining these stocks.
→ In recent years, therefore, the CAP has moved away from intervention buying in favour of reducing supply.

The jargon

Demerit good. A good whose costs are felt not only by the prime user (see page 58).

Link

Elasticity of demand: see page 12.

Take note

Unpredictable prices. Because of their low price elasticity of demand and unstable supply curves (see pages 12 and 10), prices of agricultural products can vary greatly from year to year. Unpredictable farm prices lead to unpredictable incomes for farmers.

Check the net

To check on the latest issues relating to CAP, and the EU in general, visit the EU website: http://europa.eu.int/.

Link

Overview of EU issues: see page 114.

Checkpoint 2

Suppose market price settles at a level above P_{min} in the diagram. What will the pricing authority do then?

Link

Cartels: see page 51.

Exam question (20 minutes)   answer: page 30

Aluminium is used in a wide range of products in the modern world. Suppose that a cartel of the major aluminium-producing countries decides that none of them will charge less than an agreed price for this commodity, which is well above the current free-market equilibrium price. With the help of a supply and demand diagram, discuss the economic consequences of this policy.

Maximum price controls

Link

For further explanation of the idea of price-fixing authority, see page 18.

The jargon

P_{max} = maximum price, also known as a ceiling price.

Checkpoint 1

Quantity Q_1 represents the capacity of a stadium. Explain why the supply curve could be regarded as being vertical through points Q_1 and a.

Link

If the supply curve for seats at a stadium is vertical, then this means that the seats have **zero elasticity of supply** – see page 16.

The previous topic dealt with minimum price controls. Now we use the same method of analysis to investigate some cases where a price-fixing authority decides to set a maximum price. Why are prices sometimes set deliberately below equilibrium, and what are the consequences of this?

Equilibrium prevented: price too high

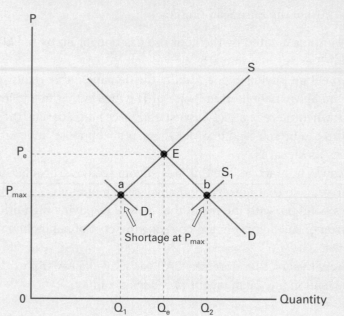

Ceiling prices

To make a ceiling price work, it is necessary either to reduce demand or to increase supply.

Tickets for a big event

The sport of football depends on stalwart fans being willing to turn out to watch lower-division teams on a wet Saturday in November. It would be very unfair if the ordinary fan had no chance of attending glamorous matches such as the FA Cup Final in an attractive location such as Cardiff or London on a sunny day in May.

The Football Association (FA) knows that it could charge very high prices indeed and still fill the Millennium Stadium or the new Wembley, but a decision is made to keep prices affordable. The problems are that:

→ An affordable price (P_{max} in the diagram) creates a shortage of tickets at that price.
→ A shortage tends to pull up prices.

So, tickets have to be rationed by some mechanism other than price, for example:

→ Selling tickets on a first-come-first-served basis to people who queue. This happens at Wimbledon: every July, you will see newspaper reports of queues winding their way around south London, full of people hoping to watch some tennis.
→ Circulating tickets to members of recognised football clubs, or, in the case of a rock concert, through fan clubs.

Such rationing has the effect of shifting the demand curve to the left, to D_1, and aims at equilibrium point a.

Merit goods

Here, the pricing authority wants a low price. But unlike point a, where supply was restricted, in this case production is positively encouraged: the supply curve is shifted to the right to S_1 by a **subsidy** and equilibrium moves to point b. Examples include dental treatment on the National Health Service (NHS) and free state education.

In both of these cases, the government ensures (or should ensure) that there are sufficient places in order to avoid shortages. In the case of university education, where places are limited, an additional rationing mechanism, such as the requirement to achieve certain A-level grades, is needed.

The jargon

Merit good. A good whose benefits are not confined to the prime user (see page 58).

Checkpoint 2

Sometimes, merit goods are supplied at zero price. In Britain, state education is provided free of charge at primary and secondary level. Why is this, and what would you predict to be the effects of charging tuition fees for higher education? Use a supply and demand diagram to help you answer.

Take note

Rationing: prices can perform a rationing function (they help to share out scarce resources). If prices are not used for this purpose, then some other method of rationing is needed. In Britain in wartime between 1939 and 1945, people were given coupons without which they could not buy basic items such as food or petrol.

The queue can be used as another method of rationing. We have seen petrol queues in the recent past: will we all be issued with petrol rationing coupons at some time in the future?

Exam question (30 minutes)   answer: page 30

Suppose a war in a major oil-producing region were to disrupt world oil supplies at a time in the near future when world oil reserves were already being used up quickly, with demand greater than supply.

(a) Explain the effects that this could have on inflation and employment in the oil-consuming countries.

(b) During the Second World War, a government rationing scheme kept down the prices of essential items and helped prevent inflation. Discuss whether a petrol-rationing scheme would be likely to be as effective today.

Parallel markets

A maximum price can be imposed only if a pricing authority has control over supply or demand or both. Where this is not the case, then a parallel market might be created.

Conditions for a parallel market

A parallel market can arise when:

→ Prices are set below market equilibrium.
→ The pricing authority cannot completely control either demand or supply.
→ People are willing to run the risks of trading unofficially (possibly illegally) in the product whose price is controlled.

Suppose the organisers of a football cup final wish to set a maximum price for tickets. They might do this to reward true fans with an affordable price; or they might be thinking of their wider TV audience, which will expect to see a full stadium as a backdrop to the televised match. The market situation is described in the diagram below.

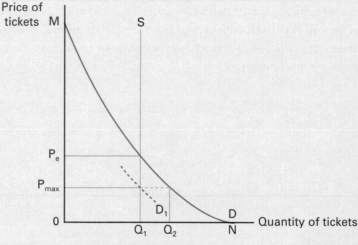

Creation of a parallel market

Let us consider the demand curve. It starts at point M, which is a price so high that nobody would come to see the match, and it descends to point N, which shows how many people would turn up if tickets were free. Between these two extreme points, the quantity demanded increases as price falls. The supply curve is vertical ($P_eS = 0$), to signify fixed capacity. If the authorities charged the equilibrium price, then tickets would cost P_e, but for reasons described above they have decided to charge P_{max}. You will see that the maximum price has created a shortage of Q_1 to Q_2. The problem becomes one of managing this shortage. Supply cannot be increased in the short run because the stadium has a fixed capacity, and so demand has to be reduced (shifted left to D_1). In other words, an extra rationing method other than price has to be employed. These rationing methods could include:

→ First come first served, for people who:
  → turn up in person and form a queue;
  → apply by post;

- → phone in;
- → buy online.
→ A ballot, or random selection, e.g. by names out of a hat.
→ Distribution through recognised sports clubs and organisations, which then decide on their own method of allocation. This could be coupled with a rota, with different clubs having tickets each year.
→ A quota – each applicant is allowed a certain number of tickets.
→ A waiting list – disappointed applicants could be given priority next time.

If the methods are not fully effective, then some tickets will end up in the hands of people who do not really want them. Meanwhile, some potential customers who were willing to pay a very high price (occupying a place on the demand curve near to M) will be without tickets. If potential buyers and sellers are willing to bend the rules or perhaps break the law, then the conditions are set for a parallel market, with its own supply and demand curves. Some tickets will end up in the hands of spivs or ticket touts.

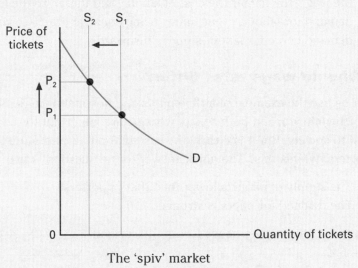

The 'spiv' market

Note the following points:

→ A vertical supply curve (only a certain number of tickets will be available through touts).
→ On the morning of the cup final, demand will be high, as ticketless fans who have travelled to the venue are desperate for tickets. If demand shifts to the right, then the fact that the supply curve is vertical means that prices can rise to very high levels. These high prices also reflect risks, as ticket touting is in a grey area of the law.
→ As the touts sell their tickets, the supply curve gradually shifts to the left, tending to increase the price of spiv tickets still further.
→ However, the touts are selling a very perishable commodity: when the event has started, demand will collapse, and so prices might fall dramatically as the kick-off time approaches, and tickets become worthless on the referee's opening whistle.

Exam question (30 minutes)   answer: page 30

Is a parallel market necessarily a bad thing? Consider both sides of the argument.

Checkpoint 1

Assess the rationing methods mentioned here. Which ones are most likely and least likely to be effective?

Checkpoint 2

A municipal car park is in demand from local residents, shoppers, commuters and tourists. Make a list of as many methods as you can think of for allocating spaces in the car park. Evaluate each method from an economic point of view.

Labour markets

Why do airline pilots earn more than hospital porters? Why do doctors earn more than nurses? Why do top sports personalities earn more than bus drivers? Market analysis can be used as a starting point in answering such questions.

What is a labour market?

A **product market** allows deals to be made that decide on prices that reflect the supply of and demand for goods and services. Similarly, a **labour market** contains prices, supply and demand.

→ **Price:** we can think of a wage as being a kind of price. It is the price of labour.
→ **Supply:** employees offer their services to employers. The higher the wage, the more willing are workers to work, and so the supply curve of labour slopes upwards.
→ **Demand:** the demand for labour comes from employers: the higher the wage, the higher the cost of labour, and therefore the lower the demand for labour, other things being equal. In other words, the demand curve for labour slopes downwards.

Why do wage rates differ?

Let us use the example of airline pilots and hospital porters. Both do a worthwhile job, and both sets of workers are important to the economy and to society. But it is clearly the case that pilots earn more than porters. Why is this? The quick answer to the question is that:

→ The supply of pilots is lower than that of porters.
→ The demand for pilots is stronger.

However, this answer needs further discussion.

The supply of pilots and porters

→ It takes many years to train a pilot. Porters can be trained far more quickly.
→ Before even applying to become a pilot, a candidate will need to attain very high levels of physical fitness and academic achievement.
→ Pilots are in a highly responsible position: one error can cost hundreds or even thousands of lives. Part of the pilot's wage can be thought of as being an extra payment for responsibility. Although modern aircraft are very safe, another part of the pilot's wage can be thought of as 'danger money'. Hospital porters cannot realistically claim these premium rates.
→ All the above mean that both the potential and actual pool of pilots is much smaller than that of porters. Not only is the supply of pilots lower, but also the supply curve is less price-elastic.

The demand for pilots and porters

→ An important point is that the demand for labour is a **derived demand**. The demand for pilots is derived from the demand for air

The jargon

Labour market. A network allowing deals on the price of labour and quantity to be made between suppliers of labour (employees) and those who have a demand for labour (employers).

Watch out!

At very high wage levels, there is the possibility of a backward-sloping supply curve for labour. This might occur if people believe that having earned enough to live on, they value their leisure time more than potential earnings from additional working hours.

The jargon

Marginal revenue product. The amount added to a firm's revenue by employing one more worker. MRP theory tells us that in a perfect labour market, an individual firm will employ workers as long as their MRP is above or equal to the wage rate. For example, if the wage rate of shop assistants is £5 per hour, and employing an extra assistant brings in £6 per hour in extra revenue, then it is worth employing another assistant.

Link

See **perfect markets** on page 42.

Checkpoint 1

To what extent can a wage rate be regarded as an **incentive** to train for a particular job? If pilots were paid the same as porters, would there be an incentive to train for six or seven years?

Link

See **derived demand** on page 8.

travel: pilots are demanded not for their own sake but because of the service they provide in helping airlines to meet the demand for air travel. Similarly, hospital porters are demanded for their role in meeting the demand for health services.

→ Airline tickets are often bought by companies rather than individuals. Firms wishing to send their executives to important meetings by business-class travel are willing to pay the price that is necessary. Hospitals, on the other hand, are usually funded by the taxpayer, and the spending power that supports higher wages is not as strong.

→ Pilots are in a more powerful position within their organisation than porters are within theirs. This is because:

→ Airlines have massive fixed costs, and the wage of a pilot, although high, is relatively small in comparison with these costs. If pilots refuse to work, then the airline is soon in trouble because it earns no revenue to cover its costs.

→ Hospitals, on the other hand, are very labour-intensive, and the wages of porters and other manual workers are a substantial fraction of total costs. If porters refuse to work, this can cause massive inconvenience, but the hospital can still function, at least for a while. It will almost certainly not go bankrupt during a porters' strike, in the same way as an airline easily could with a pilots' strike.

The overall effects of all of the above are not only that:

→ the supply of pilots is lower than that of porters while demand is stronger, but also that . . .
→ the elasticities of supply and demand are lower for pilots than for porters.

This gives a higher price or wage for pilots. It also means that any **shifts** in supply or demand will have greater effects on pilots' wages than on porters' wages.

Non-market influences on wages ●●●

The above discussion is not a complete explanation of wage differentials, as these are often caused by non-economic factors, which help explain, for instance, why women are often paid less than men. Such factors include:

→ **Social and cultural factors:** some workers have lower status in society. Hospital porters, like nurses, are respected widely for what they do, but their social status is lower than that of pilots.
→ **Union power:** some groups of workers belong to more powerful trade unions and professional bodies than do other workers.

Checkpoint 2

Draw a diagram to compare the markets for pilots and porters.

Checkpoint 3

What might cause shifts in the supply of or demand for pilots or porters?

Check the net

For labour-market information, see www.statistics.gov.uk.

Exam question (30 minutes)   answer: page 31

(a) Use supply and demand analysis to explain the very high wages earned by either of the Beckhams (David or Victoria).

(b) Is supply and demand analysis a complete explanation?

The minimum wage

In the same way as market theory can be used to help explain wage differentials (see page 24), supply and demand analysis can be used to help analyse the possible effects of a minimum wage.

(see page 24)

The jargon

Minimum wage. The minimum rate of pay for labour (usually expressed as an hourly rate), either passed into law by the government or agreed voluntarily between trade unions and employers, and designed to ensure that workers can afford some basic standard of living.

What is a minimum wage?

A minimum wage can be viewed as a type of minimum price control (see page 18). Here, the price-fixing authority is the government, which sets a wage that employers must comply with and that is usually expressed as an hourly rate. The USA, the UK and some other EU countries have minimum wages.

(see page 18)

What are the advantages and disadvantages of a minimum wage?

Advantages

A minimum wage:

➜ Acts as an incentive to unemployed people to come off benefits and seek employment, provided that the wage is set at a high enough level. In this way, a minimum wage can reduce unemployment and get people back into the habit of working. They might then be encouraged to retrain, seek promotion and move up the pay ladder.

➜ Helps to redistribute income – by raising earnings for the lowest-paid people in the community, the minimum wage reduces inequality and helps create a fairer society.

Disadvantages

A minimum wage:

➜ Raises the costs of employers.

➜ Might cause unemployment if employers shed staff as a result.

The minimum wage in the UK

Soon after winning the general election in 1997, the new Labour government adopted a minimum wage. Employers' organisations such as the Confederation of British Industry (CBI) claimed that unemployment would rise. The economic theory behind this claim is shown in the diagram below.

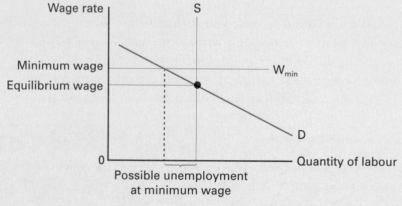

A possible effect of the minimum wage

Low-wage earners are likely to be unskilled and doing low-level tasks such as cleaning in offices and factories, waiting on tables in restaurants, washing up in hotel kitchens and stacking shelves in supermarkets. The supply curve of unskilled labour is fixed in the short run (zero wage elasticity and vertical supply curve). Meanwhile, it might be assumed that the demand for unskilled labour is wage-elastic.

The diagram shows an excess supply of labour at the minimum wage, creating unemployment that would not exist at the lower free-market wage. However, coinciding with and following the introduction of the minimum wage, unemployment in the UK has fallen steadily. Why is this so?

First, other measures have been introduced along with the minimum wage. These include the following:

→ 'Welfare to work' schemes, which are designed to encourage workers to overcome any barriers they might believe prevent them from coming off benefits.
→ A new network of employment offices, known as Job Centre Plus, to improve the information provided about job vacancies.
→ Assistance targeted at people with disabilities to help convince them, and potential employers, that they can become useful members of the workforce.
→ Training schemes to improve employability, with subsidies for employers taking on new staff.

Second, there have been favourable macroeconomic conditions in the general economy, encouraging employers to take on staff.

Third, there have been labour shortages in certain areas. It is possible that the wage elasticity mentioned above is lower than was anticipated, because employers find that they cannot manage without unskilled staff – someone has to do the washing-up in a big hotel.

In fact, many of the jobs at the minimum wage are filled by new workers coming from developing-world countries and parts of the EU where wage levels are generally lower than in the UK. Without these migrant workers, large parts of the UK economy, especially in public services and the tourism sector, would be unable to function.

Check the net

Go to www.dti.gov.uk/er/nmw and find out the current national minimum wage (note: there is a separate minimum wage for young workers). Also see www.acas.org.uk and www.lowpay.gov.uk.

Checkpoint 1

Why might it be reasonable to suppose that the demand for unskilled labour is wage-elastic?

Checkpoint 2

If the demand for unskilled labour is less wage-elastic than was thought, how might this affect anticipated unemployment?

Exam question (20 minutes)   answer: page 31

The EU has, in principle, a single labour market across its 25 member countries. Discuss how this might affect the UK government's minimum wage policy.

Answers
Market theory and applications

Production possibilities (1)

Checkpoints

1 Both are faced with many demands on scarce resources. Robinson's economy is far less complex than Gordon's, but both have to make choices, set priorities and assess opportunity costs. Both are faced with the problems of 'what' and 'how' to produce; however, only Gordon has to consider 'for whom'. Robinson lives alone and thus income distribution is not an issue until Friday arrives on the scene.

2 • **Land:** the ingredients for the cake: flour, eggs, butter, milk, sugar.
 • **Labour:** the skills and work done by Ainsley and Delia.
 • **Capital:** the kitchen and its equipment.
 • **Enterprise:** the recipe created by Ainsley and Delia, and their organisation and planning.

Exam question

(a)

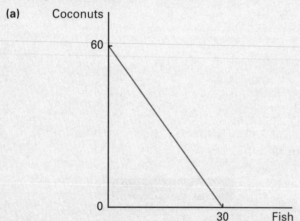

(b) The diagram is a straight line, indicating constant returns, as opposed to the usual shape, which is concave to the origin, indicating diminishing returns. In this case, factors of production are perfectly mobile: people can switch quickly, easily and effortlessly between coconut-gathering and fishing. There is no efficiency loss, and so a 50% drop in coconut production will double fish production, a 25% drop will quadruple fish production, and so on.

(c) This position is to the left of the PPF, and so there is both productive and allocative inefficiency (see pages 6–7).

(d)

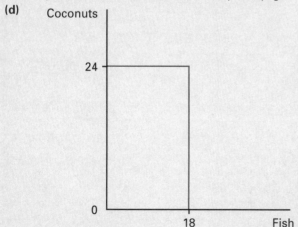

Instead of a wide range of choices between coconuts and fish, the community now has only one possible efficient combination of the two products. The moral is that an economy that is inflexible loses productivity.

Production possibilities (2)

Checkpoints

1 'Scarcity' in an everyday sense usually refers to obvious shortages, and often to natural disasters such as drought and famine. In an economic sense, everything is 'scarce', in the sense that the production of any good or service uses resources that are limited in supply: we cannot have everything we want all of the time, and so we have to make choices or 'economise' – hence, the study of 'economics'.

2 A producer is a direct user of the world's resources. A car manufacturer, for example, uses metal, plastic, glass, rubber and human resources. The producer makes choices regarding what and how to produce with these limited resources; the profits that could be obtained by producing something else are an opportunity cost. A consumer goes out to work to earn money with which to have a command over goods and services. With a limited income, buying product A means that product B is forgone, and this represents an opportunity cost.

Exam questions

1 (c). 'Fairness', like 'justice' and 'beauty', is a normative concept. People's views of fairness depend on their attitudes rather than on objective reality. (a), (b) and (d) are all statements that, in principle, can be tested objectively using methods that most reasonable people could agree upon.

2 (b). (a) might be a result of efficiency, while (c) and (d) might contribute to efficiency, but (b) relates output to the use of scarce resources and so corresponds to productive efficiency.

Demand and supply

Checkpoints

1 At each and every price, we can expect more cars to be demanded, i.e. demand shifts to the right.

2 At each and every price, we can expect fewer bananas to be supplied, i.e. supply shifts to the left.

Exam question

Transport: the demand for oil is derived from the demand for fuels used by the industry, e.g. petrol, diesel, aviation fuel. **Whole economy:** the demand for oil is derived from the demand for a wide range of oil-based products, e.g. plastics, synthetic fibres, paint, chemicals, cosmetics, certain foodstuffs.

How prices change

Checkpoints

1 A surplus means that at the current price, supply exceeds demand; this creates a downward pressure on price until the surplus is eliminated. The opposite is true of a shortage.
2 Case 4: supply shifts left, price rises, quantity demanded falls, the market contracts. It is also possible that adverse publicity will turn the public off milk: demand shifts left, price falls, quantity supply falls, the market contracts. If both of these possibilities are shown on one diagram, then we can predict that the quantity bought and sold will be less than before, but the overall effect on price is indeterminate.

Exam question

At any point in time, the number of beds available is fixed, and so this is a case of zero price elasticity of supply, i.e. a vertical supply curve in the short run (see page 16). This means that price is governed mainly by demand. In January, in the slack period after Christmas, demand shifts to the left; at weekends, when business travellers are at home, demand shifts even further left. This is especially true of some locations, e.g. lodges situated close to motorway service stations. Rather than have empty bedrooms earning nothing, it is better for the company to charge a bargain price in order to bring in some revenue.

Price elasticity of demand (1)

Checkpoints

1 400 to 200 = 50% fall in quantity demanded.
   10p to 11p = 10% increase in price.
   Using the formula PED = 50/10 = 5.
2 • **Foreign holidays and new cars:** these have a range of substitutes and take up a substantial fraction of a family budget, and so we would expect them to be relatively price-elastic.
   • **Houses:** substitutes are limited, as we all need a roof over our heads, and so this tends to reduce price elasticity. Most houses are bought with borrowed money using a mortgage; mortgages are linked closely to income, and so housing demand is more likely to be income-elastic (see page 16) rather than price-elastic.
   • **Bread:** not many substitutes; takes up a relatively small fraction of a family budget, and so we would expect a relatively low price elasticity.

Exam question

(a) If the objective really is to reduce the use of cars, then fuel taxes would need to be increased enough in order to reach the higher price levels of the demand curve, where demand is price-elastic. If taxes are imposed where demand is inelastic, then the tax acts as a revenue raiser rather than as a deterrent to car use. However, if the revenue is used in order to improve substitutes, e.g. by being invested in public transport, then this increases the price elasticity of car use and so improves the effectiveness of the policy.

(b) The objective here is to encourage the take-up of these services; this will work if demand is price-elastic.

(c) As suggested in (a), the government would normally raise the price of something partly in order to discourage its consumption. So, raising the price of university education at the same time as stating that we want more young people to go to university is inconsistent. Presumably, the government assumes that the demand for university places is sufficiently inelastic to produce revenue without losing too many 'customers'; perhaps it hopes that demand can simultaneously be shifted to the right by student bursaries and/or publicity suggesting that paying for a degree in the short run will be compensated by higher earning power in the long run.

Price elasticity of demand (2)

Checkpoints

1 The traveller has fewer travel options, i.e. fewer substitutes, and so PED falls.
2 Peak-time travellers have fewer substitutes. Off-peak travellers are not so time-constrained and can, therefore, shop around more, and so their PED is greater.

Exam question

These figures are based on actual fares of a low-cost airline. The company is clearly trying to maximise revenue by reducing price when PED is high (bookings made well in advance and for less busy weekdays) and increasing price when PED is low (bookings made at short notice and for travel before weekends).

Other elasticities

Checkpoints

1 The capacity of the human stomach is limited. This means that if your income were to, say, double, then your spending on food would less than double. In a very poor country, people spend a large fraction of their income on food, and the majority of the population are engaged in food production. In higher-income countries, such as the UK, we spend a larger amount but a smaller proportion of our income on food, and a much smaller fraction of the population is engaged in agriculture. This tendency was first noted by a statistician called Ernst Engl and is known as Engl's law.
2 • **Whisky and soda:** complements, but not necessarily close; negative, small.
   • **Cups and saucers:** close complements; negative, large.
   • **Left- and right-hand gloves:** extremely close complements; negative, very large (close to infinity).
   • **Cars and motorbikes, cars and bicycles:** substitutes in each case; therefore, CED is positive. However, if car

drivers regard a motorbike as a closer substitute, then the coefficient would be larger than for a bicycle.

Exam question

It is likely to have a high PED, since both the substitution and income effects of a price change are likely to be large and reinforce each other (see page 13). An important point that follows from the idea of substitution and income effects is that the price elasticity of demand of a product is related closely to its cross-elasticity of demand with possible substitutes and also its income elasticity of demand. In other words, a product with a high coefficient of cross-elasticity with respect to a substitute and a high income elasticity of demand is also likely to have a high price elasticity of demand.

Minimum price controls

Checkpoints

1 There is a surplus at the controlled price, and so this price will not hold unless demand is increased, supply is reduced, or a bit of both.
2 There is no need to do anything, as price is above the required minimum.

Exam question

Diagram as on page 18. Possible consequences: in order to avoid a surplus, producers must either increase demand or reduce supply. An increase in demand is possible, e.g. through an advertising campaign promoting the use of aluminium. However, more likely is that the firms will reduce supply, in effect forming a cartel (see page 51). The cartel will attempt to share out the market between them, each producing a quota of aluminium for sale at the high price. However, there is a temptation for an individual firm to cheat on the cartel, producing more than its quota. For this reason, cartels tend to break up easily.

Maximum price controls

Checkpoints

1 The capacity of the ground is fixed in the short run.
2

Quantity of school places

In most countries, school education is zero-priced. If supply (S) is insufficient, then there is a shortage (MN in the diagram). If the government makes school attendance compulsory, then it follows that the government commits itself to increasing the supply of school places to S_1 in order to eliminate the shortage. University tuition fees are discussed on page 13.

Exam question

(a) Higher prices, leading to higher inflation. Higher costs might lead employers to reduce costs by shedding labour, therefore increasing unemployment.
(b) People would have to be issued with coupons or petrol points and would not be allowed to buy petrol unless they had enough points. This might be seen to be fair, as petrol would not be restricted to those with the ability to pay; however, car use is much greater today than it was during the Second World War and the system would be under greater strain, as many more people would want extra points, claiming that they could not function without access to petrol.

Parallel markets

Checkpoints

1 Consider which methods are most/least likely to ensure that (a) tickets end up in the hands of people who really want them and therefore are less likely to be tempted to sell them on; (b) a minimum of policing is required in order to ensure that everyone accepts the outcome and sticks to the rules.
2 From an economic point of view, the most efficient method is one that ensures that there is never an empty space in the car park or a single car waiting for an empty space. This would involve finding a finely tuned market price. However, the reasons for providing a car park are not purely economic: local residents, for example, might be allowed to park free of charge, even if this upsets the delicate balance between demand and supply.

Exam question

When reporting on prices charged by ticket touts for Wimbledon, the FA Cup Final or a high-profile cricket test match, the media often assumes that parallel markets are a bad thing. However, it could be argued that by reallocating tickets so that those people who really want them pay a price to those who do not really want them, then the sum total of human welfare is actually increased.

Labour markets

Checkpoints

1 Employers are willing to pay more for skilled labour. This skills differential is the incentive for foregoing earnings during a training period in the expectation of higher earning power in the future.

2

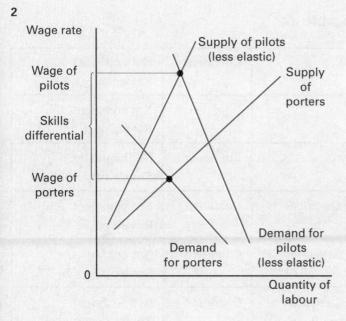

Wage rate

Supply of pilots (less elastic)

Supply of porters

Wage of pilots

Skills differential

Wage of porters

Demand for porters

Demand for pilots (less elastic)

0

Quantity of labour

3 Remember that the demand for labour is a derived demand. This can change quite quickly. The supply of labour depends on factors such as the length of training, which is a long-term variable. Sometimes, this can be shortened by migration, e.g. doctors from Asia or plumbers from Poland.

Exam question

(a) In either case, the supply curve is vertical, as there is only one of each (David and Victoria) in existence. This means that their wage is determined entirely by demand; if demand is high enough, the sky is the limit as far as the wage goes. Changes in technology have increased demand considerably in recent years: David's work on the football field, for example, is watched by millions of people round the world on satellite TV.

(b) The labour market is not a perfect market (see page 42). Supply and demand can go a long way towards explaining wage differences, but there are social, cultural and political considerations as well as economic considerations – especially when comparing male and female wages.

The minimum wage

Checkpoints

1 One group of unskilled workers can easily be replaced by another group; this gives bargaining power to the employer. On the other hand, some employers have found that unskilled workers can be hard to come by: farmers, for example, have had to 'import' crop pickers from Eastern Europe.

2 Unemployment will be lower than anticipated, as employers will be less able to do without unskilled labour.

Exam question

The single European market has three main elements: the free movement of goods and services, the free movement of capital, and the free movement of labour (see page 138). This latter element provides opportunities and threats for the UK economy. In answering this question, you should consider issues from the point of view of British employers, British workers, employers in the rest of the EU and workers in the rest of the EU. Remember that not only can foreign workers transfer easily to the UK, but also British workers can transfer easily to any of the 24 other member states.

Revision checklist
Market theory and applications

By the end of this chapter you should be able to:

1	Discuss the basic economic principles relating to the production possibility frontier.	Confident	Not confident. **Revise** pages 4–7
2	Distinguish between positive and value statements.	Confident	Not confident. **Revise** page 7
3	List the underlying conditions of demand and supply.	Confident	Not confident. **Revise** pages 8–9
4	Use supply and demand analysis to explain how market prices and quantities change.	Confident	Not confident. **Revise** pages 10–11
5	Define elasticity; write down the formula for price elasticity of demand; use the formula to calculate elasticity.	Confident	Not confident. **Revise** pages 10–15
6	Use diagrams to show the relationship between price elasticity of demand and total revenue along a straight-line demand curve.	Confident	Not confident. **Revise** pages 14–15
7	Discuss the factors affecting price elasticity of demand.	Confident	Not confident. **Revise** page 13
8	Explain the significance of → cross-elasticity of demand; → income elasticity of demand; → price elasticity of supply.	Confident	Not confident. **Revise** pages 16–17
9	Draw a diagram to show a minimum price control (floor price): → Explain why the government (or other authority) needs to either (a) increase demand or (b) reduce supply. → Discuss examples of circumstances where (a) or (b) might be chosen.	Confident	Not confident. **Revise** pages 18–19
10	Draw a diagram to show a maximum price (ceiling price): → Explain why the government (or other authority) needs to either (a) reduce demand or (b) increase supply. → Discuss examples of circumstances where (a) or (b) might be chosen.	Confident	Not confident. **Revise** pages 20–2
11	Explain how the theory of ceiling price is relevant to black-market ticket prices or other parallel markets.	Confident	Not confident. **Revise** pages 22–3
12	Discuss the relevance of supply and demand concepts to labour markets.	Confident	Not confident. **Revise** pages 24–7

Costs, competition, monopoly and market failure

This chapter considers market structures and begins by looking at markets from the point of view of the individual firm. Then we begin to consider what it is that markets *cannot* do: this is what we refer to as **market failure**.

Exam themes

→ How costs behave as output changes in the short and long run

→ Costs, revenues and profits

→ Price and output under different market conditions

→ Economic efficiency

→ Competition, monopoly, oligopoly

→ Competition and monopoly policy

→ Externalities

→ Public goods, private goods, merit goods

Topic checklist

AS ○ A2 ●	Edexcel	AQA	OCR	WJEC	CCEA
Diminishing returns and short-run costs	●	●	○	●	●
Economies of scale and long-run costs	○	○●	○●	●	●
Costs, revenue and profit	●	●	○	●	●
Alternative pricing strategies	●	●	○	●	●
Short-run and long-run equilibrium under perfect competition	●	●	○●	●	●
Economic efficiency	●	○●	○●	○●	○●
Competition and monopoly (1)	○●	○●	○●	●	○●
Competition and monopoly (2)	●	○●	●	●	●
Imperfect competition: monopolistic competition, oligopoly	●	●	○●	●	●
Price discrimination	●	●		●	●
Monopoly and competition policy	○	●	○	●	●
Market failure and welfare economics	○●	○●	○●	○	○●
Public goods, merit goods	○	○●	○	○	○

Diminishing returns and short-run costs

Firms cannot stay in business unless they make profits. We often assume that firms try to **maximise** profits. In order to know whether a firm is profitable, we need to be able to track both costs and revenues. How do costs behave as output increases? In the short run, costs are influenced by the law of diminishing returns.

Checkpoint 1

Make a list of the fixed and variable costs in a car factory.

Checkpoint 2

Using reasonable assumptions, estimate the likely time period that might be regarded as the difference between the short run and long run for the following: a supermarket, a fast-food outlet, a large hotel, an airline, a steelworks.

How long is the short run?

Within a firm, the short run is the period of time within which at least one of the factors of production is fixed in size or quantity. A farmer producing potatoes, for example, uses variable factors, such as farm workers, machines and fertiliser. The potato field, however, has a fixed size. The difference between the short run and the long run is the time it would take to acquire another field.

Diminishing returns

The law of diminishing returns tells us that when variable factors are combined with a fixed factor, eventually output will increase at a diminishing rate. This law tells us something about efficiency. Take the farmer's field for example: as output increases, efficiency goes through the following stages:

→ If only one person is employed on a very large field, then output will be low (underused capacity, low efficiency).
→ Employing twice as many people could cause output to more than double (increasing returns, output produced more efficiently).
→ Eventually, however, the field approaches its capacity limit, and output slows down. Employing twice as many people less than doubles output (diminishing returns, output produced less efficiently).
→ When the field is well over its capacity limits, extra workers might hinder each other and total output could actually decrease (falling returns, falling efficiency).

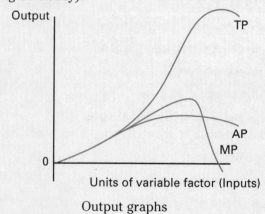

Output graphs

The diagram above shows that diminishing returns occur in the following order: marginal returns, average returns, total returns.

Classification of returns

→ **Average product:** total output divided by units of input (variable factors).
→ **Marginal product:** the amount added to total output by employing one extra unit of input.

Classification of costs

→ **Fixed costs:** those costs that remain the same at all levels of output (including zero level of output).
→ **Variable costs:** those costs that increase with output. In line with the law of diminishing returns, they increase at a slower rate than output to begin with, and then at a faster rate as diminishing returns sets in.
→ **Total costs:** the sum of fixed costs and variable costs.
→ **Average total cost:** the total cost divided by the output.
→ **Marginal cost:** the amount added to the total cost by producing one extra unit of output.

Checkpoint 3

Distinguish between variable cost and marginal cost.

How do costs behave in the short run?

If extra variable factors such as labour are taken on by a firm, and output rises faster than the increase in variable factor, then average costs will fall. Similarly, if output rises at a lower rate than the numbers employed, then average costs will rise. This means that average and marginal costs behave as shown in the diagram below.

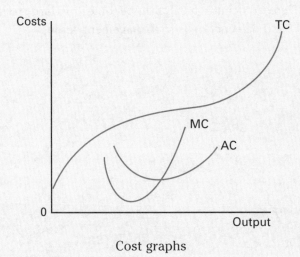

Cost graphs

Note carefully that the marginal and average cost curve shapes are a mirror image of the marginal and average product curves.

Exam question (40 minutes)   answer: page 60

(a) Calculate the fixed cost (FC), average fixed cost (AFC), average variable cost (AVC), average total cost (ATC) and marginal cost (MC) from the table below.

Units of output	Total cost	FC	AFC	AVC	ATC	MC
0	50					
1	80					
2	128					
3	180					
4	280					
5	405					

(b) Draw graphs to plot these cost curves against output.

(c) Explain what these shapes tell us about returns and efficiency.

Economies of scale and long-run costs

Whereas short-run costs are affected by the law of diminishing returns, in the long run all factor inputs are variable and costs are affected by returns to scale.

What are returns to scale? ●●●

→ Increasing returns to scale occur if output increases more than in proportion to inputs, e.g. doubling all inputs more than doubles output. Increasing returns to scale, in effect, arise from improvements in productivity that can be achieved as a firm gets larger.

→ Constant returns to scale occur when output increases in the same proportion as all inputs, e.g. doubling all inputs doubles output. If inputs are divisible (i.e. they can be increased in small quantities), then a firm can take on extra resources in small quantities and combine them in the same proportion as before. The firm then moves along the horizontal part of the long-run cost curve (see below).

→ Decreasing returns to scale occur when output increases less than in proportion to all inputs, e.g. doubling all inputs less than doubles output. This can occur when a firm becomes too large to be run efficiently and diseconomies to management set in.

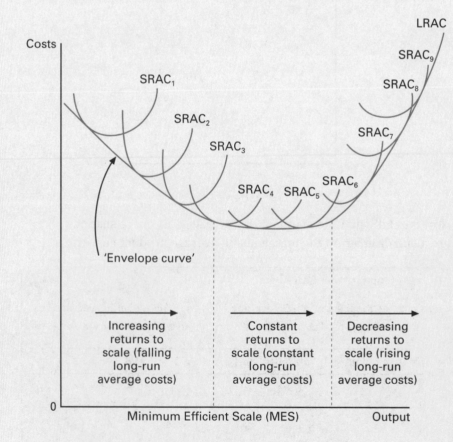

Long-run costs: the 'envelope curve'

The diagram above shows that individual production units have their own short-run cost curves, which obey the law of diminishing returns as a fixed factor becomes utilised more fully. As the enterprise gets bigger, it acquires more production units, and the firm as a whole moves along the long-run average cost envelope curve (LRAC), which touches each of the short-run curves at a tangent and shows the trend that costs follow in the long run. As output is increased through increasing both variable and fixed factors in the long run, LRAC falls, becomes horizontal and eventually rises.

What are the advantages of large firms? ○○○

Internal economies of scale enable large firms to reduce their long-run costs as they grow in size.

Type of internal economy	This economy enables a firm to . . .
Purchasing	Buy in bulk and, therefore, more cheaply
Marketing	Sell in large quantities, therefore clearing production lines quickly; offer discounts to customers; use mass advertising media
Production	Use mass production techniques, reducing unit costs; purchase large, technically advanced machinery; use division of labour; transport materials in bulk, often saving on storage costs
Financial	Borrow more easily; raise funds at favourable interest rates; use retained profits or shareholders to raise funds
Risk-bearing	Spread risks among more products; diversify and supply a variety of markets
Managerial	Employ specialist managers; use sophisticated systems to measure costs and revenues

Checkpoint 1

Explain why buying in bulk enables a firm to obtain goods and services more cheaply.

Checkpoint 2

Explain why internal economies of scale are described as 'internal'.

Check the net

For further notes on economies of scale see:
www.revisionguru.co.uk/economics/scale.htm
www.factbites.com/topics/economies-of-scale
www.bized.ac.uk

Exam question (20 minutes)   answer: pages 60–1

In view of all the advantages of large firms, how can small firms survive? Make a list of (a) things that small firms can do that large firms might find difficult; (b) ways in which small firms can fight back against large firms.

Costs, revenue and profit

Having considered how costs behave as output increases, we now consider revenue and then combine revenue and costs in order to calculate profit.

Total, average and marginal revenue

We saw on page 14 that total revenue is linked strongly to price elasticity of demand.

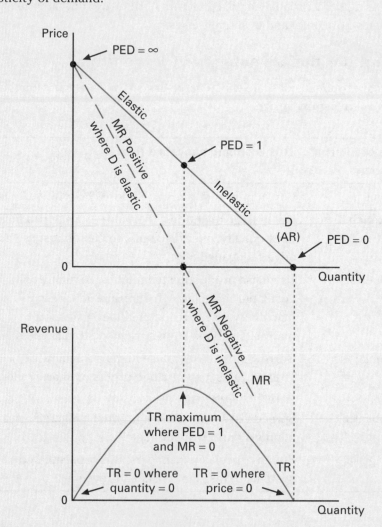

Total, average and marginal revenue

Where demand is price-elastic, a reduction in price (increase in quantity sold) increases total revenue (marginal revenue (MR) is positive). Where demand is price-inelastic, a reduction in price (increase in quantity sold) reduces total revenue (marginal revenue is negative).

A demand curve can be regarded as an average revenue line, since for any quantity sold it shows the average revenue received per unit. Average revenue, in effect, is the same thing as the price per unit.

The profit-maximising level of output ●●●

Profit can be regarded as a **remainder**: it is what is left over after total cost is subtracted from total revenue:

Total profit = total revenue − total cost

If one more unit of output is sold, then the amount added to total profit can be called marginal profit (MP):

$MP = MR - MC$

When total profit is maximised, $MP = 0$, and so

$0 = MR - MC$

or

$MC = MR$

This is the profit-maximising condition. It enables us to look at revenue and cost diagrams and identify quickly the price and level of output that give maximum profit, as in the diagram below.

Checkpoint 2

Explain why when profit is maximised, MP = 0.

The jargon

You need to know about two types of profit:
Normal profit. The basic rate of return that enables a firm to stay in business. It is best regarded as a type of cost, as it is the opportunity cost of keeping a firm in its present line of production.
Supernormal profit. Surplus profit over and above normal profit. When we use the equation TP = TR − TC, we are referring to supernormal profit.

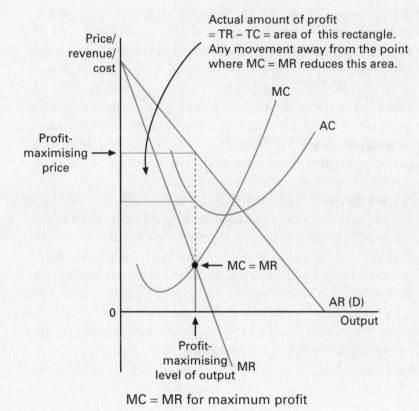

MC = MR for maximum profit

Exam question (25 minutes)   answer: page 61

Explain the role of profit in a market economy.

Alternative pricing strategies

We normally assume that firms try to maximise profits and that this is their main objective. However, firms might have other objectives, and they might conflict, at least to some extent, with the idea of profit maximisation.

The divorce of ownership and control

Due to economies of scale, many industries are becoming dominated by fewer, larger firms. Large companies are complicated organisations – far more complex than the small firms that traditional economic theory assumes exist in large numbers. Large companies employ specialist managers, and these people often receive large salaries. They might own some shares in the company, or they might not. If they do not, then they can be regarded as employees rather than part owners of the firm. They receive salaries rather than a share of profits, and it is therefore possible that they are not concerned primarily with maximising profits at all times. They might have different objectives.

How do different objectives affect prices?

→ **Market share.** Some firms aim to be the biggest provider in a particular market. The executives running a newspaper, for example, might measure their success in terms of circulation and might be more interested in increasing their share of the total circulation of newspapers in a country than in the annual profit figures. They might lower prices and sacrifice profits if they believe that this could boost circulation. Marketing experts refer to such a strategy as **penetration pricing**. Sometimes, this strategy is used to drive prices so low that some competitors are driven out of business, at which point prices might be put up again.

→ **Market foothold.** A firm that is a new entrant into a market might not yet have the productive capacity to produce up to its profit-maximising level of output. It might not yet wish to incur the costs involved in keeping stocks in large warehouses or transporting products using a wide distribution network. Also, it might not be sure of an appropriate price to charge for its product. Such a firm might put its toe into the water of a new market by charging a high price, which attracts only a few customers. Such a policy is known as **market skimming** and, if successful, might lead eventually to a lowering of price, which will bring in more customers and move the firm closer towards a profit-maximising level of output.

Checkpoint 1

Give an example of an industry that is gradually becoming dominated by fewer, larger firms, and suggest why this is happening.

Checkpoint 2

Why might the production department of a firm have quite different objectives from those of the marketing department?

→ **Sales maximisation.** It can happen that one department within a firm will have different objectives to another department. The production department, for example, might wish to produce to its maximum output as long as costs are covered. This is because employees within the department earn more overtime payments and production bonuses in this way. The sales department, on the other hand, might be paid a commission for every unit it sells, and it will want to charge a price that maximises total revenue.

→ **Managerial power and utility.** Some managers might not be terribly interested in pricing strategies at all. They might be more interested in the internal politics of a company rather than its economics. They might be seeking promotion within the company so that they can wield more power over other employees, or they might be seeking perks such as a company car or other benefits. Being wrapped up in such matters, they then ignore profitability.

→ **Cost-plus pricing.** Economic theory assumes that firms can measure and keep track of their costs and revenues. If this is not possible, some firms might make an estimate of their costs of production and add on a profit margin. If this policy is successful, then their price will give them a profit, but it might not be a maximum profit.

→ **Satisficing.** Some company bosses do not try to maximise anything at all. They might instead opt out of the stress and strain of competition and go for a quiet life. As long as their shareholders do not complain, they might get away with reasonable returns rather than maximum returns. Such managers are said to be 'satisficing'.

Although there are a number of alternatives open to firms, and it is quite possible that not all firms are profit-maximising at all times, it should be remembered that no commercial firm can exist for any length of time without profits, and so profitability is always an important consideration.

Checkpoint 3

Draw a diagram to show how the price and output of a profit-maximising firm are likely to change if it switches to revenue-maximising.

Check the net

For further information on pricing strategies, see
www.tutor2u.com and
www.marketingteacher.com

Exam question (30 minutes)   answer: page 61

Many firms claim to have an ethical dimension to their company's policies. Does this conflict with the profit-maximising objective? Justify your answer.

Short-run and long-run equilibrium under

What is meant by 'perfect competition'? Why do economists attach importance to this idea? We discuss the first of these questions here and the second overleaf.

The assumptions of perfect competition ●●●

→ A large number of firms of roughly equal size, with no large firm or firms dominating the market.
→ A homogeneous product, with no attempt to promote one brand image over another. Persuasive advertising does not exist.
→ Consumers have perfect knowledge, and they realise that the output of one firm is a perfect substitute for the output of another. There is a place for informative advertising.
→ No market barriers: new firms can freely enter a market. Similarly, existing firms can exit from a market when they wish.

These assumptions taken together lead to the conclusion that the individual firm is a **price-taker**, which means that the firm is too small a part of the market to be able to affect market price by its own actions.

Checkpoint 1

Distinguish between persuasive and informative advertising.

Checkpoint 2

Explain why a firm that is a small part of the market is more likely than a large firm to be a price-taker.

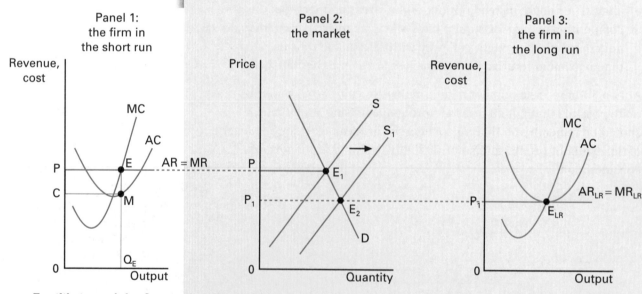

Panel 1: the firm in the short run

Panel 2: the market

Panel 3: the firm in the long run

Equilibrium of the firm in the short and long run (supernormal profits, firms entering the industry)

perfect competition

In the diagram, panel 2 shows market conditions and indicates how market forces of supply and demand decide market price.

The horizontal demand curve shows that the firm is a price-taker: no matter what output the individual firm produces, the output will be too small to affect market price by itself. Therefore, the firm can sell all of its output only if it can match the current market price. If average revenue is constant, then $AR = MR$, since the revenue from the last unit sold is equal to the revenue from all the previous units sold (the firm does not have to reduce price to sell one more unit).

In this particular example, the firm has generally low costs. At the profit-maximising level of output, it can make supernormal profits.

→ Panel 1 shows the firm's position within the wider market. This indicates how market conditions are viewed from the angle of the individual firm. The horizontal price line indicates that the firm has to react to a given market price. It does this by producing a profit-maximising output at the point where $MC = MR$.

→ Panel 2 shows how, if this firm is typical of others in the industry, supernormal profits (measured by rectangle PECM) act as an incentive to new firms to enter the market. This shifts the market supply curve to the right and lowers the market price. This happens until there is no incentive for new firms to enter, i.e. when $AC = AR$ and no supernormal profit is being made (all the excess profits have been competed away).

→ Panel 3 shows the long-run equilibrium of both the firm and the industry, with firms making normal profits only.

Link

Why is $MC = MR$ the profit-maximising condition? See page 39.

Link

What's the distinction between normal and supernormal profit? See page 39.

Exam question (20 minutes)   answer: page 62

Draw a diagram, similar to the one in this section, explaining what happens to the firm and the industry in the short and long run when the typical firm is making **losses**.

Economic efficiency

It is difficult to find many real-world examples of perfect competition. Why, then, do economists persist in discussing the idea? It is largely because the model tells us something important about efficiency.

Economic efficiency ●●●

In general terms, the idea of efficiency is linked closely to the creation of a minimum amount of waste. Economic efficiency therefore occurs when scarce resources are used in the least wasteful manner. Economic efficiency includes two important conditions: productive efficiency and allocative efficiency. In each case, efficiency can be viewed at the level of the firm and at the level of society at large.

On page 43, we noted that under perfect competition, in the long run all of the following are predicted to become equal:

$$P = MC = MR = AC = AR$$

If we take these equalities in pairs, we can see why the model of perfect competition is important.

Equality	Significance of equality
$MC = AC$	Under perfect competition, all firms in the long run are producing at the lowest point on their AC curves. Thus, we have **productive efficiency**
$P = MC$	The effort and time and costs that producers put in to making goods and services are exactly compensated for by the selling price. At the same time, the price that people pay for their goods and services reflects the benefit that people believe that they receive. Thus, under perfect competition, we have **allocative efficiency**
$MC = MR$ and $AC = AR$	Individual firms are maximising profits ($MC = MR$) in the short run but in the long run receive only normal profit ($AC = AR$). This means that although each firm acts in its own interest, then provided it exists in a competitive environment it will automatically act in the wider interests of society. Firms act in enlightened self-interest

If we move away from perfect competition towards any other kind of market, there may well be some advantages, but there will always be the disadvantage that it becomes impossible for all five elements in the above equation to be equal at the same time. Thus, there is always some disadvantage in terms of a loss of economic efficiency.

Watch out!

If you are asked a question about 'efficiency', generally you need to be able to describe both productive and allocative efficiency. Sometimes, however, you might be asked about one of the two specific types, so read the question carefully.

Checkpoint 1

Distinguish between productive and allocative efficiency.

Link

We dealt with efficiency at the level of society on page 6 using the production possibility frontier. Here, we deal with the efficiency of **firms**.

Checkpoint 2

Is perfect competition always the 'perfect' way of doing things?

Consumer and producer surplus ●●●

When economic efficiency is reduced, we can see one group in society benefiting at the expense of the other.

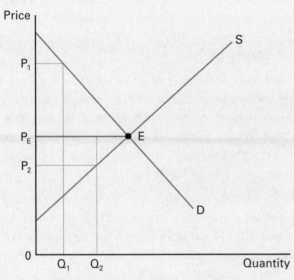

Consumer and producer surplus

The demand curve above shows the prices that consumers are willing to pay. For example consumer Q_1 is willing to pay a price P_1. The horizontal price line shows that this consumer only has to pay P_E. Therefore, this consumer's surplus is $P_1 - P_E$. The total consumer surplus of all consumers is the area shaded (///).

The supply curve shows the prices at which producers are willing to sell. For example, producer Q_2 is willing to pay a price P_2. The horizontal price line shows that this producer actually receives PE. Therefore, this producer's surplus is $P_E - P_2$. The total producer surplus of all producers is the area shaded (\\\).

Suppose that this market is taken over by a monopolist, who forces up the price. The horizontal price line P_EE moves upwards, and some consumer surplus now becomes producer surplus. One section of society has benefited at the expense of another, and thus economic efficiency has been lost.

The jargon

Producer surplus. The additional revenue received by a producer when it is able to sell at a price higher than the minimum price at which the producer is prepared to accept. This is related to (but not quite the same as) supernormal profit (see page 39).

The jargon

Consumer surplus. The utility or satisfaction that is received free of charge when buying a product at a price below the maximum that the consumer would have been prepared to pay.

Link

See the discussion of **monopoly** on page 46.

Exam question (20 minutes)   answer: page 62

Explain carefully why a firm that is making losses in the short run might make profits in the long run and increase its own output, while the output of the industry as a whole falls. Give some actual examples and refer to 'efficiency' in your answer.

Competition and monopoly (1)

We might think it is obvious that monopoly is a 'bad thing'. We can use economic theory to demonstrate the problems posed. Economic theory shows that monopoly has disadvantages or costs; but under certain circumstances, we might predict advantages or benefits.

What is a monopoly? ●●●

In theory, a monopoly is a single seller in a market for a product where a substitute is not available. In practice, a firm does not need to supply 100% of a market in order to be a monopolist. Monopoly law varies from country to country, but usually a monopoly needs to be supplying only about 25% of a market in order to be regarded as a monopoly.

Barriers to entry ●●●

How do monopolies come into existence? They arise from **barriers to entry**, which make it difficult or even impossible for new firms to enter a market. These barriers include:

→ **Natural barriers**, including the uneven distribution of natural resources. The fact that oil is concentrated in certain countries assists in the creation of oil monopolies.
→ **Cost barriers:** economies of scale might be so important in some industries that in order to compete a company must be large. This makes it difficult for smaller firms to compete.
→ **Legal barriers:** some monopolies are protected by law. A national government might argue that this is in the public interest, e.g.
  → The mail-service monopoly ensures that a single-price stamp will guarantee delivery to addresses anywhere in the country. The monopoly enables cheap local deliveries to cross-subsidise loss-making deliveries to remote places.
  → The fact that dentists, doctors, lawyers and teachers have to belong to a professional body creates a type of monopoly but ensures that standards are maintained.
  → Patents, copyright, intellectual property: if new ideas could simply be pirated, there would be no incentive to be creative. Why be the first to write a piece of music, a book or a computer program or the first to invent a machine or a new medicine if others can use your idea without payment?
→ **International distances** can be a barrier, and sometimes trade barriers such as tariffs and quotas have the effect of protecting monopolies.

The jargon

A **simple** monopoly is a single dominant firm. A **complex** monopoly might act together (or collude) in order to dominate a market, for example through a **cartel**, which fixes prices.

Watch out!

Do not confuse **natural factor endowments**, such as oil, with **natural monopoly**. They are not quite the same thing.

The jargon

A **natural monopoly** exists where the average costs of production actually rise with competition. For example, in the UK the supply of water is a natural monopoly. Water is plentiful in the UK and of low value in relation to its volume. It would be wasteful to have two or more water companies flooding valleys for reservoirs and laying parallel water pipes through city streets.

Checkpoint 1

Explain how international trade barriers such as tariffs can lead to monopoly.

The model of monopoly

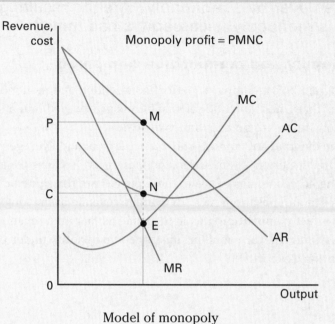

Model of monopoly

Points to note about the diagram above:

→ Under monopoly, the firm is the same thing as the industry. Therefore:
  → There is no market supply curve that is separate from the MC curve.
  → The demand curve is in effect the firm's AR curve.
→ The monopolist has reduced output in order to push up price:
  → The price charged is always in the upper half (the price-elastic part) of the demand curve.
  → The fewer substitutes available, the less choice there is for the consumer, the steeper (less price-elastic) the demand curve, and the greater the price that can be charged.
→ Efficiency has been reduced:
  → MC > AC. Therefore, we have productive inefficiency.
  → P > MC. Therefore, we have allocative inefficiency (consumers have lost and producers have gained).
  → Society in general has also lost out, because monopolists do not make the best use of scarce resources; this is known as a **deadweight loss**.
→ Unlike under perfect competition, any profits earned in the short run will still be earned in the long run.

Checkpoint 2

Explain why an absolutely pure monopoly would have zero price elasticity of demand for its product (a vertical demand curve), and why the demand curve in the diagram is not vertical.

Examiner's secrets

Candidates often make the mistake of saying that a monopolist can charge any price they wish. In fact, the monopolist can decide either output or price, but not both. Consumers may, of course, have very few options, but they usually have some choice.

Exam question (30 minutes)

answer: page 62

(a) Identify the main costs of monopoly.

(b) Are monopolies always profitable?

Competition and monopoly (2)

What happens when a perfectly competitive industry is taken over by a monopoly? Are the results good or bad? Is monopoly necessarily a bad thing?

Watch out!

Exam candidates often assume that a monopoly is bound to be a large firm. Although we can normally expect a monopoly to be large, it is quite possible to have a small-scale monopoly. For example, a corner shop might be the only shop on a remote housing estate, or a small specialist firm might be the only firm that supplies a certain product.

Link

See the model of perfect competition on page 42.

Examiner's secrets

This diagram can be very useful as a focus for exam answers and is worth practising so that it can be drawn quickly and accurately under exam conditions. A good technique is to rotate the horizontal curve AR$_{(PC)}$ to its new position AR$_{(MON)}$ using E$_{(PC)}$ as a pivot point. This helps the rest of the diagram to work first time.

Checkpoint 1

Explain why a falling AR line leads to a falling MR line.

Monopoly and competition compared

The diagram below compares perfect competition and monopoly. It assumes that when a number of small firms are merged into a large monopoly, there are **no economies of scale**.

In the diagram, MC and AC show the marginal and average cost curves under perfect competition and monopoly. Because we are assuming no economies of scale, these curves are the same both before and after monopolisation. AR$_{(PC)}$ is average revenue in the long run under perfect competition; this is the same as marginal revenue MR$_{(PC)}$. E$_{(PC)}$, P$_{(PC)}$ and Q$_{(PC)}$ are equilibrium, price and quantity under perfect competition, respectively.

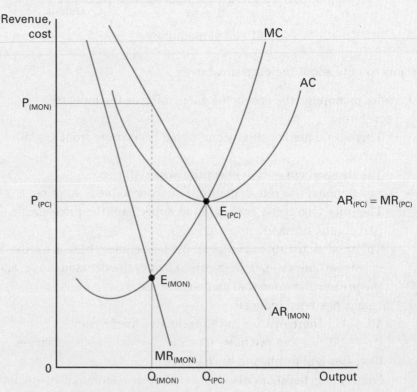

Perfect competition and monopoly compared

Following monopolisation, the horizontal demand curve (the industry's market demand curve perceived from the point of view of the individual firm) is replaced by a downward-sloping demand curve. This is because the individual firm now *is* the industry.

Since average revenue AR$_{(MON)}$ is falling, marginal revenue MR$_{(MON)}$ is lower than average revenue and falls faster.

Comparing the new equilibrium E$_{(MON)}$, price P$_{(MON)}$ and quantity Q$_{(MON)}$ with their corresponding levels under perfect competition, we see clearly that consumers are paying a higher price than necessary for a lower quantity than they really want and society is wasting resources through increased costs.

Monopoly and economies of scale ●●●

An important defence of monopoly is that although it might lead to economic inefficiency, there might be economies of scale, and these economies might actually reduce prices and increase quantities over those available when a market is supplied by a large number of small firms.

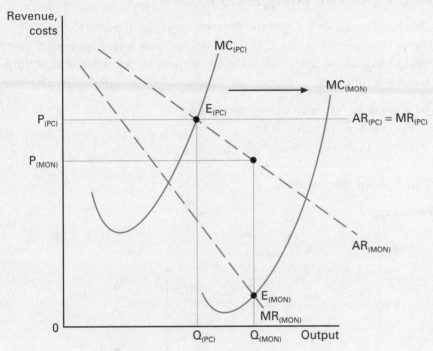

Monopoly and economies of scale

To show economies of scale, we shift the $MC_{(PC)}$ curve downwards and rightwards to $MC_{(MON)}$. $P_{(MON)}$ is now *lower* than $P_{(PC)}$, and quantity $Q_{(MON)}$ is now *higher* than $Q_{(PC)}$.

Contestable markets ●●●

It can be argued that a monopolistic market can operate efficiently without competition, provided that the market is contestable. In other words, firms can benefit from large-scale production and consumers benefit from fair prices, provided that there is the **threat** of new entrants into the industry. If firms potentially can be replaced by new firms, then existing firms will be content with normal profits as opposed to monopoly profits. For a market to be fully contestable, new entrants would have to face costs similar to those of existing firms, and firms leaving the market would need to be able to recoup most of their capital costs. A possible example in the UK would include the national lottery, where an operator is kept on its toes by the possibility of losing the contract.

Exam question (30 minutes)   answer: page 62

A monopoly is broken up into a large number of competing firms. Evaluate the consequences from the point of view of consumers.

Examiner's secrets

To make this diagram easier to draw under exam conditions, the AC curves have been left out.

Checkpoint 2

Give some examples of situations where monopolies can benefit consumers through economies of scale.

Imperfect competition: monopolistic

We can think of perfect competition and monopoly as occupying two extremes on a spectrum of competition, with perfect competition representing maximum and monopoly minimum levels of competition. There are two intermediate market structures: monopolistic competition and oligopoly.

Monopolistic competition ●●●

This combines some aspects of both monopoly and perfect competition. For example, the Mars company has a monopoly over the brand name of the Mars Bar, but it faces considerable competition from makers of other chocolate brands. The main market conditions are:

→ Many firms, some of which may be large.
→ Few barriers to entry or exit.
→ Product differentiation.

The firm in the market

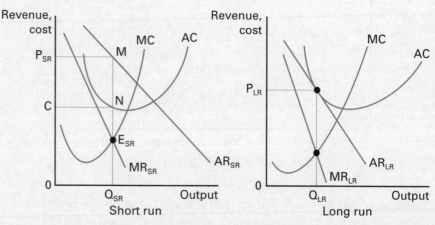

Monopolistic competition

Customers have preferences for the product of a particular firm, but they are aware of substitutes. The demand curve therefore has some elasticity.

The firm is in equilibrium, where MC = MR and is making supernormal profits of PMNC. These supernormal profits attract new entrants. As competitors enter the market, the share of the market supplied by each firm gets smaller, so from the firm's point of view the demand curve shifts to the left, until it just touches the AC curve. At this point, MC = MR and AC = AR, so in the long run firms make normal profits.

Oligopoly ●●●

This is where there are only a few suppliers and the actions of one firm affect other producers. They are interdependent – firms making pricing decisions must consider carefully how rivals will react.

The firm in the market

One way of analysing an oligopolistic market is to assume that firms view their demand curve as being kinked around the current market price.

The jargon

Product differentiation is when sellers use persuasive advertising to create a brand image for their product. The purpose is to try to persuade customers that rival products are a poor substitute.

Checkpoint 1

Give examples of products that are supplied in the UK through oligopolistic markets.

Checkpoint 2

Compare the efficiency of monopolistic competition with that of perfect competition and monopoly.

competition, oligopoly

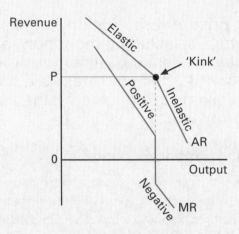

Kinked demand curve

This means that an increase in price will reduce total revenue (because rival firms might decide *not* to increase their prices) and a reduction in price will also reduce total revenue (because rival firms might decide that they *will* reduce prices and perhaps enter a price-cutting war). The results are:

→ **Price stickiness:** firms tend to keep their prices at one level for long periods of time and then all change their prices at the same time.
→ **Non-price competition:** firms tend to play down the importance of their prices and concentrate on brand image and other aspects of their product for marketing purposes. Products, therefore, are usually highly **differentiated**.
→ **Price leadership:** firms will look to their rivals for a cue as to when to alter price. This can occur because of:
  → **Dominant firm price leadership**, where smaller firms follow the lead of a larger one.
  → **Barometric price leadership**, where a smaller firm is known to have the best entrepreneurs, marketing people, economists and accountants, so that they are one step ahead of the rest of the market.
→ **Games play:** the theory of games is often useful in oligopolistic market analysis. For example, where there is:
  → **Pure conflict:** the gains made by one player are the losses of another.
  → **Mixed conflict and cooperation:** players may cooperate to increase their joint payoff, but conflict arises about how to share it out. This leads to the possibility of:
→ **Collusion:** in order to reduce the strain of uncertainty, firms might do secret deals with each other to reduce competition. Hence, the need for laws on competition (see page 54).

Checkpoint 3

Think of an example of dominant-firm price leadership and barometric price leadership.

The jargon

Cartel. When firms conclude to fix prices.

Exam question (30 minutes)   answer: page 63

Use the theory of the kinked demand curve to help explain:

(a) why petrol prices do not always move in step with the world price of oil;

(b) how car manufacturers are likely to react to a sudden increase in the demand for new cars.

Price discrimination

The idea of price discrimination is linked to several other major topics, including monopoly, oligopoly and price elasticity of demand. It is not only a piece of abstract theory: it attempts to explain aspects of the behaviour of some producers in the real world of imperfect competition.

What is price discrimination?

Price discrimination occurs when consumers are charged different prices for the same product and price differences cannot be justified fully by cost differences. Suppose a travel agency sells identical holidays to two different families at different prices – this might be a case of price discrimination.

The purpose of price discrimination is to increase company revenues and, hence, to increase profits. It is profitable only if all three of the following conditions exist:

→ There must be some degree of monopoly power. The supplier needs some ability to make rather than take prices.
→ It must be possible to identify different markets and to keep these markets separate from each other. Markets can be separated by:
  → **Distance:** a manufacturer might sell products more cheaply in low-income countries than in high-income countries.
  → **Time:** a hotel might charge high rates to business customers during the week but offer bargain breaks to tourists at the weekend.
  → **Type of customer:** customers might be classified by age, sex, income, occupation, age or some other criterion. Senior citizens might travel at reduced rate on buses, for example.
→ Each separate market needs to have a different price elasticity of demand. This enables the supplier to try to charge different customers whatever price their market will bear.

Perfect price discrimination

Here, each unit is sold for the maximum obtainable price. In this way, the seller obtains all the consumer surplus.

Imperfect price discrimination

Here, the seller splits one market into two or several separate markets, each with its own price elasticity of demand. Within each separated market, all customers pay the same price. The seller therefore gains extra revenue.

Checkpoint 1

Is the difference between the prices of first class and standard class rail travel a case of price discrimination?

Disadvantages of price discrimination

→ It represents a transfer of welfare from consumer to producer.
→ If we were all forced to pay the maximum we were willing to pay for everything we bought, so that we never received consumer surplus, then our incomes would purchase fewer goods and services and there would be a massive drop in our living standards.

Advantages of price discrimination

→ It can sometimes turn a loss-making business into a profitable business. A loss-making railway line, for example, might be valued more highly by some passengers than others. If those who are willing to pay more actually do pay more, then the line might make a profit.
→ It can support a product that would not otherwise be available. Before the days of the NHS, doctors would charge people what they thought they could afford. The vet James Herriot charged the rich dog owner a different price to the poor dog owner. This enables more people to receive the service.
→ The principle of price discrimination is linked to the idea of yield management, which is used by companies such as budget airlines to charge people different, cheaper prices for booking early. This principle has revolutionised the travel industry and increased competition.

Checkpoint 2

Students whose parents have low incomes pay lower tuition fees than students from high-income families. Is this a case of price discrimination?

Exam question (20 minutes)   answer: pages 63–4

The marketing department of a company identifies two separate markets for its product. Use the idea of price discrimination to explain how this knowledge can be used to increase profits. Include a diagram in your answer.

Monopoly and competition policy

Monopolies have advantages and disadvantages, or benefits and costs. Competition is usually regarded as desirable but is not always the best option. Monopolies are not all necessarily bad. Thus, national governments must have policies in place to regulate monopoly and encourage competition where appropriate. Rather than rely on market forces, all developed countries have policies and institutions in place for this purpose.

Policy options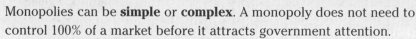

Monopolies can be **simple** or **complex**. A monopoly does not need to control 100% of a market before it attracts government attention.

Monopolies can be **actual** or **potential**.

If several firms dominate a market and it is difficult for other firms to enter, then we have a type of **market failure**.

From a government's point of view, monopolies can be either **ended** or **amended**:

→ **Ended – or simply banned:** this would, however, lose not only the disadvantages of monopoly but also any advantages.
→ **Amended – or controlled:** this would aim to preserve the advantages and regulate the disadvantages.

An instructive way of evaluating UK competition policy is to compare and contrast it with the USA. Compared with what has traditionally happened in Britain, US monopolists have always been treated more strictly. The philosophy in the USA is that where companies conspire to charge the consumer a higher price than they would otherwise pay, then that is a form of theft, and theft is a crime. Furthermore, those facing the sanctions of the criminal law are the people at the very top of the company. So, when Microsoft is accused of monopolistic practices, it is Bill Gates who appears in court and who could end up in prison if found guilty.

Dealing with monopoly

Legal means (the US model)	Administrative means (the traditional UK model)
Court of law	Committee or quango, e.g. the Competition Commission
Tightly defined jurisdiction: the court has no discretion as to which cases to hear	Wide-ranging jurisdiction: the Commission can choose which monopolies or proposed mergers to investigate
Public proceedings	Private proceedings
Rules of precedence	Case-by-case consideration
Attempts to measure monopoly objectively	Subjective view of public interest
Binding decisions	Recommendations
Criminal sanctions	Politicians decide whether to implement recommendations

Link

The difference between a simple and a complex monopoly is discussed on page 46.

The jargon

An **actual monopoly** is one that already exists. A **potential monopoly** is one that might come about, either through the expansion of a company or through a merger or takeover.

The jargon

Market failure. When the market system brings about an inefficient allocation of resources.

Evaluation of UK policy

UK policy is more flexible than US policy, but the former generally is weaker and less consistent. US companies can be clearer about where they stand; they know in advance when they are likely to fall foul of the competition laws and can build this into their business plans.

In the UK, politicians often appear to be tougher on monopolies and mergers just before elections compared with just after elections. There is also a wide variety of institutions and quangos involved, including the Office of Fair Trading, the Department of Trade and Industry, the Competition Commission, trading standards offices and consumer groups.

However, in recent years attempts have been made to toughen up UK competition policy and to make it in some ways more 'American'. For example, some private-school headteachers were accused of price-fixing their fees among themselves and were threatened with a court case and even a possible prison sentence.

The European dimension

Companies over a certain size, measured in terms of turnover in euros per annum, can now be investigated by the competition authorities of the European Commission.

Proposed mergers between firms can also be prevented if those firms wish to operate within the single European market. The offices of cross-Channel ferry operators have been raided by EC officials, looking for evidence of price-fixing on the Channel Tunnel and sea routes. This type of action applies to European and non-European firms alike; a giant US electronics company, for example, was told that it could not take over a rival company if it wished to sell within the EU. Microsoft faced court action not only from the US authorities but also from the European Commission. Although the EC cannot send monopolists to prison, it can fine companies a percentage of their turnover, which is a significant sanction.

Checkpoint 1

Give one important advantage and one important disadvantage of the UK's flexible approach.

Checkpoint 2

Does the existence of such a wide range of interested organisations strengthen or weaken anti-monopoly policy?

The jargon

Quango. Quasi-autonomous non-government organisation: a semi-independent agency sponsored by the government either in an advisory role or with some executive function.

Check the net

For further information on anti-monopoly and pro-competition policy, see:
www.dti.gov.uk
www.competition-commission.org.uk/our_role
www.oft.gov.uk
www.europa.eu.int/comm/competition

Watch out!

In the USA, and sometimes in the EU, monopolies are known as trusts and competition policy is called anti-trust policy.

Exam question (30 minutes)   answer: page 64

In the past, utility industries, such as the postal service, electricity and gas, have been heavily protected by entry barriers. Evaluate the effects on efficiency and resource allocation of removing these barriers.

Market failure and welfare economics

As we have seen, the idea of a perfect market assumes a minimum amount of government intervention in the economy. However, governments *do* intervene in the economy at both the macro-level (see page 67 onwards) and the micro-level in relation to competition policy (see page 54). Here we begin further consideration of government micro policy.

Market failure

In reality, all economies are mixed to some extent, in that there is no such thing as a purely planned economy or a complete free-market economy with no government intervention. Even in Western democracies, traditionally described as mixed economies, there has been fierce debate about the degree of planning and the extent to which prices should be freely determined.

The strongest case for government intervention in the micro-economy arises from market failure. Market failure occurs for three reasons known widely to economists:

→ There is the resource misallocation that stems from any departure from perfect competition and the fact that monopolists seek to dominate markets and exploit consumers.

→ There is the slowness of markets to react to disequilibrium. Workers made redundant by the failure of one industry, for example, need government support during their transition period of retraining and seeking work in an alternative sector.

→ There are externalities. As economic development takes place, there is bound to be an increase in both the production and the consumption of goods and services. Production and consumption both involve the creation of costs and benefits; these costs and benefits can be internal or private (experienced only by the individual producer or consumer) or can be external or public (side effects experienced not only by the producer or consumer but also by the community at large). So, the full costs to society (social costs) of any act of production or consumption will consist of both the private costs and the public side effects, which could be positive or negative.

Welfare economists suggest that efficiency and welfare are increased if negative externalities are taxed (for example, the 'polluter pays' principle) and positive externalities are subsidised (for example, free primary education).

These actions internalise the externalities and force the producer or consumer to consider the full social costs (or benefits) of their actions. Thus, a firm polluting a river, for example, and relying on the taxpayer to pay for its dirty work could be forced by taxation to reflect the pollution costs in higher prices and/or lower profits. The 'polluter pays' idea receives a great deal of support today (in principle at least) from economists and politicians alike.

Checkpoint 1

What is meant by a 'mixed economy'?

The jargon

Internal or private costs and benefits. Those experienced only by the individual producer or consumer.

External or public costs and benefits. Side effects experienced not only by the producer or consumer but also by the community at large.

Social costs and benefits. The full costs and benefits to society of any act of production or consumption, consisting both the internal (private) costs and benefits and the external (public) side effects, which could be negative (costs) or positive (benefits).

Checkpoint 2

Give an example of a 'polluter pays' tax.

Cost–benefit analysis

Acts of production and consumption produce both benefits and costs:

→ **Benefits** can be defined as anything that adds to human welfare.
→ **Costs** can be defined as anything that subtracts from human welfare.

Some benefits and costs are easily quantifiable; some are more difficult to quantify. Cost–benefit analysis (CBA) is a method of appraising investment projects to see whether the long-term benefits outweigh the costs. CBA involves techniques such as:

→ **Shadow-pricing:** attempting to attach money values to such things as a nice view (a benefit) or a traffic jam (a cost).
→ **Discounting:** reducing the value of future costs and benefits to their present day equivalent.

The basic principle of CBA is that:

→ Internal benefits + external benefits = social benefits.
→ Internal costs + external costs = social costs.
→ Social benefits – social costs = net social product (NSP).

If a project appears to yield a positive NSP, then the economist's recommendation is likely to be that the project should go ahead, provided that costs and benefits are distributed fairly and justly. However, economists are often not very good at discussing 'fairness' and 'justice', and so CBA should properly be viewed as a means of putting more information in the public domain, so that those actually making decisions (business leaders, politicians) can make better-informed decisions, can be called upon to justify those decisions and can, therefore, be made more accountable.

Exam question (30 minutes)   answer: pages 64–5

Under what circumstances do markets fail? Where markets fail, do governments always succeed?

Public goods, merit goods

Should the railways be run for the national good or for private profit? Should university students receive grants or pay fees? Should the NHS be privatised or be run by the public sector? Understanding the key concepts of public goods theory helps you debate such questions from the economist's perspective.

Public goods and merit goods

Public goods are usually regarded as being best provided by the state because they are:

→ **Non-excludable:** individuals cannot be stopped from consuming them.
→ **Non-diminishable/non-rival:** one person's use does not deprive that of another.

Examples are national defence, law and order, and public-health measures such as clean air and the eradication of infectious diseases. Provision at all means provision for all, and it is unlikely that their provision could be achieved by any supplier other than the state, which has access through taxes to the funds necessary to provide them. Because of non-excludability and non-diminishability, no private supplier would offer a public good because it would be unable to exclude free riders.

Governments also find it necessary to intervene to provide goods and services that do not respond very well to price signals. These goods and services would be underconsumed at market price, because they are expensive but not wanted at all times. They are known as **merit goods**, and their essential feature is that they are high in positive externalities: that is, they benefit both the user and the non-user. Education and hospital treatment are examples. Spending on education and health produces a literate, numerate, physically fit workforce with consequent benefits in labour productivity.

Conversely, some goods are **demerit goods**, and their use imposes costs on the non-user: the effects of passive smoking on non-users of tobacco is an example.

Checkpoint 1

What do we mean by 'free riders'? Give an example.

The jargon

Economists often use the phrase 'public goods' when actually they are talking about services.

The effects of externalities

Main features	Public good	Mixed good (merit/demerit)	Private good
Diminishability/rivalry	Non-diminishable/non-rival	Diminishable/rival	Diminishable/rival
Excludability	Non-excludable	Excludable, but: → society decides that as many people as possible should be encouraged to be included (**merit goods**) → the price mechanism by itself does not sufficiently discourage people from using them (**demerit goods**)	Excludable
Examples	National defence, law and order, public health (e.g. mass vaccinations, sanitation), lighthouses	**Merit goods:** health (hospital treatment), education, environmentally friendly modes of transport **Demerit goods:** road transport, alcohol, tobacco, gambling	Televisions, clothes, baked beans, cornflakes, entertainment, holidays
Benefits	Communal (mainly positive externalities)	**Communal and individual** **Merit goods:** strong positive externalities **Demerit goods:** strong negative externalities	Individual (mainly internalities)
Provided by	Usually the government	Mixture of government and private sector	Usually the private sector
Financed by	Usually taxation (the 'ability to pay' principle)	Mixture of taxes and prices	Usually prices (the 'beneficial' principle)

The jargon

Taxes are generally based on the ability to pay (they are progressive, or increase with income). This means that better-off taxpayers contribute more to public services, even though they use them no more than less well-off taxpayers (in fact, the former might well use the services less). When public services are charged for, the people who benefit from them most are made to pay for them (the 'beneficial' principle).

Checkpoint 2

Is university education a merit good or a private good? Should it be financed by the ability to pay or by the beneficial principle?

Exam question (30 minutes) answer: page 65

What is meant by privatisation? What are the arguments for and against further involvement of the private sector in the provision of public services?

Answers
Costs, competition, monopoly and market failure

Diminishing returns and short-run costs

Checkpoints

1 • **Fixed:** rent, business rates, interest payments, most wage costs.
 • **Variable:** fuel, energy, raw materials, some wage costs, e.g. production bonuses.

2 It would normally take a matter of months to build an extension to a supermarket or a hotel. It is said that four or five fast-food outlets open somewhere in the world everyday, and once land is purchased and planning permission granted they have been known to be built in less than a week. It used to take about seven years for a steelworks to build a new blast furnace; this timescale has been reduced to two or three years by new building techniques. An airline might be able to purchase or lease an additional aircraft very quickly; the time taken to find landing and takeoff slots at established airports is another matter and might take years.

3 They are related closely. Variable costs are costs that vary directly with output. Marginal cost is the extra variable cost added to total cost by a small increase in output.

Exam question

(a)

Units of output	Total cost (£)	FC	VC	AFC	AVC	ATC	MC
0	50	50	0	∞	0	∞	–
1	80	50	30	50	30	80	30
2	128	50	78	25	39	64	48
3	180	50	130	16.7	43.3	60	52
4	280	50	230	12.5	57.5	70	100
5	405	50	355	10	71	81	125

(b)

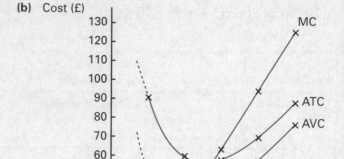

Cost (£)

Output (units)

(c) The falling ATC graph shows increasing efficiency, as greater use is made of productive capacity and there are increasing short run returns. The rising ATC graph shows falling efficiency, when productive capacity is overstretched and there are diminishing short run returns. Optimum use of existing productive capacity is made at the point where ATC is minimised; this can be identified as the point where MC = ATC.

Economies of scale and long-run costs

Checkpoints

1 Look at this from the point of view of the supplier. In one order they can clear production lines more quickly than from multiple orders, and with less paperwork, administration and transport costs. These efficiencies can be passed on to the customer in a discount.

2 These economies arise from within the firm, from the way in which the firm itself is organised. There are also **external economies**, which are cost-reducing influences that come from outside a firm, as the industry to which the firm belongs expand or a group of firms cluster in a particular region. Silicon Valley is a prime example of a cluster that enables firms to benefit from transport links, educational institutions, etc.

Exam question

(a) Let us take an example: small shops versus supermarkets. Small shops can give personal service; they can get closer to the customer, use smaller, more local suppliers, react quickly to changes in the market, and supply niche markets.

(b) Small firms can, sometimes, act together in order to obtain some economies of scale, e.g. the Spar and NISA organisations enable small retailers to buy in bulk and operate mass marketing. Small firms can also make use of changes in technology. Economies of scale depend on technology being **indivisible**, and as time goes on some technologies become more **divisible**. Computer technology is a clear example – it used to be available only to very large companies; now even the smallest firm can easily use more computer power than only a huge organisation could afford 20 years ago. The Internet, through developments such as eBay, enables small traders to supply niche markets. Some economists claim that the future lies in supplying millions of markets of dozens rather than dozens of markets of millions. Amazon.com makes more than half its profits from selling books whose market is too small for high-street bookshops to be interested in stocking them.

Costs, revenue and profit

Checkpoints

1 If P = price, TR = total revenue, Q = quantity demanded and AR = average revenue:
TR = P × Q (by definition)
But:
AR = TR/Q (also by definition)
Substituting for TR:
AR = P × Q/Q
Therefore:
AR = P

2 Marginal profit is the amount added to total profit by selling one more unit. Where total profit reaches its maximum, no more can be added; so MP = 0.

Exam question

In market theory, profit acts as an **incentive**: the existence of profit will motivate new firms to enter a market; the lack of profit will encourage loss-makers to leave a market (here, you need to discuss normal and supernormal profit). Profits are also an important factor in the growth of firms: the vast majority of business investment comes from retained profits being ploughed back.

Alternative pricing strategies

Checkpoints

1 The car industry. Partly this is due to the idea of minimum efficient scale (MES). This is the point on the long-run average cost curve where constant returns sets in. The further to the right this point occurs, the less room there is in the world for separate firms. In order to sell mass-produced family cars at an affordable price, the cars must be produced by the million, and so the MES for cars has moved to the right. There used to be over 20 separate car-makers in the UK alone; now about 20 mass car-makers

exist in the global market around the world. There are other factors as well as economies of scale: there could be more petrol producers in existence, still working beyond their MES, but 'barriers to entry' (see page 46) are being used to reduce competition. In some industries, new divisibilities (see above) are moving the MES to the left and enabling smaller firms to compete.

2 The production department wishes to produce maximum output at minimum cost; the marketing department might have little knowledge of costs, but will wish to maximise sales.

3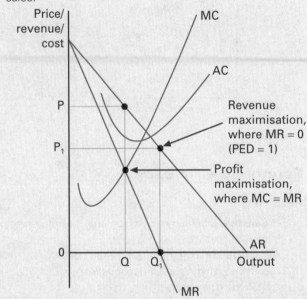

Price falls from P to P₁; quantity increases from Q to Q₁.

Exam question

Ethical policies are likely to add to costs: organic farming, for example, is more costly than non-organic farming. On the other hand, ethics can be used as a marketing tool: the answer to the question depends on whether the extra revenue produced outweighs the extra costs.

Short-run and long-run equilibrium under perfect competition

Checkpoints

1 Informative advertising conveys facts about a good or service. Persuasive advertising (**product differentiation** in economic jargon) tries to convince consumers that product A is in some way better than product B. The differentiation might be based on real or imaginary attributes of the product.

2 A small firm could, say, double its output and have no effect on the overall market price; equally, it could go out of business without any effect on price. This is not true of a large firm with a significant share of the market.

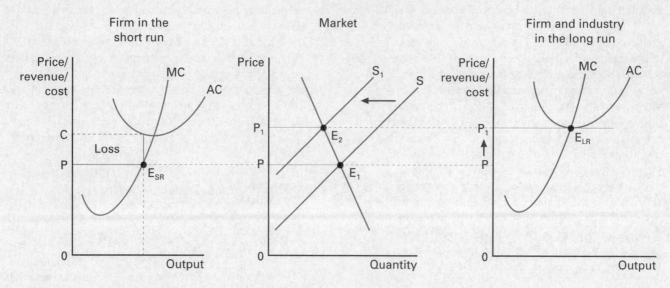

Firm in the short run — Market — Firm and industry in the long run

Economic efficiency

Checkpoints

1 • **Productive efficiency:** any given output is produced at minimum cost.
   • **Allocative efficiency:** changing existing resource allocation would make somebody better off and somebody else worse off.
2 Not necessarily. Some goods and services are subject to market failure (see page 56).

Exam question

Refer to the diagram in the answer to the previous exam question. Where costs are high in relation to market price, firms will leave the industry. Those firms that can produce most efficiently will remain. So while the industry as a whole contracts, individual surviving firms might expand. Examples include surviving companies in the UK coal and steel industries.

Competition and monopoly (1)

Checkpoints

1 Tariffs (taxes on imported goods) reduce international competition and can protect high-cost monopolies in the domestic market.
2 A pure monopoly would have absolutely no substitutes and, therefore, zero PED. In practice, even the strongest monopolies have some degree of substitution for their product and, therefore, some PED.

Exam question

(a) The basic cost is that monopolists raise the price by restricting output. This reduces productive efficiency (AC is no longer minimised). But allocative efficiency is also reduced: welfare is transferred from consumers to producers, who receive higher profits than before; and society as a whole suffers from an inefficient use of its scarce resources (known as a **deadweight loss**).

(b) Monopoly profits are not guaranteed. Simply having a monopoly does not mean that people will automatically buy your product. How profitable would a company be if it acquired a monopoly in supplying mud to the Glastonbury Festival? There are plenty of examples of loss-making monopolies. The Royal Mail, for example, has made losses in spite of its monopoly in delivering letters.

Competition and monopoly (2)

Checkpoints

1 Remember that AR = price. A falling AR means that the seller has to reduce price in order to sell each extra unit. In other words, MR is less than AR.
2 Examples:
   • A pharmaceutical company needs to invest huge amounts of money into research to develop a new medicine or cure. The promise of a number of years of monopoly on the formula is an incentive to make the investment.
   • The Royal Mail monopoly on letter delivery creates economies of scale in delivering to large population centres. Some of the revenues can then be used to cross-subsidise deliveries to rural areas and remote places.

Exam question

• **Advantages:** lower prices, higher output, increased efficiency.
• **Disadvantages:** loss of economies of scale; smaller firms might eventually be swallowed up by larger firms, creating a new monopoly. This has happened, for example, where private bus companies have replaced public-sector transport monopolies.

Imperfect competition: monopolistic competition, oligopoly

Checkpoints

1 Petrol, cosmetics, breakfast cereal, paint, newspapers.
2 Monopolistic competition is less economically efficient than perfect competition, as output is lower and price is higher. However, there are normal profits in the long run, and so efficiency is greater than under monopoly, where supernormal profits can continue into the long run.
3 • **Dominant:** British Airways on long-haul services out of Heathrow.
  • **Barometric:** easyJet on short-haul services from regional airports.

Exam question

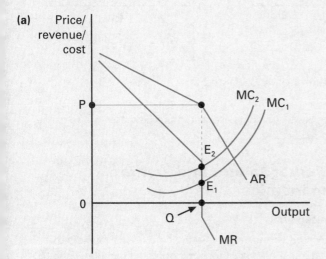

(a)

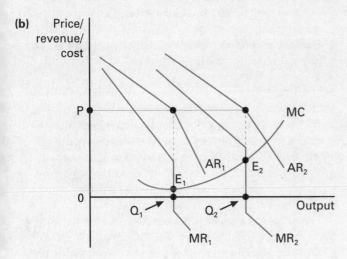

(b)

The diagrams show that oligopolistic companies can, at least for a time, avoid altering prices by:
• Absorbing cost changes and accepting different profit margins.
• Reacting to a change in demand by varying output.

Price discrimination

Checkpoints

1 Up to a point. There are two separate markets here, with different PEDs. Many first-class passengers are travelling on expenses, with tickets bought by their companies, and so PED is lower than in standard class, where more passengers buy their own tickets. However, it can be argued that the two sets of travellers are not buying the same product: they are travelling to the same destination, but in different surroundings. In first class, for example, the seats are larger and there is more leg room; passengers get 'free' coffee and newspapers, and so the train company's costs are higher. If the difference in ticket prices is not entirely explained by cost differences, then there is an element of price discrimination.
2 'Yes' is a reasonable answer. Universities incur the same costs whatever the income of the student's family, and these are identifiable separate markets with differing PEDs.

Exam question

The diagram overleaf shows two distinct markets, A and B, and the overall demand curve of the combined market, C. In market C, the equilibrium output is Q_C and this is sold at price P_C. Profit is shown by the area Z. If this monopolistic market can now be split into two, each segment with different PEDs at any given price, and if customers can be kept separate, then part of the output can be sold on each separate market, and two different prices will operate (the consumers with the lower PED paying the higher price). The marginal cost and the average cost of production will be determined on the combined market, and so the output and price on the separate markets will depend on where MC for the combined output is equal to MR for the individual market. The supernormal profit from market A is shown by area X, and from market B by area Y. Price discrimination is worthwhile for the producer if $X + Y > Z$.

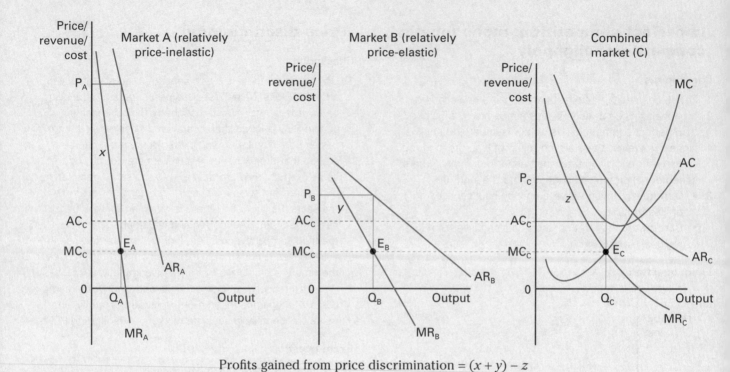

Market A (relatively price-inelastic) · Market B (relatively price-elastic) · Combined market (C)

Profits gained from price discrimination = $(x + y) - z$

Monopoly and competition policy

Checkpoints

1 • **Advantage:** monopolies can be dealt with on a case-by-case basis. For example, if it is considered that closing down a monopoly would create an unacceptable level of unemployment in a particular town or region, then policy can be softened.
  • **Disadvantage:** uncertainty and inconsistency are created. Growing companies do not know exactly where they stand in relation to competition policy; action is open to political interference.
2 On the one hand, a wide range of interested observers means that monopolies are subjected to constant scrutiny and vigilance. On the other hand, responsibility is diluted and action against monopoly therefore is weakened.

Exam question

One of the main entry barriers was a legal barrier: the telephone monopoly of the General Post Office (GPO) and later British Telecom (BT) was protected by law. It now seems unthinkable that BT should be the only telephone provider and that in those days we had to join a long waiting list for telephones (nowadays there is cut-throat competition, with companies falling over themselves to supply us with mobiles and networks). Prices have fallen, supply has increased and efficiency has improved. However, it is very doubtful whether replacing a nationalised monopoly with a privatised one will do anything for efficiency and resource allocation. In those utilities where efficiency has clearly increased, there have been technological changes that have helped break up the natural monopoly; for example, in the telephone market, the dependence on copper-wire technology has been replaced by microwave radio and satellite technology, allowing more new entrants to gain a foothold in the market.

Market failure and welfare economics

Checkpoints

1 **Mixed economy:** one with some use of markets to address the basic problems of production (see page 58), together with some use of centralised planning and government intervention.
2 **Fuel tax escalator:** the arrangement by which taxes on petrol and diesel increase each year.

Exam question

Market failure can be predicted to occur where there is monopoly, oligopoly, externalities, public goods and communal property rights (property owned by society as a whole). In such cases, decisions made by individuals might not result in the most efficient outcomes for the wider community, and so the use of market forces might not be the best way of allocating resources.

The existence of market failure provides an argument for government intervention to correct the failure, e.g. by taxing negative externalities, subsidising positive externalities and providing public goods. However, it should by no means be assumed that governments always get things right: due to inadequate information, lack of resources or sheer incompetence, there is the possibility of **government failure**. We do not have a straight choice between perfect governments and imperfect markets; at the same time, neither is it a case of 'markets: good; and governments: bad'. Instead, we have to decide on the balance between methods of resource allocation, which are always bound to be imperfect. Ultimately, this is not a purely economic problem but is concerned with the type of society in which we live. For example, prisons used to be run entirely in the public sector, but now we have some privatised prisons. These might or might not be economically efficient, but many people feel that there is something morally wrong with the idea of paying companies to imprison people for profit.

Public goods, merit goods

Checkpoints

1 **Free riders:** people who benefit from a public good, a merit good or a positive externality without contributing to it themselves. For example, the car driver who does not fit an efficient exhaust system but benefits from the fact that everyone else has done so.

2 On this point, some politicians have spoken with forked tongue. The argument that the country needs to increase the university population to a target figure, such as 60% of school-leavers, suggests a public good and is an argument for the ability to pay principle (payment through taxes). On the other hand, the suggestion that graduates should pay more because of their higher potential earning power suggests a private good and is an argument for the beneficial principle (tuition fees). Some politicians have used both arguments at once.

Exam question

Privatisation has involved several features:

- The conversion of nationalised businesses into public limited companies with shareholders, e.g. BT, British Gas, British Airways, coal, steel.
- The opening up of some public services (in whole or part) to private-sector contractors, e.g. prisons, school meals, train services, bits of the NHS.
- Deregulation, allowing greater competition in areas previously protected by law, e.g. bus services, mail delivery.
- Market testing and contracting out, whereby some public service departments have to compete with private sector contractors, e.g. RAF aircraft maintenance, local-authority refuse collection.

Arguments for and against further privatisation, from the point of view of an economist, should be made by relating specific examples to the general principles discussed in this and previous sections: public goods, private goods and mixed goods; externalities; the ability to pay and the beneficial principles; market failure and government failure.

Revision checklist
Costs, competition, monopoly, market failure

By the end of this chapter you should be able to:

1	Explain how short-run cost curves are related to the law of diminishing returns.	Confident	Not confident. **Revise** pages 34–5
2	Explain the effect on long-run costs of returns to scale.	Confident	Not confident. **Revise** pages 36–7
3	Discuss the importance to firms of profits.	Confident	Not confident. **Revise** pages 38–9
4	Evaluate alternative objectives of firms.	Confident	Not confident. **Revise** pages 40–41
5	Explain how perfect competition leads to short- and long-run equilibrium.	Confident	Not confident. **Revise** pages 42–3
6	Discuss the implications of perfect competition to economic efficiency.	Confident	Not confident. **Revise** pages 44–5
7	Draw a diagram to show what happens to price and quantity when a perfectly competitive market is monopolised. Explain what happens to efficiency.	Confident	Not confident. **Revise** pages 46–9
8	Draw a diagram to show what happens to price and quantity if a monopoly results in economies of scale. Explain what is meant by the term 'natural monopoly'.	Confident	Not confident. **Revise** pages 48–9
9	Give a list of reasons why monopoly may be undesirable. Give a list of circumstances where monopoly can be defended.	Confident	Not confident. **Revise** pages 46–9
10	Explain why governments control monopolies. Explain the difference between legal and administrative means for controlling monopolies. Discuss the effectiveness of UK anti-monopoly policy.	Confident	Not confident. **Revise** pages 54–5
11	Explain the implications of price discrimination.	Confident	Not confident. **Revise** pages 52–3
12	Distinguish between monopolistic competition and oligopoly.	Confident	Not confident. **Revise** pages 50–51
13	Define the following terms and give examples: internality, externality, internal cost, external cost, social cost, internal benefit, external benefit, social benefit, net social product.	Confident	Not confident. **Revise** pages 56–7
14	With the help of as many examples as possible, explain the difference between public goods and private goods in terms of rivalry/diminishability and excludability.	Confident	Not confident. **Revise** pages 58–9
15	Give examples of mixed goods. Explain the difference between merit and demerit goods.	Confident	Not confident. **Revise** pages 58–9
16	Explain the difference between the beneficial principle of payment for goods and services and the ability-to-pay principle.	Confident	Not confident. **Revise** pages 58–9

We now consider the whole economy as a system, and appraise economic policy at the national and international level.

Exam themes

→ The nature of macroeconomics; relationships between variables

→ Aims of macro-policy

→ Demand management and supply-side policy

→ Economic indicators and their uses

→ Macro-problems: causes, consequences, policies

→ The European dimension

→ International issues

Topic checklist

AS O   A2 ●

	Edexcel	AQA	OCR	WJEC	CCEA
Micro, macro, the circular flow of income				O	O
Macroeconomic indicators	O	O	O	O	O
Traditional aims of macroeconomic policy	O●	O●	O●	O●	O●
Supply side: microenvironment of macro-policy	O●	O●	O●	O●	O●
Rules-based budgetary policy	O●	O●	O●	O●	O
Inflation targeting, interest-rate policy, output gaps	O●	O●	O●	O●	O●
Relationships in macro-theory	O●	O●	O●	O●	O
GDP, AD and AS in the UK	O	O	O	O	O
Uses and limitations of GDP league tables	O●	O●	O●	●	O●
Underlying concepts: saving, investment, multiplier	O	O	O●	O	O
Economic growth and sustainability	O	●	●	●	●
Definitions and measures of inflation	O	O●	O	●	
Consequences (costs) of inflation	O●	O●	O●	O●	O
Demand pull and cost push inflation	O●	O●	O●	O●	O
Measures of unemployment	O●	●	O	●	O
Causes of unemployment	O●	O●	O●	O●	O
Consequences (costs) of unemployment	●	●	O	●	O
Stop–go policies	O●	O●	O●	O●	O●
The simple Phillips curve tradeoff	●	●	●	●	
Expectations-augmented Phillips curve	●	●	●	●	
The nature and importance of international trade	O	●	●	●	●
Free trade versus protection	●	●	O●	O●	●
Fixed and floating exchange rates	●	O●	O●	O●	
EU issues		●	●		
Potential costs and benefits of UK membership of the euro	●	●	●	●	●
The eurozone's Growth and Stability Pact	●	●	●	●	
International institutions	●		●	●	●

Micro, macro, the circular flow of income

Macroeconomics has changed considerably in recent years. The good news is that in many ways it has become less complicated. Before we can understand and evaluate government macroeconomic policy, we need to understand some basic concepts. When we move from microeconomics to macroeconomics, we move from studying parts of the economy towards studying the economy as a whole.

Micro and macro

The table below summarises the main differences between microeconomics and macroeconomics.

	Micro	Macro
From the Greek	*Mikros*, meaning small	*Makros*, meaning large
Deals with	Sectors, markets	Aggregates, totals
Focuses on	Individual consumer choices, business decisions	Government policy, international economic relations
At the level of	Localities, regions, firms, industries	Nations, international organisations, global institutions
Typical questions include	What determines the price of potatoes? What determines the demand for labour in the steel industry? What determines the distribution of income?	What determines the rate of inflation? What determines the national level of employment/ unemployment? What determines the level of national income?

The distinction between microeconomics and macroeconomics should be regarded as a way of making the study of economics more manageable. It is a convenience, but there are many overlaps between micro and macro. For example:

→ The **level** of income and wealth (a macro-concept) is linked closely with the **distribution** of income and wealth (a micro-concept). In economies where a small percentage of the population holds a large proportion of the country's assets, then these inequalities may well become dysfunctional, with industrial conflict and social unrest reducing economic growth and development.

→ **Unemployment** traditionally is viewed as a macro-problem. These days, most of the long-term solutions to this problem are viewed as residing at the micro-level; these include policies for competitiveness, education and skills.

Checkpoint 1

Think of another way in which the level of income and wealth might be linked to their distribution.

The circular flow of income

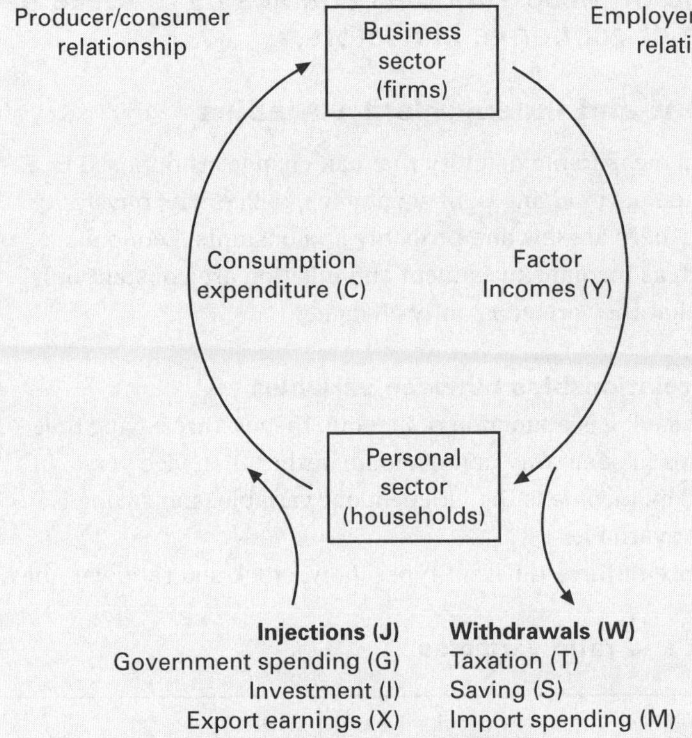

Producer/consumer relationship

Employer/employee relationship

Business sector (firms)

Consumption expenditure (C)

Factor Incomes (Y)

Personal sector (households)

Injections (J)
Government spending (G)
Investment (I)
Export earnings (X)

Withdrawals (W)
Taxation (T)
Saving (S)
Import spending (M)

Circular flow of income

Checkpoint 2

The diagram shows only two sectors in the economy, and shows only money flows between these sectors. Identify three other sectors, and describe the real flows that correspond to the money flows in all five sectors.

In the diagram above, businesses and households react in two ways:

→ **Producers and consumers:** household expenditure (C, consumption) flows to firms to pay for goods and services.
→ **Employers and employees:** incomes (Y) flow from firms to households to pay for the services of factors of production (wages, interest, rent and profit pay for labour, capital, land and enterprise, respectively).
→ Money not passed on in the circular flow is known as a withdrawal:
  → S = saving
  → T = taxation
  → M = import spending
→ Money entering the circular flow is known as an injection:
  → I = investment
  → G = government spending
  → X = export earnings

Exam question (25 minutes)   answer: page 122

(a) Explain the statement: 'One person's spending is another person's income.'

(b) Discuss what is likely to happen to national income if injections differ from withdrawals.

Macroeconomic indicators

Analysis of the circular flow of income involves examining relationships between economic variables. Knowledge of these variables enables us to make use of a range of economic indicators.

Checkpoint 1

Cast your mind back to the physics or maths that you studied earlier as part of the National Curriculum. Give an example of a constant with which you have worked. Why is it unlikely that there are many constants in economics?

Dependent and independent variables ●●●

A variable is a measurable quantity that can change, as opposed to a constant, which never changes. In economics, unlike, say, physics or mathematics, there are few and probably no constants. Economic variables such as income, investment and inflation are constant only in the sense that they are constantly changing.

Functional relationships between variables

If we say that saving is a function of income, then we are saying that saving depends in some way upon income, rather than vice versa. In this relationship, income is the independent variable, and saving is the dependent variable.

Variables are of three different types, flow, stock and ratio variables.

Flow, stock and ratio variables

Examiner's secrets

Very often in economics exams you need to give a definition of a term. Often, candidates define terms very badly. A good way to start any definition is to state whether the concept is a stock, flow or ratio concept. If it is one of the items in the circular flow of income, then you should also state whether it is an injection or a withdrawal. For example: 'Investment is a flow variable, measured over a time period. It is an injection into the circular flow. It measures spending on capital goods.'

	Flows	Stocks	Ratios
Main feature	Have a time dimension: measured per hour, per week, per year, etc.	Have no time dimension: measured at a point in time	Are neither simple stocks nor flows. Might or might not have a time dimension. Calculated by multiplying or dividing flows and flows, stocks and stocks, or flows and stocks
Everyday example	Speed of a car: measured by mph = distance covered over time	Weight of a car: measured by tons or kilos, at a point in time	Fuel consumption of a car: measured by mpg = the number of miles covered over a time period, divided by the volume of petrol over the same time period, i.e. the division of two flows
Examples from economics	Income, investment, production, saving	Wealth, capital, savings	Inflation, unemployment rate, productivity, exchange rate

Leading indicators and lagging indicators

A lead indicator is an indicator that can tell us something about the future. For example, if interest rates are reduced, we can predict that national income will increase. Refer to the circular flow diagram on page 69. A higher interest rate will affect this diagram in several ways, for example:

→ **Lower consumption:** many major household purchases are financed by borrowings. A higher mortgage rate, for example, leaves families with less disposable income for consumption purposes.
→ **Lower injections:** investment will fall as the cost of financing business investment rises.
→ **Higher withdrawals:** higher interest rates make saving more attractive.

Taking these points together, the diagram shows us clearly that we can expect the flow of national income and, therefore, national spending (in total, the level of economic activity) to decrease.

A lagging indicator tells us something about how the economy has behaved in the recent past. For example, a fall in the inflation rate suggests that demand may have declined recently.

Indicators can often be **leading** and **lagging** at the same time. For example, if a fall in the unemployment rate is announced, then this suggests that in the recent past injections have increased and/or withdrawals have fallen, so that the level of economic activity has increased, and so has the demand for labour, in order to produce the output being demanded. Looking ahead, we can predict that this extra level of demand might pull up the rate of inflation at some time in the future.

Checkpoint 2

How might a higher interest rate affect imports and exports?

Check the net

UK economic indicators are updated every week on the Treasury website: www.treasury.gov.uk.
International indicators can be investigated at www.nationmaster.com.

Exam question (15 minutes)   answer: page 122

Choose the correct answer, explain why it is correct, and explain why the alternatives are incorrect:

Close to £20 billion is expected to be spent using credit cards by the end of December, a 10% increase on the same period last year. BBC News

The most likely consequence of this increase in spending is a rise in:

(a) imports

(b) unemployment

(c) household savings

(d) exports

Traditional aims of macroeconomic policy

Macroeconomic policy has changed considerably in recent years, leaving most textbooks at least slightly out of date.

In order to be able to comment critically on current macroeconomic policy, it is necessary first to make sure you understand the main objectives and methods of traditional policy.

Stabilisation policy

When we say 'traditional', we are referring to the way in which Western governments tried to control their economies in the 30 years or so following the Second World War; that is, from the late 1940s to the 1980s. Governments were using Keynesian techniques, i.e. policies influenced by the economist John Maynard Keynes.

Macroeconomic policy is sometimes referred to as stabilisation policy. This is because it is recognised that the economy is affected by the booms and slumps of the business cycle, and that governments have a role in stabilising or smoothing out the peaks and troughs of economic activity.

→ A **boom** (or recovery) occurs when an economy's output is growing, unemployment is falling and incomes are rising.
→ A **slump** (or recession) occurs when output is falling, unemployment is rising and incomes are falling.

The four main aims of traditional stabilisation policy are usually given as:

→ Stable prices.
→ Balance of payments equilibrium.
→ Full employment.
→ Steady growth.

Stable prices are important for a country's competitiveness and so are linked closely to the balance of payments. Full employment is linked closely to economic growth, since one is difficult to achieve without the other. It is possible to reduce these four problem areas to two key issues: inflation and unemployment.

In recent years, the objectives of government policy have changed, as have government priorities. Whereas it used to be thought that the government's first priority should be to tackle unemployment, now inflation is an overriding concern, and it is widely believed that tackling inflation in the first instance will lead eventually to the solving of other problems.

Until the end of the 1970s, the policies that governments used to achieve their objectives were known as demand-management techniques. These are essentially short-run techniques. They take the supply-side conditions of the economy, such as its productive capacity, as being given and attempt to increase employment or reduce inflation by increasing or decreasing total demand in the economy. Total demand in the economy is known as **aggregate demand**.

Aggregate demand can be increased or decreased in two broad ways:

→ **Monetary policy** affects the supply of money in the economy by influencing the amount of lending by banks and other institutions and the price of credit or the interest rate. A **restrictive** monetary policy consists of credit controls and high interest rates. An **expansive** monetary policy consists of easy credit and low interest rates.

→ **Budgetary policy**, sometimes known as fiscal policy, affects demand by working on taxation and government spending. A **deflationary** budgetary policy consists of lower government spending and higher taxes. Higher taxes reduce people's disposable incomes and, therefore, reduce consumer demand. A **reflationary** budgetary policy consists of higher government spending and lower taxes. Lower taxes increase people's disposable incomes and, therefore, increase consumer demand.

Traditional stabilisation policy used monetary policy to set the scene or to establish the general atmosphere (restrictive, thus discouraging spending, or expansive, thus encouraging spending). Budgetary policy was then used to fine-tune the economy; that is, to attempt to hit particular inflation or employment targets with either a deflationary or reflationary budget.

An important problem with reflationary budgets is that they can also be inflationary. With higher government spending at the same time as lower taxation, there might be a budget deficit. Critics of deficit financing, as it is called, accuse governments of causing inflation by, in effect, 'printing money' to cover their deficits.

Conflict between policies ●●●

A major problem with trying to influence short-run demand is that objectives can conflict. For example, lower unemployment might lead to increased inflation. This could occur for demand-pull or cost-push reasons (see page 94).

Another tradeoff is between the internal and external economies. Full employment at home will lead to higher incomes; however, higher incomes can lead to balance-of-payments difficulties. This has been a major cause of the stop–go policies that Britain has traditionally suffered from, or, as politicians tend to say nowadays: 'Boom and bust.'

Checkpoint 1

In the early 1970s, a massive increase in the world price of oil was said to be inflationary and deflationary at the same time. Explain why.

Link

We shall see on page 74 onwards that this has changed completely in recent years. In the short term, day-to-day monetary policy is governed by the interest rate; in the medium term, budgetary policy is rules-based; in the long run, supply-side policies are used to boost productivity and output.

Checkpoint 2

Explain why higher incomes are likely to lead to balance-of-payments difficulties.

Exam question (20 minutes)   answer: page 123

Evaluate the consequences of a sustained high rate of economic growth.

Supply side:
microenvironment of

Today there is considerable overlap between micro- and macro-policy. Whereas the Treasury used to be concerned solely with matters such as taxes, public spending and interest rates, now the Chancellor of the Exchequer takes a close interest in productivity and comments regularly on matters such as efficiency and skills, which used to be the sole preserve of ministers with responsibility for trade, industry, employment and education.

Microeconomic environment ●●●

The main features of New Labour supply-side policies are:

→ **Active labour-market policies:** these policies support flexible working practices as opposed to the flexible labour markets favoured by the previous Conservative government.

→ **Welfare to work:** whereas measured unemployment is at record low levels, there are large numbers of people claiming incapacity benefit. Until the mid 1990s, most doctors' certificates for incapacity stated that people were unfit for work due to musculoskeletal problems; today, most incapacity claims are for mental health problems. In effect, backache has been replaced by stress as the main reason why people claim they cannot work. Trying to convince people who have been off work long-term, 'on the sick', is now a major challenge for government policy-makers.

→ **Productivity:** Britain's productivity is approximately 20% lower than that of France and Germany, and 30% lower than that of the USA. The UK's total output is comparable to that of France and Germany, but this is achieved through our long-hours culture. In other words, French and German workers can achieve similar living standards to those of British workers, but with a shorter working week and with longer holidays. Britain has the worst of both worlds: it has US-style working hours with below-European productivity levels.

The jargon

Supply-side. Policies aimed at improving the productivity and output of the economy. Such policies often focus on what is called **human capital**, e.g. policies for improving education and training. In their widest sense, supply-side policies also include policies for increased competition and investment in infrastructure such as transport. In the 1980s, supply-side policy was interpreted in a narrower way, to signify policies to enable employers to hire and fire without trade-union resistance.

Checkpoint 1

Explain the difference between flexible working practices and flexible labour markets.

Checkpoint 2

Suggest possible economic reasons why stress has replaced backache as a major cause of incapacity.

macro-policy

→ **Competition and monopoly:** attempts to make Britain more competitive are part of supply-side policy. Many experts believe that competition policy in the UK has traditionally been too weak, and this is summarised by the phrase 'rip-off Britain'. The USA has always had much more vigorous anti-monopoly laws. However, the EU now has a major role in this area.

Effects of supply-side policy ●●●

Supply-side policies, if successful, increase the **productive capacity** of the country. They take time to work, and therefore they are essentially long-run policies. They shift the aggregate supply curve to the right, and this generally takes longer than shifting the aggregate demand curve, which is the aim of demand-management policy in the short-run.

Checkpoint 3

Distinguish between production and productivity.

Link

See monopoly and competition policy on page 54.

Exam question (30 minutes) answer: page 123

What is the more effective way of running the UK economy: demand-management or supply-side policy?

Rules-based budgetary policy

Economists used to talk about discretionary budgetary policy. Now they talk about budgetary policy as being rules-based. What has changed?

Fiscal and budgetary policy

The word 'fiscal' refers to anything to do with taxation. The word 'budgetary' refers to anything to do with taxation and public spending. Strictly speaking, then, the term 'budgetary policy' is a wider concept than 'fiscal policy'. However, economists generally use these phrases interchangeably.

The end of discretionary budgetary policy

Some economics textbooks will tell you that budgetary policy is used for stabilisation purposes, i.e. to increase or decrease the level of aggregate demand.

In Britain, this is no longer the case, and such textbooks are out of date. Discretionary budgetary policy had the following problems:

→ **In times of recession:** taxes would be reduced and government spending would be increased in order to boost aggregate demand. Higher spending together with lower taxes would put the government's budget into deficit; this deficit led to government borrowing. This government borrowing had several effects:
  → Some critics argued that government borrowing and spending would crowd out the private sector. In other words, the only overall difference to the economy would be that the government sector got bigger while the business sector got smaller.
  → At some stage, the government would have to repay its debts and would be tempted to do this by, in effect, printing more money. This would be inflationary.
  → Even if the government could repay its debts without printing money, the chances were that lower taxes now would lead to higher taxes later. So, future generations would pay the price of our current spending.
→ **In times of boom:** taxes would be increased and public spending would be reduced. This would help to reduce inflationary pressure, but:
  → Government projects might have to be curtailed, but the idea of half-finished motorways or abandoned new school building sites was never a very attractive option.
  → Long-term planning would be harmed by a stop–go or boom and bust cycle.

Link

See the section on interest-rate targeting on page 78.

Checkpoint 1

Suppose the government decided that it would reduce taxes in order to boost the economy. How would the Monetary Policy Committee of the Bank of England react?

The new rules

In the late 1990s, Chancellor Gordon Brown replaced discretionary budgetary policy with the following budgetary rules:

→ **The 'golden rule':** this states that over an economic cycle, the government will borrow only for investment purposes. In effect, this means that over a period of years, government borrowing will be cancelled out by government surpluses (apart from borrowing for investment).

→ **The 'sustainable investment' rule:** this states that government borrowing should never exceed 40% of GDP.

Points to note

→ These so-called 'rules' are self-imposed: nobody has forced the Chancellor to adopt them. Their main purpose is to give international money markets the confidence that the UK is serious about controlling inflation and stabilising the exchange rate of the pound.

→ There is some debate about the meaning of the phrase 'economic cycle'. The success of budgetary policy during one cycle depends on when it is decided that the cycle starts and ends. This can affect the success of the next cycle.

→ There is nothing special about the 40% figure. In the eurozone, the European Central Bank's members have chosen a figure of 60%.

Checkpoint 2

The Chancellor of the Exchequer often uses the phrase 'boom and bust'. Exactly what does this phrase mean?

Exam question (30 minutes)   answer: pages 123–4

(a) Explain the main economic reasons for government spending.

(b) To what extent is it important for the UK government to maintain a balanced budget?

Inflation targeting, interest-rate policy, output gaps

Most advanced economies around the world use inflation targeting as their main macroeconomic policy, with interest rates as the main weapon of monetary policy. The **output gap** is an important indicator used in setting interest rates.

Link

The index of consumer prices method of measuring inflation. See page 90.

Checkpoint 1

The target is a symmetrical one, meaning that the MPC is allowed to hit a level of inflation one percentage point either side of the target. What reasons are there for having a symmetrical target?

Contemporary macroeconomic policy management ●●●

→ Since 1992, both Conservative and Labour governments in the UK have used the interest rate as their most important tool of monetary policy in order to achieve a target rate of inflation set by the Chancellor.

→ Since 1997, interest rates have been set independently of the Treasury at the monthly meetings of the Bank of England's Monetary Policy Committee (MPC). Shortly after becoming Chancellor of the Exchequer in 1997, Gordon Brown handed responsibility for setting interest rates to the MPC. The MPC's brief is to target inflation at an annual rate of 2.0%.

→ In order to achieve this target, the MPC has to consider various economic indicators. One important indicator is known as the **output gap**.

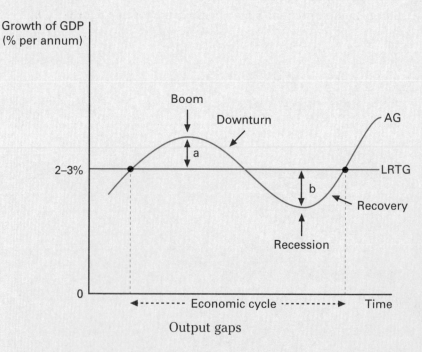

Output gaps

→ Output-gap theory compares actual output with potential or **non-inflationary output**. The latter is shown as a **trend growth** line. Based on UK performance over the past 100 years or so, it is believed that in the UK a growth rate of between 2% and 3% per annum is sustainable without excessive inflation. In the diagram, LRTG is long-run trend growth and AG is actual growth.

→ It is assumed that inflation is demand-led and that demand is affected by interest rates.

Checkpoint 2

Why would a change in interest rates affect demand?

→ When there is growth above the trend line, we have an output gap (overstretched capacity), where inflation is likely due to supply bottlenecks. We can expect interest rates to be increased. The output gap is a maximum at a in the diagram.
→ Where there is growth below the trend line, we have a negative output gap, or spare capacity. The negative output gap is a maximum at b in the diagram. We can expect interest rates to be reduced. However, it might be believed that there may be inflationary trends even with spare capacity, depending on the actual amount of spare capacity, the speed with which the output gap is being closed, and the extent to which spare capacity is usable, given such things as skills shortages.

How effective is inflation-targeting policy?

For the first time in over 200 years, Britain has had more than a decade of:

→ uninterrupted economic growth, with
→ low inflation, and
→ falling unemployment.

However:

→ Interest rates in the UK are higher than in the eurozone, the USA and Japan.
→ The 'single golf club' of the interest rate has several associated problems, for example:
  → It increases the cost of living through its effect on mortgage rates, so that an immediate effect of anti-inflation policy is actually to increase the measured rate of inflation.
  → It increases industrial costs when companies need to borrow in order to re-equip.
  → It pulls up the exchange rate and makes exporting more difficult.
  → It hits the less prosperous regions such as the north-west harder than more prosperous areas such as the south-east.
  → It hits certain sectors, such as manufacturing and domestic tourism, harder than others, such as clothing retailers.
→ The MPC is sometimes accused of paying too much attention to the overheated housing market in the south-east.

Link

See the section on the housing market on page 148.

Check the net

www.treasury.gov.uk
www.bankofengland.co.uk
www.ons.gov.uk

Exam question (30 minutes) answer: page 124

'The UK has a stable economy, but it is an unbalanced economy.' Discuss.

Relationships in macro-theory

Here, we bring together four important tools of macro-economic theory, which are dealt with separately on other pages. It is important that you are able to see how these different items of macro-theory link up with each other.

Theoretical tools in macroeconomics ●●●

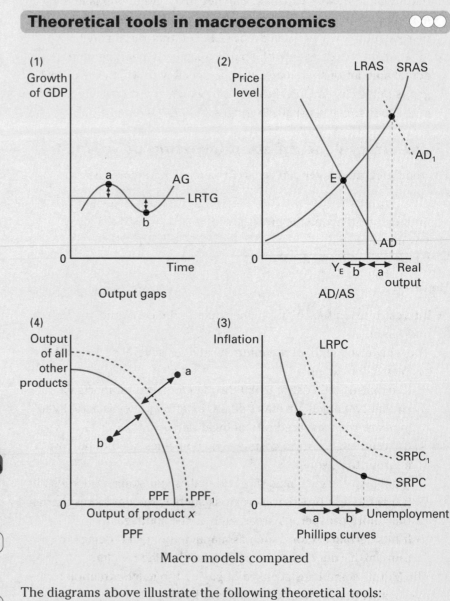

Macro models compared

The diagrams above illustrate the following theoretical tools:

1 Output gap diagram.
2 AD/AS analysis.
3 Phillips curve.
4 Production possibility frontier (PPF).

Each of these diagrams can be used to show potential output, actual output, output gaps, the effect of short-run demand management (interest-rate policy) on actual output, and the effect of long-run supply-side policy on potential output (productive capacity).

Checkpoint 1

Distinguish between an output gap and a negative output gap.

Link

See AD/AS analysis on page 94.

Link

See the Phillips curve discussion on page 104.

Link

The production possibility frontier was discussed as part of microeconomic theory on page 4. It is also useful in macroeconomics.

Diagram	1	2	3	4
Potential output indicated by	Horizontal line LRTG (long-run trend growth)	Vertical line LRAS (long-run aggregate supply)	Vertical line LRPC (long-run Phillips curve)	PPF
Actual output indicated by	Cyclical line AG (actual growth)	Equilibrium level of income, Y_E, where AD = AS	Economy's position on the short-run Phillips curve (SRPC)	Economy's position within the PPF
Output gap indicated at point **a**, where	AG is greater than LRTG	AD is beyond LRAS	Unemployment is below level of LRPC	Planned demand is beyond productive capacity
Negative output gap indicated at point **b**, where	AG is less than LRTG	AD is below LRAS	Unemployment is above level of LRPC	There is underutilised productive capacity
Purpose of demand-management policy in the short run is to	Reduce the difference between AG and LRTG by reducing the size of the troughs (lower interest rates) and peaks (higher interest rates) in AG	Shift AD to the right (lower interest rates) or to the left (higher interest rates)	Move the economy along the SRPC, to the left (lower interest rates) or to the right (higher interest rates)	Change the degree of utilisation of capacity, moving the economy outwards (lower interest rates) or inwards (higher interest rates)
Purpose of supply-side policy in the long run is to increase productivity and potential growth and hence	Shift the horizontal line LRTG upwards	Shift the vertical line LRAS to the right	Shift the vertical line LRPC to the left	Shift the PPF outwards

Checkpoint 2

Notice that the short-run Phillips curve (SRPC) is a mirror image of the short-run aggregate supply curve (SRAS). Explain why this is so.

Exam question (15 minutes)   answer: page 124

Refer to the production possibility diagram. In what sense might it be said that point a is unattainable?

GDP, AD and AS in the UK

National-income figures are used widely in tracing the economic progress of a country and in making international comparisons. Here we look at some of the basic concepts. You need a good knowledge and understanding of these concepts before you can apply them.

Gross domestic product at factor cost

National income can be defined in three ways. It is the total value of:

→ output of goods and services; or
→ incomes earned; or
→ expenditure

... in one country in one year.

An important part of economic theory is the principle that on a national level the following aggregates or totals are equal to each other: output, income and expenditure. The basic principle is quite simple: one person's spending is another person's income, and it is also another person's output. For example, if I buy a new bicycle, then my expenditure represents income for the people selling the bike, and what I am buying is part of the output of the bicycle industry.

A common statistic used to measure national income is gross domestic product (GDP) at factor cost. Let us break down this phrase.

→ **Gross** = before depreciation. If an allowance is made for depreciation or wear and tear of productive assets, then the figure is **net**.
→ **Domestic** = produced within the geographical boundaries of the home country. The gross **national** product includes earnings from UK-owned assets, regardless of where they are located.
→ **Factor cost** = cost measured in terms of the cost of resources used up, as opposed to measured in terms of **market prices**, which might be increased by taxes or reduced by subsidies.

The components of aggregate supply and aggregate demand

GDP, in terms of output, can be described as aggregate supply (AS). This comes from the output of different industrial sectors: the primary sector (agriculture, mining, quarrying and energy), the secondary sector (manufacturing and construction), and the tertiary sector (services, distribution and tourism).

In the circular flow of income, AS = AD, and so:

$$Y = C + I + G + (X - M)$$

The components of aggregate demand (AD) are consumption expenditure, investment, government spending and exports (net of imports, which create AD for the exporting country).

Checkpoint 1

Give an example of depreciation in the national income process.

Checkpoint 2

Is gross domestic product likely to be larger or smaller than gross national product?

Checkpoint 3

Why is factor cost a more true reflection of national output than market prices?

Link

Refer to the circular flow of income on page 69.

These components are in turn affected by several variables, including income levels, interest rates, taxes, exchange rates, and consumer and business confidence. The main relationships are not difficult to work out. For example:

→ Higher incomes can be predicted to lead to higher consumption and, therefore, higher AD.
→ Taxes, which reduce disposable income, can be predicted to reduce AD.
→ Higher interest rates can be expected to increase saving and, hence, reduce consumption, while reducing borrowing for investment purposes.
→ Government spending will depend on short- and long-term political decisions, the state of the economy, and the level of taxation and government borrowing.
→ International trade depends largely on incomes and spending power in the exporting and importing countries. Higher exchange rates will reduce a country's exports (by making them dearer to foreign buyers) and reduce imports (by making them cheaper to domestic buyers).

In round figures, the value of total AD (and, therefore, for AS) for the UK is approximately £1000 billion, or a trillion pounds (which is an easy number to remember). This makes the UK economy about the fourth largest in the world.

Link

Refer to economic indicators on page 70.

Check the net

To investigate international comparisons of GDP, try www.nationmaster.com.

Exam question (15 minutes) answer: page 125

My car cost £10 000 when new. I sell it to a garage for £3000. After servicing it and doing it up a bit, the garage sells the car for £3500. How much has been added to the national income?

Uses and limitations of GDP league tables

National-income statistics are quoted in the media on a daily basis. As with any statistics, they have to be treated with caution: they tell a truth, but it is not the whole truth.

Uses of GDP

GDP statistics (and related measures such as GNP) can be used for:

→ **Single-country comparisons**, e.g. tracing the economic progress of the UK over time.
→ **International comparisons**, e.g. comparing the current economic performance of the UK with that of other countries.

There are close links between GDP, living standards and quality of life. Most people would prefer to live and work in a country with good facilities for such things as health, education, transport, housing, pensions, leisure and community facilities. Such **social capital** is both created by and helps create national income. People generally would prefer to live in a high-income country rather than a low-income country. However, the methods of measuring income need some evaluation.

Limitations of GDP

When making single-country comparisons, it is necessary to use real income figures (nominal income adjusted for inflation). If measured national income doubles merely because prices have doubled, then there has been no real increase in national output. Similarly, international comparisons need to take account of the spending power of income by making a cost-of-living power adjustment.

In order to make meaningful comparisons of GDP between countries of differing sizes, it is necessary to measure GDP per head or per capita.

However, GDP per head has limitations. It takes no account of the following important considerations:

→ **Distribution:** GDP per head is an arithmetic mean measure of average income. Averages can be very misleading and can disguise important differences. Two countries can have similar GDPs per head, but one might have a small elite of very high-income earners, with a huge amount of people in dire poverty, while the other country may have fewer extremes and a very large proportion of middle-income families. Economic deprivation in large sections of the community can be hidden by the average. Contrary to popular belief, not everyone in the USA lives in Beverly Hills. When Hurricane Katrina hit the coast of Louisiana and Mississippi in 2005, the results were described by commentators as resembling a 'third-world disaster area' and highlighted stark divisions in US society. It was the people of the poorest areas of New Orleans who suffered most, as they did not have the means to get out of harm's way.

Link

Refer again to the differences between GDP and GNP on page 82.

Checkpoint 1

Explain what is meant by social capital.

Checkpoint 2

Explain the statement 'Social capital is both created by and helps create national income.'

The jargon

Purchasing power parity (PPP). A method of comparing GDP, making an allowance for the prices of everyday goods and services in each country.

Check the net

In international comparisons in terms of GDP, the UK is near the top of the league tables, being located between fourth and seventh place, depending on how GDP is measured (the USA and China are numbers 1 and 2, respectively). In terms of GDP **per head**, however, the UK falls to somewhere around number 24, with Luxembourg at number 1, the USA at number 2 and China way down at number 122. International GDP league tables can be constructed using www.nationmaster.com.

→ **Range of goods and services:** one country might devote huge amounts on military expenditure, while another might have a larger proportion of GDP devoted to household consumption.

→ **Social wage:** countries with strong public services have a hidden income that benefits all citizens. In Europe, for example, 40–50% of national income is spent by government and used largely for welfare purposes; in the USA, taxes are equally high, but a much larger proportion is spent on military purposes and people have to pay out of their disposable (after-tax) income for such things as medical insurance.

→ **Externalities:** high-income countries might have higher social costs, such as pollution and stress levels. These are not accounted for in GDP figures.

→ **Intangible factors:** many influences on living standards and quality of life are intangible; in other words, they tend to be less obvious than factors that directly affect people's material wellbeing, such as the consumption of retail goods. These include:

  → **Leisure time:** If everyone worked an 80-hour week, national income per head would increase but human welfare might well decline, due to stress levels, family problems, etc.

  → **Self-sufficiency:** If grandad and granny do some babysitting, this makes no difference to measured GDP, but a registered childminder's fees will find their way into national statistics. Countries with stronger family and communitarian values might well have lower incomes than countries that are stronger in commercial terms but weaker in other ways. Similarly, the value of vegetables produced in your own garden are not counted in national income, but expenditure on carrots from the supermarket is counted (while the environmental damage from any pesticides used might not be costed). Housework, voluntary work and many other important activities are underrecorded in GDP figures.

  → **Climate and other factors:** People in Sweden have much higher incomes than people in Barbados but have to spend more on heating and lighting their homes. On the other hand, Swedish education and healthcare are more likely to be taken care of by the state than in Barbados. People in Cuba have low incomes but benefit from high standards of education and health.

Check the net

The New Economics Foundation has calculated that in terms of quality of life, 1977 was the best year to live in the UK, even though incomes were relatively low, compared with the worst year in recent times, 1988, when the economy was stronger but social costs, including unemployment and stress levels, were higher.
See www.neweconomics.org

Exam question (40 minutes)   answer: page 125

Country X has twice the GDP of country Y. Does this necessarily mean that the average citizen of X is twice as well off as the average citizen of Y?

Underlying concepts: saving, investment,

The circular flow of income is not static. It is a dynamic model, meaning that it helps us to understand changes in the economy. Here we look at important factors determining an increase in the levels of national income, output and employment.

Saving and investment

Saving and investment are flow concepts, saving being a withdrawal from the circular flow of income and investment an injection.

→ **Saving** is income that is not spent on consumption.
→ **Investment** is expenditure on capital goods.

These economic definitions differ from everyday definitions:

→ For saving to take place, it is not necessary for money to be placed in any account. It simply has to be withdrawn from the circular flow, e.g. placed in a box under the bed.
→ Investment involves more than the movement of money around financial institutions. For investment to take place, a real productive asset has to be purchased.

In everyday language, the buying of shares in a company is often described as 'investment'. To an economist, however, buying shares is, strictly speaking, a form of 'saving'. Only if or when the company uses shareholders' money to buy a real productive asset does it become investment.

Saving is generally regarded as a good thing. However, in the short run, an increase in saving can reduce investment, as saving reduces consumer demand and can, therefore, depress output and employment. For this reason, the Japanese government has tried to discourage saving. However, economists and governments generally agree that in the long run, saving ought to be encouraged, since a willingness to postpone present consumption creates funds for investment in industry, social infrastructure and important social provision such as pensions. The UK Chancellor of the Exchequer has often spoken of the need to improve the **savings ratio** of the UK. In practice, the UK's saving ratio has deteriorated in recent years. In fact, many British families are **dis-saving** (spending more than they earn), and there has been a very worrying increase in **personal debt**.

The multiplier

Look at the circular flow diagram on page 69. If a sum of money, say £1 million, is injected into the circular flow of income, by how much will national income increase? The multiplier principle predicts that it will increase by more than £1 million.

If a change in an injection (ΔJ) leads to a greater change in national income (ΔY), then:

$$\Delta Y > \Delta J$$

Link

Stocks, flows, injections, withdrawals: see pages 68 and 70.

Checkpoint 1

Define and give some examples of capital goods.

Watch out!

Individuals can save (withdraw money from the circular flow), and so can firms. Saving by firms is known as 'plough back', 'retained profits' or 'internal financing'. In fact, the largest proportion of business investment comes from this source.

The jargon

Saving ratio. The fraction of national income that is saved.

Check the net

Saving ratios of different countries can be compared using www.nationmaster.com.

Checkpoint 2

Identify one important cause and one important effect of an increase in personal debt.

The jargon

The multiplier. A measure of the effect on national income of a change in some component of aggregate demand.

multiplier

or

$$\Delta Y = K \Delta J$$

where K is greater than 1
or

$$K = \Delta Y / \Delta J$$

K is known as the multiplier coefficient. For example, if an investment of £2 million increases national income by £4 million, then the value of the investment multiplier, K_I, is £4 million/£2 million = 2.

Why does the multiplier principle work? It is because money is spent more than once. Suppose people tend to spend 75% of their income and save the other 25%, and there is an injection into the local economy of £1 million: the building of a new factory, for example. The people receiving the £1 million will spend £750 000 on goods and services, the people selling these goods and services will in turn spend 75% of £750 000, and this money will in turn be recycled into the economy, creating incomes of 75% of 75% of 750 000%. This process will continue until the money being recycled becomes very small and 'disappears'.

It should be clear from this example that the multiplier effect from any injection is increased by a tendency to spend on consumption and is reduced by saving or another withdrawal from the economy, such as taxation or spending on imports.

Exam question (30 minutes)   answer: page 126

Why would a knowledge of the multiplier be useful as a guide to government policy?

Economic growth and sustainability

Here we take a further look at GDP and examine its relationship with economic growth. We also introduce the idea of sustainable development.

What is economic growth? ●●●

There are two types of economic growth:

→ **Potential growth:** the steady process of increasing the productive capacity of a country.
→ **Actual growth:** utilising productive capacity so that national income increases over time.

There have been long periods in British history when hardly any economic growth took place at all. Over the past 200–300 years, however (since the Industrial Revolution), we have become used to the idea of constant growth – so much so that no politician would dare to go into an election promising less growth. However, nothing in economic history has ever grown forever, so one day (if, for example, an important contributor to growth, like the supply of oil, runs out) we might have to change our ideas about the nature and desirability of economic growth.

Economic development

While growth focuses on quantity, development also considers quality. Development involves not only growth of GDP but also fundamental changes in economic structure, typically the increasing importance of manufacturing and services as opposed to agriculture, migration of labour from rural to urban areas, a diminishing reliance on aid, and the opening up of markets to international trade.

Human development

American economists Nordhaus and Tobin have developed a measure of economic welfare (MEW) that consists of:

→ National income.
→ **Plus** an allowance for leisure, non-marketed goods and services (such as housework), and public amenities such as roads.
→ **Minus**
  → 'Bads', such as pollution.
  → 'Regrettables', such as military spending and time wasted commuting to work.

They argue that generally, MEW grows at a slower pace than GDP.

The United Nations Development Programme (UNDP) has developed a Human Development Index (HDI) based on the assumption that the purpose of economic development is to raise the living standards and general wellbeing of all of the people, and not just an elite few. The HDI is an index combining:

Link

See the discussion of economic development on page 140.

Checkpoint 1

Give examples of countries that have shown rapid development recently, focusing in particular on international trade, together with investment in educational provision.

Checkpoint 2

Suggest why MEW grows at a slower rate than GDP.

→ GDP, to give a measure of people's command over material things, goods and services.
→ Life expectancy, which is assumed to be linked closely to quality-of-life factors such as good diet, health services and proper housing.
→ Adult literacy, which is an indicator of educational standards, employment prospects and general 'life chances'.

When GDP league tables are adapted to become HDI tables, then materialistic aggressively free-market countries, such as the USA, tend to be demoted, as are countries where there is discrimination against sections of society (where women, for example, are treated as second-class citizens). Countries with socialised markets and strong welfare systems, such as Canada, the UK and other western European countries, tend to be promoted in league tables based on HDI.

Sustainable development ●●●

The idea of sustainable development takes into account environmental and natural resource considerations. When Britain and other colonial powers were having their industrial revolutions, they were able to use resources from other parts of the world that they had conquered. Now that ex-colonial countries are independent sovereign states, industrialised countries do not have access to such, cheap resources and might be tempted to borrow (or steal) from future generations, producing now and postponing the tackling of environmental problems until some future date. The idea of **sustainable development** draws attention to this problem and is defined as development that takes place in the present without reducing the ability of future generations to achieve human development.

Checkpoint 3

Why is it difficult to make international comparisons of educational attainment?

Check the net

Further information on the HDI is on www.undp.org.int. HDI league tables can be constructed and compared with GDP league tables using www.nationmaster.com.

Exam question (20 minutes)   answer: page 126

Which of the following are essential for economic growth and development? Investment, aggregate demand, exports, public spending.

Definitions and measures of inflation

Watch out!

Inflation is not always bad. Low inflation rates do have benefits. It is when inflation rates rise that problems really occur.

Check the net

For further information on inflation check the following sites:
www.bankofengland.co.uk
www.oecd.org
www.statistics.gov.uk

The jargon

Other measures of inflation include the following:

RPIX. Retail Price Index X – Excludes mortgage interest payments.

RPIY. Retail Price Index Y – Excludes mortgage interest payments, indirect taxes, excise duties and other specific taxes.

Tax and price index. Seeks to measure the income of the average person before tax.

Producer price index. Estimates the price of goods produced by manufacturers (factory gate prices).

The rate of inflation measures the annual percentage increase in prices. The government produces a range of consumer price indices, which provide useful indicators regarding the performance of the UK economy. The two main consumer price indices used in the UK are the retail prices index (RPI) and the consumer prices index (CPI).

The government's inflation targets are based on the CPI.

Retail prices index

The RPI measures the change in a wide range of prices, from cars to food. The index measures the price change of a typical basket of more than 650 goods and services. The RPI represents the average change in a range of products and reveals the underlying trend in prices. Often, prices move in different directions. For example, the price of coffee may be falling due to overproduction, while the price of chicken may be rising due to increased consumption.

Items in the basket of goods are given a weighting to reflect their importance in the budget of a typical household. For example, some households contain smokers while others do not; the system of weighting takes account of this.

The basket of goods is adjusted over time to reflect changing tastes and preferences and the introduction of new products. Over time, the proportion of money spent on food has fallen while spending on electrical goods has increased.

It is important to remember that the price index measures changes in prices and not in price levels.

Base year
The base year for the RPI is 1984. This means that 1984 is given a value of 100 in the index. Price changes are measured relative to this year, e.g. January 1984 = 100 January 2004 = 183.1 **Calculation** $183.1 - 100 = 83.1$ In other words, the price of the basket of goods has increased by 83.1%.
Annual rate of change
The annual rate of inflation is the percentage change in the index from one year to the next, e.g. January 2003 = 178.4 January 2004 = 183.1 **Calculation** $183.1 - 178.4 = 4.7$ $4.7/178.4 \times 100 = 2.6$

The consumer prices index

The government inflation targets are based on the consumer price index. The target was set in December 2003 at 2% per annum.

The principal advantage of the CPI is that it allows international comparisons to be made, because it uses a standard method of calculation.

The data used to prepare the CPI are broadly the same data used to produce the RPI. The data do not include the cost of:

→ Council Tax.
→ Housing costs.

The data do include the cost of some services.

The cumulative effect of these differences is that the CPI inflation rate will always be lower than the RPI rate of inflation.

Problems of measuring inflation

The method of collecting data using a basket of goods has problems. Over time, new goods are launched and old goods are removed from sale. These changes are reflected in the basket of goods. This means that it is difficult to compare price levels over a long period. Comparing prices in 2005 and with those in 1975 means that the price of a computer in 2005 must be compared with the price of an electric typewriter in 1975. Most people would consider a computer to be preferable to a typewriter and would be prepared to pay more for a computer. In the RPI, this would be shown as an inflationary price rise. In this way, inflation may be overstated.

Watch out!

The Bank of England inflation target of 2% is expressed in terms of an annual rate of inflation based on the CPI.

Checkpoint 1

Identify two limitations of the measures used to calculate inflation.

Checkpoint 2

What advantages does the CPI have over the RPI?

Checkpoint 3

Explain what you understand by the term 'inflation'.

Watch out!

The Bank of England is charged with achieving the lowest possible inflation rate. An inflation rate of less than the target rate of 2% is judged to be just as bad as inflation above the target rate. The inflation target is symmetrical.

Exam question (minutes 15 each)   answer: pages 126–7

(a) How would a sharp fall in inflation be likely to affect household expenditure?

(b) Assess the impact of house price inflation on consumer borrowing.

Consequences (costs) of inflation

Most countries in the developed world experience inflation. Inflation in developed countries is typically around 2–3%. This level of inflation is generally not felt to be a cause for concern. Higher rates of inflation may create winners and losers.

The impact of inflation

→ **Loss of international competitiveness:** if the inflation rate in the UK is higher than the inflation rate in trading partners, then UK-produced goods may be less competitive.
→ **Planning uncertainty:** firms may be reluctant to invest if they are uncertain of the cost of a project.
→ **Shoe-leather costs:** consumers and firms will try to shop around for the best price.
→ **Pensioners** and people on fixed incomes may see a fall in their real incomes.
→ **Menu costs:** firms will have to pay to reprice goods and reprint brochures.
→ **Falling real returns for investors:** interest rates may lag behind inflation rates. This will benefit borrowers but may discourage saving.

Inflation may also lead to a wage-price spiral

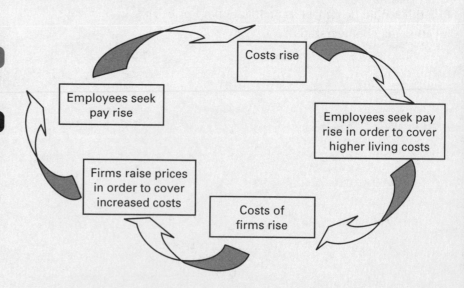

Measures to control inflation

Various policies are available to the government in order to control inflation. The choice of policy will depend to a large extent on the cause of inflation.

Watch out!

Statistics published by the Office of National Statistics (ONS) show that the factors affecting UK inflation are complex. Inflation has fallen for the first time since September 2004. The ONS suggests that a fall in bank charges and fuel prices contributed to a reduction in the rate of inflation. Increasing supplies of fresh vegetables such as onions, cauliflowers and tomatoes were also cited as a factor in the reduction of inflation.

Checkpoint 1

Which groups are likely to be winners as inflation rises? Which groups are likely to be losers?

Examiner's secrets

In reality, inflation often has more than one cause.

Checkpoint 2

Will the use of the Internet cut 'shoe-leather' costs?

Checkpoint 3

Will menu costs be affected for exports?

Examiner's secrets

The government can take advantage of inflation as a stealth tax while firms can use inflation to reduce the real wages of staff.

The government may 'forget' to change the tax brackets after a period of inflation and so the average person could end up paying higher taxes.

Employers can choose not to raise their employees' wages as much as inflation, thereby giving them a decrease in real pay.

During the 1980s, the Conservative government employed supply-side policies in order to reduce the power of the trade unions. Legislation introduced during the period weakened the trade unions and made it harder for unions to take strike action.

Supply-side policies could also be used to increase the number of job-seekers by reducing benefits paid to the unemployed.

Aggregate demand could be reduced by the use of fiscal policy. Taxes could be raised in order to reduce disposable income. Government may also choose to reduce government spending. Such a decision may have important tradeoffs, such as cuts in services and hardship for the poorest people in society.

Prices and incomes policy

Attempts have been made to use a prices and income policy during the post-war years. The strategy has met with mixed success. Governments tried to restrict price increases and to limit pay settlements in order to reduce inflationary pressure.

There are a number of reasons why this approach has proved unsuccessful:

→ Trade unions may use their bargaining power to obtain settlements breaking the limits set by the government.
→ A prices and incomes policy may distort the market economy, creating labour shortages because firms are unable to attract the labour they need.
→ Firms may pay benefits in kind, such as company cars.

Exchange rate policy

Governments could intervene in the foreign currency markets. In an effort to reduce inflationary pressure, the government could buy up sterling in order to increase the value of sterling, thus reducing the relative price of imports while at the same time reducing the demand for exports.

The jargon

The Bank of England's Monetary Policy Committee (MPC) is made up of nine members: the governor, two deputy governors, the bank's chief economist, the executive director for markets, and four external members appointed by the Chancellor.

Watch out!

When the Bank of England changes the official interest rate, its aim is to influence the level of expenditure in the economy. When the level of expenditure grows faster than the volume of output produced, inflation is the result. By changing interest rates, the level of expenditure can be reduced.

The jargon

Fiscal policy. The expenditure a government undertakes in order to provide goods and services and the way in which the government finances these expenditures.
Aggregate demand. Total demand for goods and services produced in the economy over a period of time.
Supply-side policies are designed to improve the quality and quantity of the supply of labour available to the economy.

Exam question (10 minutes)   answer: page 127

Assess the measures that the UK government might adopt in order to reduce wage price inflation.

Demand pull and cost push inflation

Inflation is a sustained rise in prices that is measured on a monthly basis. There are two causes of inflation: demand pull inflation and cost push inflation.

Checkpoint 1

What is the difference between cost push inflation and demand pull inflation?

Demand pull inflation ●●●

Demand pull inflation is caused by too much demand in the economy. Basically, there is too much money chasing too few products. This occurs when demand increases and firms cannot produce enough output and then raise their prices in order to ration supply.

Watch out!

Inflation is a sustained rise in prices that is measured by various indices. Small rises of up to 2% are generally thought acceptable, but significant increases in inflation can damage the economic prospects of a country.

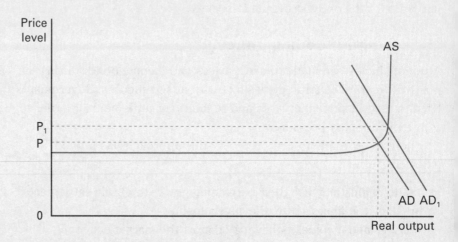

An increase in income may cause a shift in aggregate demand, shifting the aggregate demand curve to the right from AD to AD_1. As demand shifts, firms are unable to increase supply as the equilibrium moves towards full capacity. As a result, prices will rise from P to P_1.

Checkpoint 2

What are the basic differences between Keynesian and monetarist beliefs?

Checkpoint 3

What effect may inflation have on living standards?

Keynesian and monetarist analysis ●●●

In Keynesian analysis, demand pull inflation is one of the causes of inflation. According to Keynesian analysis, demand pull inflation can occur only at full employment, when an increase in aggregate demand cannot be matched by a rise in output.

Monetarists believe that demand pull inflation is the only cause of inflation. As Milton Friedman said: 'Inflation is always and everywhere a monetary phenomenon.'

Watch out!

Tax rises can create inflationary pressure. Cost push inflation may be temporary, occurring as a result of short-term shocks such as a poor harvest.

Cost push inflation ●●●

The UK is an open economy. The UK imports and exports goods and services. The import of goods and services can bring with it inflationary pressure. A sudden increase in the price of crude oil can lead to a rise in prices in the UK for petrol and a range of other products, as higher petrol prices lead to increased transport costs.

Examiner's secrets

The use of appropriate AS and AD curves to support your answers will strengthen analysis.

Cost push inflation may occur as a result of a rise in the costs of production. Firms may increase prices in order to maintain profit margins. Firms may also use their monopoly power in order to make bigger profits by forcing up prices.

Wage push inflation can also lead to cost push inflation, where trade unions force wages levels to rise independently of the demand for labour. Wages account for around 70% of national income. In consequence, wage increases are likely to be the most significant cause of increased production costs.

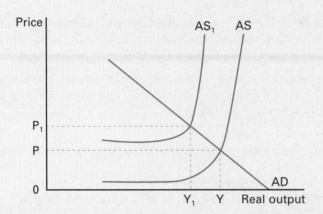

A rise in cost will cause a shift in the aggregate supply curve to the left (AS to AS$_1$). The effect of this is to increase prices from P to P$_1$. The quantity demanded will as a result move from Y to Y$_1$.

Watch out!

A wage price or cost push spiral describes the process whereby increases in wages lead to an increase in costs and an increase in prices.

The jargon

Keynesian economics. A theory of total spending in the economy (called aggregate demand) and of its effects on output and inflation.
The principal belief of **monetarists** is that a sustained growth in the money supply in excess of the growth of output produces inflation. In order to end inflation or to produce deflation, money supply growth must fall below the growth of output.

Examiner's secrets

Use your revision time effectively. Don't postpone difficult topics. Don't just read. Make notes, and summarise and condense notes. Discuss topics, after revising them, with your classmates. Use diagrams wherever possible.

Watch out!

The Keynesian theory of cost push inflation suggests that there are four main sources of cost push inflation:
→ Wages and salaries.
→ Imported goods.
→ Profits: the more price-elastic demand is for a firm's goods and services, the less an increase in price will affect demand.
→ Taxes and subsidies: increasing indirect rates of taxation and a reduction in levels of government subsidy result in an increase in costs.

Exam question (15 minutes)   answer: page 127

(a) Discuss two strategies for controlling the rate of inflation.

(b) Explain the link between wage push inflation and cost push inflation.

Measures of unemployment

It is possible to use government data to analyse the state of the labour market. Three possible indicators are available:

→ LFS employment survey.
→ Claimant unemployment.
→ Economic activity rate.

Checkpoint 1

Explain why the number of people in employment rose by 334 000 (September 2005) while the numbers unemployed also rose by 41 000. Use the following link to help you: www.statistics.gov.uk.

Checkpoint 2

What effect would a rise in the number of people staying in education have on the economic activity rate?

Three labour market indicators ●●●

The Labour Force Survey

The Office for National Statistics compiles the Labour Force Survey (LFS). The LFS is a survey of households using internationally recognised procedures laid down by the International Labour Organization (ILO) . The survey draws on demographic data such as age, gender, ethnic origin and skills levels. LFS surveys are conducted throughout the EU and in OECD countries, allowing international comparisons to be made.

According to LFS criteria, someone who is unemployed must:

→ have made efforts to find work within the past four weeks; or,
→ be waiting to return to a job that they were previously laid off from; or,
→ be preparing to start a new job within the next 30 days.

Claimant unemployment

The claimant count measures unemployment according to the number of people who are eligible for, and claim, unemployment-linked benefits, such as jobseekers' allowance. This measure can be influenced by government policy and changes in benefit entitlement. This measure does not include young people aged 18 years or under and excludes married women returning to work after a period of absence from the labour market. When employment is high, the gap between the numbers recorded as unemployed using the LFS method and the claimant count method tends to widen. This happens because some of those who were jobless people and not previously seeking work start to do so. By seeking work, they may become classified as unemployed under the ILO definition. If these people are not in receipt of jobseekers' allowance, they will not appear in the claimant count.

The Economic Activity Rate

The number of people who enter the workforce is an indicator of the willingness of people of working age to take up employment. The economic activity rate is the percentage of the working-age population who are members of the workforce.

$$\text{Economic Activity Rate} = \frac{\text{Workforce}}{\text{Working-age population}} \times 100$$

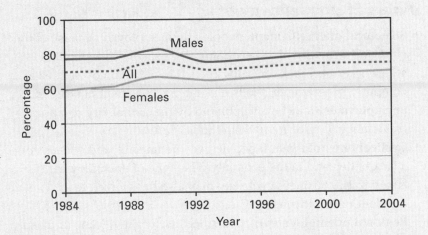

The UK male working-age employment rate was 79% in spring 2004. This was largely unchanged from spring 1984. Over the same period, the female rate rose gradually from 59% to 70%, reflecting the growing importance of women in the workplace. This trend is likely to continue for the foreseeable future. Women are becoming a more significant force in the labour market. Firms are working much more imaginatively to find ways of keeping women in the workforce and to combine childrearing with employment. Increasing the participation rate of women in the workforce is an important part of the government's strategy to reduce child poverty.

Checkpoint 3

Which measure of unemployment might an opposition party use when challenging the government on unemployment?

Checkpoint 4

Examine the importance of women in the workforce as the UK population continues to age.

Examiner's secrets

Make sure that you read data tables and graphs carefully. Marks can be thrown away in an exam by not paying careful attention to headings and the labelling of axes.

Exam question (10 minutes)   answer: page 127

Explain the value of gathering data on unemployment.

Causes of unemployment

Check the net

The following sources will provide additional information on the different types of unemployment and statistical data.
www.bized.ac.uk/virtual/economy/policy/outcomes/unemployment/unempth2.htm
www.statistics.gov.uk
http://news.bbc.co.uk/1/hi/business/4441570.stm
Follow the link above for some unemployment news from the BBC
http://news.bbc.co.uk-BBC

Check the net

In a strong economy, it can be difficult to fill seasonal jobs. The UK has become increasingly dependent on immigrant labour to fill vacant jobs in the agricultural and tourism sectors. Follow the links below for news stories linked to this topic:
http://news.bbc.co.uk/1/hi/scotland/633921.stm
http://news.bbc.co.uk/1/hi/england/southern_counties/4176826.stm
http://news.bbc.co.uk/1/hi/uk/3535629.stm

Checkpoint 1

Identify a solution to frictional unemployment.

Checkpoint 2

What type of unemployment is caused by a lack of aggregate demand?

Checkpoint 3

Explain what is meant by the term 'natural rate of unemployment'.

Watch out!

It would be simplistic to assume that a single cause for unemployment may exist within a particular geographic area. For example, structural unemployment was at the heart of rising unemployment levels within Wales in the 1980s and 1990s. As structural unemployment rose during this period, so did regional unemployment.

Unemployment occurs when there are people who want to work at the going wage rate but are unable to find jobs. High levels of unemployment mean that human capital is being wasted. There are a variety of causes of unemployment: structural, cyclical, regional, seasonal, frictional unemployment, residual unemployment and the natural rate of unemployment.

Types of unemployment

→ **Structural unemployment:** people are unemployed because of the changing structure of the economy. For example, a redundant steelworker may lack the skills needed to gain employment as a computer programmer (skills mismatch). The effect of structural unemployment may be accentuated by the immobility of labour (reluctance to relocate to where jobs are available).

→ **Cyclical unemployment:** people become unemployed because of a lack of demand in the economy. This type of unemployment is linked to the business cycle and may also be referred to as demand-deficient unemployment.

→ **Regional unemployment:** occurs because of the decline or closure of a major employer in a particular area. For example, the closure of steelworks and coalmines in South Wales and the contraction of the automotive industry in the Midlands has created a pool of unemployed workers in these areas.

→ **Seasonal unemployment:** this has become less significant over time, but it applies mostly to workers in the tourist sector, construction industry and agricultural work. Much of this type of work has been taken up by migrant workers.

→ **Frictional unemployment:** occurs where people are between jobs. They may have left one job and are waiting to start another job.

→ **Residual unemployment:** occurs when people are unwilling to work or are not able to work due to disability. Employment statistics published in November 2005 showed considerable growth in employment (up by 330 000 over the previous year). Margaret Hodge, Minister for Employment and Welfare Reform, believes that the rise in employment reflects people who previously had not looked for a job are moving back into work.

Changing levels of unemployment ●●●

High levels of unemployment are likely to have implications for the demand of goods and services. Unemployment is likely to reduce levels of disposable income and change consumer purchasing patterns, e.g. influencing where they shop and what goods they buy.

For firms, increasing levels of unemployment may create a wider choice of labour. This does, however, assume that people who are unemployed have the skills that firms want. It may also weaken the bargaining position of existing employees.

Unemployment levels will have an impact on the investment decisions of firms and upon the attitude of employees to change.

Natural rate of unemployment ●●●

There are always some people who are unemployed. The natural rate of unemployment is the rate of unemployment when all markets are in equilibrium. The natural rate of unemployment is the rate of unemployment that produces a stable (unchanging) rate of inflation. The natural rate of unemployment is not static; it may change over time. For example, the natural rate of unemployment was estimated to be 10.5% in 1980. By 1998, it had fallen to less than 6%. The natural rate of unemployment arises from the existence of structural and frictional unemployment.

Some economists believe that restrictive practices adopted by trade unions and real increases in the benefits paid to unemployed people can increase the natural rate of unemployment. They attribute the fall in the natural rate of unemployment to the introduction of labour-market reforms in the 1980s.

> **The jargon**
>
> The government may intervene into the market in order to reduce unemployment. The government may use:
> → **Supply-side policies.** These policies would increase the ability of people to accept work (reducing structural unemployment), by increasing opportunities for training, reducing benefits and thus forcing people to accept jobs, and thus adjusting the tax and benefits system in order to increase the rewards from work.
> → **Demand-side policies.** These may help to increase demand (reducing cyclical unemployment) by reducing interest rates, cutting taxation and increasing government taxation.

Exam question (20 minutes)　　　　　　　　　　answer: page 128

(a) Examine the impact of an economic downturn on the labour market.

(b) Assess two possible government policies to deal with unemployment.

Consequences (costs) of unemployment

Unemployment brings significant personal and social implications. The extent of the impact will depend upon a number of factors, including the size of the pool of labour, the skills of the labour force, and the mobility of the workforce.

Checkpoint 1

What can the government do to massage the unemployment rate?

Checkpoint 2

What effect do housing costs have on individuals seeking employment?

Checkpoint 3

Identify two costs of unemployment for the government.

Examiner's secrets

The diagram opposite assumes that the labour market is uniform and that the pool of labour has common skills. In reality, unskilled and manual jobs may experience periods of excess supply and excess demand according to the state of the economy. Demand and supply of skilled labour are likely to be less elastic. Skilled labour may be geographically and occupationally mobile.

The pool of labour

The relationship between the supply and demand for labour will determine how many people are without work (see page 24). If there is a surplus of workers in the economy, then wage levels may be depressed. This can be illustrated in the following diagram:

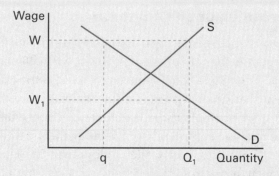

At wage level W, the supply of labour will exceed the demand for labour in the market. The available labour could find employment only if it were to accept a wage reduction to W_1. Competition for employment will depress wage rates until a new equilibrium is achieved at the point where the market supply of labour is equal to the market demand. Where there is a disequilibrium in the labour market, this can be corrected only by an adjustment in the supply of or the demand for labour. The government may choose to intervene in the labour market by increasing the supply of skilled workers needed by firms or by stimulating demand for workers by increasing demand for goods and services.

The skills of the labour force

The skills level of the workforce will influence the degree to which workers are affected by unemployment. Unskilled workers are likely to experience more long-term unemployment than skilled workers. People with transferable skills are more likely to find alternative employment.

The mobility of workers

The ease with which workers are able to move from one area to another will influence the degree to which they are affected by unemployment. Workers who are mobile (usually younger, more highly skilled people) can relocate to areas with better employment prospects. Workers who lack transferable skills or who are tied to an area by family commitments, e.g. aged relatives or school-age children, may find it harder to relocate.

The private cost of unemployment

The private costs of unemployment can be seen in terms of relative poverty and social exclusion. People experiencing unemployment even for relatively short periods may have problems with debt management and financial hardship.

In the UK today, one million children live in poverty, the majority in families where the principal breadwinner of the family is not in full-time employment.

Individuals facing unemployment are more likely to live in sub-standard housing, to experience physical and mental health problems and to experience marital breakdown.

Statistics indicate that the longer an individual is unemployed, the harder it will be for that person to re-enter the workforce.

The social costs of unemployment

The social costs of unemployment can be seen in a loss of skills through disuse and in areas of social deprivation.

Areas of high unemployment in the UK, such as parts of the north-east, are characterised by urban decay. Infrastructure decays, and the most employable people within an area may migrate in search of work. The effect may be seen in surplus housing and a fall in house prices. Once housing becomes vacant, it becomes a target for vandalism and the cycle of decay accelerates. House prices become depressed. In areas such as Burnley, Newcastle and parts of Durham, whole districts and villages have become uninhabited. In terms of the provision of public services such as schools, libraries and healthcare, this creates a misallocation of resources. In parts of Durham and Burnley, the decision has been taken to relocate residents and bulldoze communities.

Areas of urban decay and high unemployment have a higher incidence of crime. There is also a link to drug and alcohol abuse.

Failing schools are often to be found in areas of high unemployment, helping to create a cycle of social deprivation.

Unemployment is distributed unevenly. There are likely to be hotspots that require government assistance. Unemployment is also higher among ethnic minorities, and this may give rise to social unrest.

The jargon

Poverty trap. This occurs when the income received from benefits is greater than the income that might be received from employment. This acts as a disincentive to work. Strategies to reduce the poverty trap include:
→ Reduce the level of benefits in order to increase the attractiveness of employment.
→ Use benefits to top up low pay in order to make employment more attractive.

Absolute poverty. Measures the number of people whose income level means that they are unable to afford certain basic goods and services.

Relative poverty. Measures the extent to which a household's financial resources falls below an average income threshold for the economy. Living standards and real incomes have risen in the UK due to higher employment and sustained economic growth over recent years. Despite this, the gains in income and wealth have been distributed unevenly across the population.

Social exclusion. A relatively new term in British policy, referring not only to poverty and low income but also to some of their wider causes and consequences. The government has defined social exclusion as 'what can happen when people or areas suffer from a combination of linked problems such as unemployment, poor skills, low incomes, poor housing, high crime, bad health and family breakdown.'

Exam question (20 minutes)   answer: page 128

(a) Assess the impact of inward investment to the west of Scotland on employment.

(b) Assess the view that the higher the price of labour, the less will be demanded.

Stop–go policies

Increasing levels of employment might be considered to be beneficial for the economy. As with other policy objectives, achieving full employment may well create tradeoffs. One tradeoff may be balance-of-payment difficulties.

Checkpoint 1

Explain how rising manufacturing costs and increased prices will affect the value of sterling.

The jargon

Balance of Payments (BOP). An account of all transactions between one country and its trading partners. Transactions are measured in terms of receipts and payments.
Current Account. Records the difference between a nation's total exports of goods, services and transfers, and its total imports of them.

Benefits of rising employment levels

Increasing employment is generally considered to be desirable. As employment levels rise, this may be expected to lead to an increase in aggregate demand.

Aggregate demand may increase as a result of investment increasing productive capacity or increased government expenditure to improve infrastructure. Aggregate demand may also increase as a result of higher levels of consumer spending, arising from increased employment.

If increased employment coincides with improved efficiency, then UK exports may be able to exploit a cost advantage.

Downside of rising employment levels

As unemployment levels are reduced, labour shortages may start to occur. Upward pressure on wage levels to rise may increase, causing the costs of firms to rise. Firms will have two choices – to absorb the higher costs themselves or to pass on the cost to customers.

The choice taken will be determined by the availability of substitutes and the price elasticity of demand. For exporters, rising costs may erode their competitiveness, making it harder for them to sell their products abroad. Importers may find it relatively easier to sell their products in the UK.

Rising costs and erosion of international competitiveness are likely to be reflected in the current account of the balance of payments and influence exchange-rate movements. Rising costs and higher-priced goods may reduce demand for sterling. At the same, imported goods may become relatively cheaper, leading to increased demand for foreign currencies. The cumulative effect may be seen in sterling depreciation and a deficit in the balance of payments. Firms may choose to invest in countries where economic policies are more stable and where labour costs are lower. This is most likely to occur in the manufacturing sector.

Government intervention

The government can also use macroeconomic policies to increase the level of aggregate demand. These policies might involve lower interest rates or lower direct taxes. It might also encourage foreign investment into the economy from foreign multinational companies.

The UK government has found it necessary to adopt stop–go policies in the past in order to address the problem of balance-of-payments deficits. Records reveal that when the UK economy starts to grow, the balance of payments moves into deficit. The government has been forced to curb demand using fiscal and/or monetary policies. The problem of rising levels of employment leading to adjustments in the balance of payments and exchange rates reinforces the point that economies do suffer from inherent instability. As a result, economic growth and other macroeconomic indicators tend to fluctuate.

During the 1950s and 1960s, successive governments experienced difficulty in maintaining low levels of unemployment. The economy shifted from recession to boom to recession in a stop–go cycle.

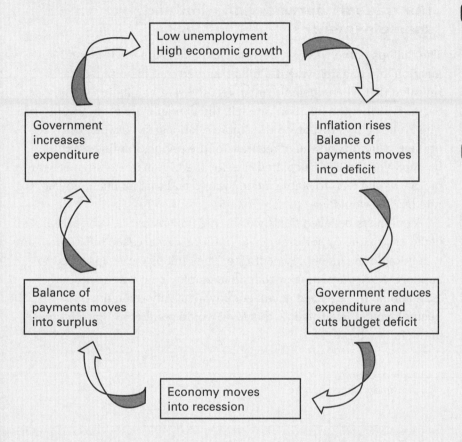

Checkpoint 2

Does the government have to intervene in order to correct a balance-of-payments deficit?

Examiner's secrets

Show that you appreciate that government policy may have adverse consequences, e.g. reducing a balance of payments deficit could lead to unemployment.

Watch out!

Britain's unprecedented economic expansion, combined with the absence of stop–go policies, has helped to generate a period of sustained growth and prosperity.

Exam question (10 minutes)   answer: page 129

(a) Explain the relationship between rising employment levels and aggregate demand.

(b) Explain how labour shortages may result in loss of competitiveness.

The simple Phillips curve tradeoff

Governments have a number of macroeconomic objectives. Two objectives of national governments are full employment and stable prices. AW Phillips, while working at the LSE during the 1950s, sought to explain the relationship between unemployment and inflation.

The tradeoff between inflation and unemployment

The Phillips curve was first used in 1958 to explain the tradeoff between inflation and unemployment. Phillips argued that historical data revealed that when unemployment fell, the rate of inflation would rise. Similarly, when the inflation rate fell, the unemployment rate would rise. The Philips curve displayed the stable relationship between the rate of wage inflation and the percentage of the population that was unemployed. Philips calculated that for the UK, an unemployment rate of 5.5% would lead to stable money wages and that an unemployment rate of 2.5% would lead to zero inflation.

Economists believed that by using the Phillips curve, the government could assess the opportunity cost, in terms of increased inflation, of any reduction in the unemployment rate. The Phillips curve appeared to support the Keynesian view that an unemployment rate of around 1.5% should be regarded as full employment. Any reduction in unemployment levels below this level would result in a sharp increase in the inflation rate.

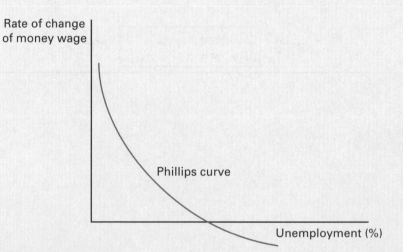

In Phillips' study, the wage increases were around 2% higher than price increases. It is, therefore, possible to draw a parallel curve showing the tradeoff between price inflation and unemployment.

The Phillips curve has been used by economists to show the impact of changes in aggregate demand relative to potential output. If aggregate demand rose in relation to output (see diagram below), then inflation

Checkpoint 1

How might a rise in interest rates reduce inflation?

Examiner's secrets

Take time to look at previous exam papers. The papers will help you to see how examiners phrase the questions and will help you appreciate the spread of knowledge you require to answer the questions. The questions sometimes contain clues that will help you solve them – remember the sort of clues that crop up and look out for these in your exam.

Checkpoint 2

What might cause an increase in aggregate demand?

Examiner's secrets

Make sure you know how many questions you have to attempt and how long you have to answer them. A recurring frustration for examiners is the candidate who insists on answering every question on the paper rather than just some.

would rise and unemployment would fall. This would lead to an upward movement along the Phillips curve. On the other hand, if there was a reduction in aggregate demand, then this might be expected to lead to a downward movement along the aggregate demand curve.

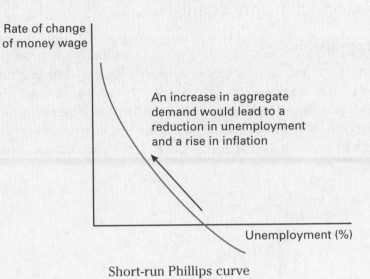

Short-run Phillips curve

Consider a scenario where prices in the economy are stable and there is an increase in aggregate demand. As a result, the aggregate demand curve shifts to the right. This will result in a new AS/AD equilibrium at point B. The new equilibrium will mean that aggregate supply will have to increase. Increasing supply is likely to increase demand for labour and reduce unemployment, creating a tradeoff between inflation and unemployment.

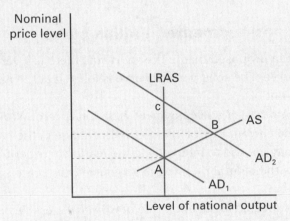

In the long run, the economy will move back to c.

Checkpoint 3

How might a fall in the inflation rate reduce unemployment?

Checkpoint 4

Why should an unemployment rate of 1.5% be regarded as 'full employment'?

Examiner's secrets

Make sure you use your time in the exam effectively. Plan in advance how much time you have for each question.

Watch out!

Milton Friedman's analysis of the Phillips curve makes a distinction between short-run and long-run Phillips curves. As long as inflation remains fairly constant (as occurred in the 1960s), inflation is related inversely to unemployment. When the average rate of inflation changes, however, unemployment returns after a period of adjustment to the natural rate (as occurred in the 1970s).

Exam question (20 minutes)   answer: page 129

(a) Discuss whether it is possible to control inflation while maintaining a high level of employment.

(b) Explain the effect of a reduction in aggregate demand on unemployment and inflation.

Expectations-augmented Phillips curve

The early 1970s saw a growing level of unemployment. At the same time, inflation rates increased. This appeared to indicate the breakdown of the Phillips relationship, which cast doubt on the cost push and demand pull theory of inflation.

Stagflation ●●●

During the 1970s, the relationship between unemployment and the rate of inflation broke down. The oil crisis of 1973 resulted in high levels of unemployment and high rates of inflation. The UK economy found itself facing high inflation and a stagnant economy. A monetarist economist sought to explain what had happened using the expectations-augmented Philips curve.

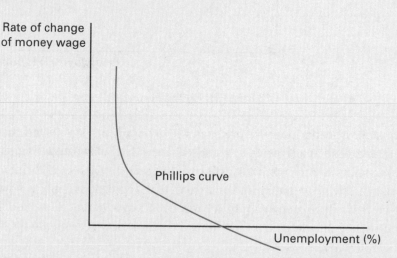

Expectations-augmented Philips curve ●●●

Milton Friedman proposed that in the short run, there is a vertical long-run Phillips curve. The solid vertical curve is located at the natural rate of unemployment.

At the natural rate of unemployment, inflation is zero. Workers may believe that the current rate of inflation will continue in the future. The government may choose to intervene in the market in order to reduce inflation below the natural rate. These actions may increase aggregate demand.

If workers expected an inflation rate of 6% and excess demand was to cause demand pull inflation of 3%, then the actual inflation rate would be 9%. The workers' expectations of the inflation rate will influence their pay demands: this is called the **money illusion**. An increase in aggregate demand will push the inflation rate upwards and will mean that workers are relatively cheaper. Firms will demand more labour, which will pull up wages, reducing unemployment from A to B. Eventually, workers will recognise that the inflation rate is 9% and will increase their pay demands, allowing the prices and wages to converge.

Checkpoint 1

Explain what we mean by 'tradeoff' in the context of the Phillips curve.

Checkpoint 2

What is an alternative name for stagflation?

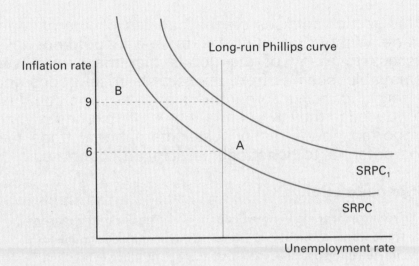

The expectations-augmented Phillips curve may be expressed as:

$$P = f(1/U) + Pe$$

P, the rate of price inflation, is a function (f) of the inverse of unemployment (1/U) plus the expected rate of inflation.

The expectations-augmented Phillips curve is a fundamental element of almost every macroeconomic forecasting model now used by government and business. The tradeoff between unemployment and inflation influences forecasts of how fast an economy can comfortably grow over the medium term. This information is vital for a government when it is deciding on its key **fiscal policy** decisions.

Checkpoint 3

What do we mean by the term 'money illusion'?

Examiner's secrets

Don't try to revise topics as isolated pieces of knowledge. Look for the links, e.g. unemployment and inflation.

Examiner's secrets

Candidates often make the mistake of writing more for a four-mark question than for an eight-mark question – don't!

Exam question (20 minutes)   answer: page 129

(a) Explain what is meant by the natural rate of unemployment.

(b) Explain whether it is possible to maintain an unemployment rate which is below the natural rate of unemployment.

The nature and importance of international trade

This section focuses on the benefits of international trade. Without international trade, we would not have access to many of the goods that make our lives enjoyable, such as fruit, textiles, electrical goods and foreign holidays. Some goods such as wine could be produced in the UK but might be more expensive than imported goods or services. International trade has the potential to benefit all participating countries.

Checkpoint 1

What is a current-account deficit?

Checkpoint 2

Identify three benefits of international trade.

Checkpoint 3

Identify two factors that may have contributed to the UK's current-account deficit.

Watch out!

The end of country quotas on textile exports is a major development in the world economy and illustrates the impact of comparative advantage on trade. The Multi-Fibre Agreement (MFA) was put in place in 1974 to protect textile industries in the USA and Europe. The USA is expected to lose a large number of jobs in the textile industry. In 1974 there were 2.4 million workers in the textile sector in the USA. By 2000, 40% of these jobs were gone. Global textile exports are worth nearly $500 billion a year. The ending of quotas is expected to boost global exports to more than £1200 billion by 2010. China and India are expected to benefit enormously. Foreign-exchange earnings will increase, growth will be boosted and unemployment should fall.

Examiner's secrets

The theory of comparative advantage assumes that specialisation will bring benefits. Less developed countries (LDCs) specialising in primary sector have experienced falling real prices since the Second World War. Barriers to trade, unequal bargaining strength and high transport costs have eroded the benefits of specialisation.

Specialisation

The reasons for trade between countries are similar to the reasons for trade within a country. In the same way that it is desirable for an individual to specialise rather than try to produce everything for themselves, so it is beneficial for a country to specialise.

Firms that specialise in producing particular goods can achieve economies of scale. Countries also specialise, producing more than they need of certain goods. The surplus can be exported. Revenues from exports can be used to buy imports. Countries must decide which goods to produce. The logical decision would be for a country to concentrate on the goods in which it has a comparative advantage.

Law of comparative advantage

Countries have different factor endowments. The workforce of a particular country will have particular skills, the climate varies from country to country and the available raw materials are different in different countries. These resources will be relatively immobile. Due to variation in resources, the relative cost of producing goods will vary from country to country.

For example, country A could produce one flat-screen television for the same cost as three tonnes of wheat or four DVD players. It is this difference in relative cost that provides the basis for trade.

At this point, it is appropriate to distinguish between absolute and comparative advantage.

Absolute advantage

A country has an absolute advantage over another country in the production of a good if it can produce the good using fewer resources than the other country. If France can produce wine using fewer resources than the UK, and the UK can produce whisky using fewer resources than France, then France has an absolute advantage in wine production and the UK has an absolute advantage in whisky production. Production of both wine and whisky will be maximised by each country specialising and then traded with the other country.

Comparative advantage

The law of comparative advantage states that a country that is able to produce all goods more efficiently than other countries will still benefit from trade if it specialises in those products in which it is relatively

most efficient. Producers that are less efficient will gain from trade
if they specialise in producing those products in which they are
comparatively least inefficient.

Production possibilities for two countries

		Flat-screen televisions	DVD players
Country A	Either	1	4
Country B	Either	2	32

Despite country B having an absolute advantage in both flat-screen
televisions and DVD players, country A has a comparative advantage
in flat-screen televisions because flat-screen televisions are relatively
cheaper in country A. Only four DVD players have to be sacrificed in
order to produce a flat-screen television. In country B, 16 DVD players
have to be sacrificed in order to produce one flat-screen television. In
other words, the opportunity cost of flat-screen televisions in country B
is higher (16/1 compared with 4/1). On the other hand, the opportunity
cost of DVD players is relatively lower (1/16 compared with 1/4).

Summary

Countries have a comparative advantage in those goods that can be
produced at a lower opportunity cost than in other countries.

If countries are to gain from trade, then they should export those
goods in which they have a comparative advantage and import those
in which they have a comparative disadvantage.

Checkpoint 4

Identify two advantages of specialisation.

Examiner's secrets

It is more important that you are
able to explain the principles of
comparative advantage than give a
numerical example. Under exam
conditions, students often get
numbers muddled.

Checkpoint 5

Draw a table similar to the one opposite.
This time assume that the figures are
country A, two flat-screen televisions or
six DVD players; country B, three flat-
screen televisions or 30 DVD players.
What are the opportunity cost ratios now?

Exam question (15 minutes)   answers: page 130

(a) Discuss two policies that the government may adopt in order to improve a
deficit in the balance of payments.

(b) Explain how UK membership of the EU might stimulate inward investment.

Free trade versus protection

Here we examine the potential tradeoffs associated with free trade and the implications of protecting domestic markets from imports.

Checkpoint 1

Give possible reasons for the decline of the UK shoe industry.

The jargon

Free trade area. Group of countries that remove trade barriers between member countries but retain their own trade policy with other countries, e.g. the North American Free Trade Agreement (NAFTA) allows free trade between Canada, Mexico and the USA.

Watch out!

Members of free-trade areas do not trade on a level playing field. For example, many Mexican farms have gone bankrupt since the NAFTA agreement was signed in 1994. Mexican import tariffs have been removed while the USA has maintained subsidies to its farmers.

Check the net

Follow the links below to find out about two free trade areas, their members and the aims of the organisations:
www.caricom.org
www.ftaa-alca.org

Free trade

The theory of comparative advantage illustrates that trade can be beneficial if the relative costs of production differ. The gains from trade are likely to be greatest when economies of scale are significant and transport costs are low.

Specialisation makes it possible for world production to be higher than it otherwise would. Specialisation and trade lead to resources being used more efficiently. With greater efficiency, the price of goods may be expected to fall. Lower prices will benefit consumers, increasing their real incomes and providing a wider range of goods.

Free trade should benefit producers. Firms will have access to larger markets, enabling them to benefit from economies of scale. The growth of firms should bring growth to the economy and raise living standards.

Free trade will inevitably mean that there will be winners and losers because of different factor endowments and different levels of efficiency. Comparative advantage may change over time, resulting in structural change as circumstances change.

Free trade may benefit strong countries and strong firms more than weak countries and firms. Well-established producers can move into new markets, enabling them to produce on a larger scale and sell at relative low prices. The danger of this is that overseas producers can eliminate weak domestic producers.

It is perhaps unsurprising that the most developed nations are the strongest advocates of trade liberalisation.

Should domestic markets be protected?

Few countries have adopted a policy of unrestricted free trade. Governments recognise that trade involves costs as well as benefits. When governments decide their policy on trade, they should consider the marginal benefits as well as the marginal costs of changing limits on trade.

Reducing barriers to trade may increase consumer choice. Conversely, a reduction in barriers to trade may make it difficult for some domestic producers to compete. This may have a knock-on effect upon domestic output and employment figures.

Ways of restricting trade ●●●

Customs duties or **tariffs** are taxes on imports. These taxes are often *ad valorem* (i.e. the tax is a proportion of the import). Tariffs can reduce demand if demand is elastic. Demand for goods is likely to be elastic when there are close domestic substitutes.

Tariffs can be a way of raising revenue for the government. Revenue-raising tariffs may be used when demand for a product is inelastic.

Tariffs can be used in order to prevent unfair competition. Tariffs have been used in the USA in order to prevent dumping in the US steel industry.

Quotas can limit the quantity of a particular good imported. In some instances, voluntary agreements are made with exporting countries in order to restrict exports.

Governments may choose to put an embargo on goods that are not felt to be in the public interest.

Firms importing goods could be required to apply for **import licences**. If the process is made very bureaucratic, this could limit imports.

Checkpoint 2

What are the arguments for developed countries protecting their industries against unfair competition from developing countries?

The jargon

Customs union. Free-trade area allowing unrestricted trade between member countries while operating a common trade policy to countries outside the union, e.g. the EU.

Checkpoint 3

What do you understand by the terms 'trade creation' and 'trade diversion'?

Checkpoint 4

Identify two possible costs of international trade.

Check the net

Follow this link for articles and video clips on protectionism: http://news.bbc.co.uk/1/hi/business/4230714.stm.

Exam question (25 minutes)   answer: pages 130–1

(a) Explain the costs and benefits of trade liberalisation.

(b) Assess whether trade liberalisation might reduce inequalities between countries.

(c) Examine the reasons for the UK government's commitment to improving competitiveness of British firms.

Fixed and floating exchange rates

The exchange rate is the value of a currency measured in terms of another currency. The exchange rate may be determined by free market forces of supply and demand, or governments may intervene in order to influence the exchange rate by buying or selling currency.

Checkpoint 1

Explain why the percentage increase in exports may be less than the percentage decrease in the value of sterling.

Examiner's secrets

When explaining how exchange rates are determined in a free market, bear in mind that the value of one currency can be measured only in terms of another currency.

Checkpoint 2

Draw a diagram to show the effect of sterling appreciation.

The jargon

When the value of sterling falls relative to a foreign currency, this is described as **sterling depreciation**.
When the value of sterling rises relative to a foreign currency, this is described as **sterling appreciation**.

Floating exchange rate

Exchange rates exist because countries wish to trade goods and services and countries use different currencies for internal trade. The exchange rate of a currency is its external price measured in terms of another currency.

Individuals may buy and sell currency for a number of reasons:

→ To pay for trade goods.
→ To move capital for investment purposes.
→ Speculators may wish to profit from short-term currency movements.

The value of the British pound is influenced by the forces of supply and demand. If overseas firms want to buy British goods to sell in their own countries, then they will need to demand pounds.

British firms wanting to buy foreign goods will have to buy foreign currency. In this way, foreign firms will demand sterling and British firms will buy sterling.

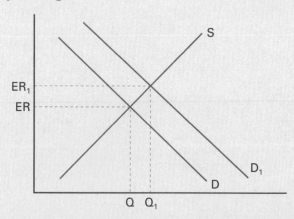

Quantity of pounds traded on the foreign exchange market

If the demand for exports increases, then the demand for pounds will increase, shifting the demand curve above to the right, from D to D_1 and raising the sterling exchange rate from er to er_1.

If we assume that foreign currency is acquired in order to finance trade, then the slope of the supply and the demand curve will be determined by the value of the exports and imports required at each exchange rate. If the sterling exchange rate falls, then UK exports will become more competitive as their relative cost falls. This will increase demand for pounds on the international exchange markets. The desire for imported goods will ensure that there is a supply of pounds.

A depreciation in sterling will reduce the competitiveness of foreign goods. If the demand for imports is elastic, then a fall in the exchange rate will result in fewer pounds being offered.

Fixed exchange rates ●●●

A fixed exchange rate system is one where a country's currency is fixed against other currencies by the central bank.

Intervention in the market ●●●

If the supply and demand of the domestic currency on foreign currency markets are not in equilibrium, then the central bank will be forced to intervene in order to adjust supply or demand. If there is excess demand for a country's currency, then the central bank will be forced to release more of its own currency on to the market.

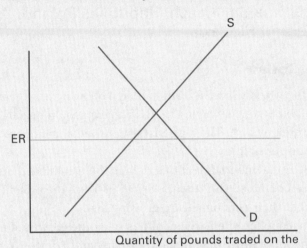

Quantity of pounds traded on the
foreign exchange market

In a fixed exchange rate system, the government undertakes to maintain the exchange rate at or near an agreed level (see the diagram above). Often, the currency value may move slightly above or below its agreed value (er). By allowing limited movement of the currency, the government does not have to constantly intervene in the market in order to maintain the exchange rate.

There are a number of advantages associated with fixed exchange rates. The principal benefits are:

→ A fixed exchange rate offers certainty.
→ The exchange rate encourages a discipline upon the economic management of firms and national governments.

The disadvantages of a fixed exchange rate are:

→ The fixed exchange rate may be incorrect and lead to currency being undervalued or overvalued.
→ Incorrectly valued currency could result in a trade imbalance.

Exam question (30 minutes)   answer: page 131

(a) Examine the likely consequences of a strong pound for British firms.

(b) Explain why a fall in the value of sterling may give UK manufacturers a competitive advantage.

(c) Assess the impact of the common agricultural policy (CAP) on cane-sugar producers.

Examiner's secrets

When examining the effect of an exchange-rate movement on firms, students often forget that the impact of exchange-rate movements will often depend upon price elasticity of demand.

Checkpoint 3

Explain why sterling appreciation may have good and bad effects on UK manufacturers.

Watch out!

Economic analysts have argued that China has kept its currency pegged against the dollar at an artificially low level in order to make its exports more attractive and fuel its rapid economic growth. Criticism has been strongest in the USA, where many analysts blame China for the decline of US manufacturing.
In July 2005, China abandoned this system for a floating exchange rate measured against a basket of currencies. It would be worth keeping an eye on the Chinese economy to see what effect this has on the economy.

EU issues

Ten new states joined the EU on 1 May 2004, increasing the number of states to 25. May 2005 saw a series of referendums, within member states. EU commissioners hoped that this series of votes would enable further progress on political integration. Twelve of the twenty-five member states approved the new constitution but Holland and France both rejected the constitution. Without unanimous agreement, political integration cannot proceed. Politicians continue to look for a way forward but rapid progress is unlikely.

The new EU members are Cyprus, Malta, Estonia, Latvia, Lithuania, Czech Republic, Poland, Hungary, Slovenia and Slovakia.

Checkpoint 1

The article identifies the ten new EU members. Who are the other 15 EU members?

The jargon

Common agricultural policy (CAP).
Set up to appease France, which wanted a system of agricultural subsidies as its price for agreeing to free trade in industrial goods. The aim of CAP was to:
→ increase productivity;
→ ensure fair living standards for the agricultural community;
→ stabilise markets;
→ ensure availability of food;
→ provide food at reasonable prices.
CAP costs EU members £50 billion euros annually and has led to some of the highest food prices in the world.

Europe today

The EU is the world's largest trading bloc. Following enlargement, there are 455 million people living in the EU. The expansion in 2004 increased its surface area by 25%. The new Eastern European members form an important power bloc.

The new EU members are not as rich as the established members. They have a combined GDP that is less than 5% of the other 15 EU members, but their economies are growing fast.

One consequence of enlargement has been the growth of migrant workers, most notably from Poland. Germany and France have tried to stem the flow of migrants by imposing limits on migration from new member countries. Quotas have been imposed on migrant workers in certain professions.

The UK, Ireland and Sweden have chosen to reduce barriers to their labour markets. More than 123 000 nationals from eight of the new member states obtained work permits to work in the UK between May and December 2004. The Home Office estimates that these workers generated £240 million worth of economic activity during that time. Migrant workers appear to have given a boost to the economy. Migration appears to have reduced labour shortages without increasing unemployment levels.

Concerns remain that migrant workers could exacerbate the problems of some of Europe's largest economies, struggling with high unemployment and expensive welfare systems.

Migration from new member states could damage their long-term growth prospects. Most migrant workers are aged under 34 years. Many are university-educated, prompting concerns of a 'brain drain'.

Europe tomorrow

The president of the European Commission, Jose Manuel Barroso, believes that enlargement has helped to consolidate political and economic stability, democracy and human rights, strengthening the EU's international position. Despite this, there are concerns about the EU's future identity and future growth and how it should function in the future.

France and Germany are not happy about the tax advantages of the new states and are concerned about social dumping as populations migrate in search of a better life in the major EU economies. Fears of an invasion of migrant workers have so far proven unfounded.

These concerns have prompted a review of future plans for expansion. France is particularly concerned about the shifting balance of power away from the Franco-German alliance towards a grouping of new member countries that prefer English as their second language. The French are likely to reject the new European Constitution which was intended to bring greater political integration. Further expansion of the EU may be delayed.

The French government is particularly concerned about allowing Turkey to join the EU. Apart from concerns about human rights and equal opportunities, there is concern that Turkey is a largely Muslim state and has a high birth rate: By 2020, it is estimated that Turkey would have a population of more than 100 million people. This would make it the largest state within the EU. If Turkey were to join the EU, then political power would slip away from France and Germany. Turkey is engaged in talks to join the EU but entry is at least 10 years away.

Heated debate is also likely to centre on the reform of the CAP and rebate given to the UK because of the size of its contribution to EU funds.

Examiner's secrets

You need to know about the major EU policies and legislation and you need to be able to discuss their economic impact.

Watch out!

Europe's rate of population growth is slowing, while the inhabitants are ageing. This raises a major question: who will produce the wealth to sustain the retired population?
Some analysts believe that immigration could be the magic bullet that will solve Europe's labour market and welfare-state problems.

Exam question (20 minutes)   answer: page 131

(a) Examine the implication of economic migrants on EU members.

(b) Assess the reasons why new members of the EU may have wished to join.

Potential costs and benefits of UK membership of

Watch out!

The rate of growth in the eurozone is expected to rise during 2006 and 2007. The European Commission expects growth of 1.9% in 2006 and 2.1% in 2007. Unemployment is expected to fall as domestic demand increases. Capital investment is also expected to rise. Despite the positive indicators, it is unlikely that the positive economic indicators will influence the UK's position regarding joining the euro.

The debate over whether the UK should join the eurozone is complex and extremely heated. Those who wish to join the euro offer promises of more trade, more jobs and lower transaction costs. Those who argue against the UK's membership of the euro suggest that membership would create a straitjacket for the UK economy and would tie economic policy to that of the rest of Europe.

Detailed below are the main arguments for and against joining the euro.

Arguments for joining the euro

The existence of different currencies across Europe is seen by some politicians and economists as a major obstacle to trade, in the same way as tariffs and quotas restrict trade. Supporters of the euro argue that it will bring considerable economic benefit to member countries, increasing trade through the elimination of exchange rate fluctuations. Costs for industry will be lowered because firms will not have to buy euros for use within the eurozone.

Membership of the eurozone would also encourage economic stability, as countries are required to move towards economic convergence. Governments are no longer able to relax economic policy in the run up to an election in an attempt to win over voters. The European Central Bank (ECB) will determine interest-rate policy in order to ensure stable prices.

For consumers, there is a clear benefit of comparability. Prices of products can be compared easily, encouraging the purchase of goods across borders and moving markets closer to a state of perfect knowledge.

Checkpoint 1

Which countries have adopted the euro?

Check the net

www.euro.gov.uk
www.xe.com/euro.htm
http://news.bbc.co.uk/1/hi/uk_politics/2981479.stm

Gordon Brown's five tests for entry into the euro

→ Are UK and eurozone economies and interest rates converging?

→ Is there sustainable long-term compatibility? In other words, if things go wrong, is the system flexible enough for the government to be able to deal with any problems?

→ Will the UK benefit from increased foreign investment by joining the euro?

→ Would the financial services sector benefit from joining the euro?

→ Would membership of the euro stimulate growth and employment?

the euro

Arguments against joining the euro ●●●

Joining the euro would mean that the UK government would give up its right to manage economic policy. Decisions about interest rates and public spending would be taken by unelected officials. A single economic policy does not meet the needs of all member countries, causing high unemployment and more boom and bust.

The UK has fared well outside the euro, with the lowest unemployment and inflation for a generation, and a stable economy.

Key arguments against joining the euro

→ The UK's ability to set taxes and control spending would be affected as the eurozone seeks to harmonise all aspects of economic policy.

→ The Bank of England can react to domestic or international conditions. It could reduce interest rates in order to ease or reduce the effects of a global downturn. In contrast, the ECB must balance the conflicting needs of the 12 Eurozone members.

→ The public spending policy of countries in the eurozone is limited by the Stability and Growth Pact. The pact's guidelines are inflexible. The UK could be asked to reduce its budget deficit, resulting in cuts in public services.

→ The UK has benefited from remaining outside the eurozone and has, according to the OECD, the best outlook of any G7 country. GDP per head in the UK is higher than in Germany or France. The UK also has the lowest inflation and has some of the highest take-home pay in the EU.

→ UK unemployment is at the lowest level for 25 years and is almost half the eurozone average rate. Since leaving the ERM in 1992 and resuming control of its own monetary policy, Britain has created over two million jobs.

Checkpoint 2

Which types of business would be most affected by the introduction of the euro?

Checkpoint 3

Will a single currency end price discrimination across Europe?

Examiner's secrets

When answering a question, take time to consider the question. Look at how the marks are allocated and allocate your time appropriately – and stick to it! Too often, candidates spend too long trying to gain a few marks, thereby wasting time that could be spent on questions with a greater mark allocation. It is better to answer three questions fairly well rather than answering one very well and failing to answer two others. Underline key words in the question to help you focus your thoughts.

Exam question (20 minutes)   answer: page 132

(a) Assess the economic arguments for the UK joining the euro.

(b) Explain why economic problems in Greece, France and Germany could result in economic slowdown throughout the eurozone.

The eurozone's Growth and Stability Pact

The Growth and Stability Pact states that a country's budget deficit must not exceed 3% of its gross domestic product (GDP). Countries that exceed this limit would face financial penalties imposed by the European Central Bank (ECB). The agreement limits the size of a nation's budget deficit and has been criticised for not letting governments boost economic growth by spending more.

A fiscal straitjacket

France and Germany have pushed for the Growth and Stability Pact to be changed. The deficit limit would stay at 3% of GDP, but countries would be allowed to break that level in special circumstances and only for a limited period. France and Germany have breached the 3% deficit limit in every one of the past three years, and along with Italy they are calling for greater freedom to increase state spending. They argue that the rules were put in place when economic growth was stronger and make no allowance for more difficult times. The governments of France and Germany are having to pay out more in benefit payments.

Greece has admitted it joined the euro in 2001 on the basis of figures that showed its budget deficit to be much lower than it really was. The budget deficit of Greece has exceeded the 3% limit since 1999 due in part to the £4.8 billion cost of hosting the 2004 Summer Olympics.

The ECB is currently telling Eastern European member states hoping to join the euro that they must adhere strictly to the 3% rule, despite the fact that ten of the EU's 25 members are currently in breach of the deficit rule.

Despite initial tough talk, the Stability and Growth Pact has delivered neither growth nor stability. The whole point of the pact is that it is supposed to guarantee against spendthrift governments' lax fiscal policies undermining the euro.

It was hoped that the launch of the euro and the creation of the ECB would create a unified monetary policy, while the pact would ensure a unified fiscal policy. This has not happened.

The revised pact maintains the existing limits on spending: budgets deficits should be no more than 3% and public debts should not exceed 60% of GDP or economic output. Governments can now use a variety of excuses for breaking the Growth and Stability Pact, including the costs

---

Checkpoint 1

Greece produced misleading figures for its budget deficit. Why might this become a problem for the eurozone?

Checkpoint 2

Italy is experiencing rising unemployment and falling productivity. What are the implications of this?

of development aid, measures to increase employment, reforming pension systems and the cost of European unification. The latter criterion allows Germany to exclude the costs of German reunification (1989) from budget-deficit calculations. Governments can now spend their way out of an economic slowdown without the threat of penalties from the European Commission.

Qualitative judgements must now be made regarding budget deficits. Will a budget deficit of 3.9% be acceptable? What about 4%? The answer is likely to depend on whether it is Germany or Greece with the deficit.

A spokesperson for the ECB said: 'Sound fiscal policies and a monetary policy geared to price stability are fundamental for the success of the economic and monetary union.' Building up large deficits could undermine confidence in the euro. The USA has shown how promoting growth by deficit spending can lead to currency depreciation.

Changes in the Stability and Growth Pact have given governments increased flexibility to manage their own fiscal policies. It has also created a two-tier system, which could cause divisions in the future. Germany and France have been protected from penalties. Other countries may not be so fortunate in the future. The ECB also has the capacity to increase interest rates if a member country breaks the limits set on budget deficits. This could cause an economic slowdown across the eurozone, damaging the economies of financially prudent economies.

Checkpoint 3

The EU has created a two-tier system with special considerations being given to France and Germany. What problems may this cause in the future?

Check the net

http://news.bbc.co.uk/1/hi/world/europe/4082610.stm
http://news.bbc.co.uk/1/hi/business/4119282.stm
http://europa.eu.int/comm/economy_finance/index_en.htm

Watch out!

The Growth and Stability Pact has been criticised as being inflexible and needs to be applied over the economic cycle rather than in any one year. Eurosceptic commentators argue that it promotes neither stability nor growth and remark that it has been applied inconsistently.

The jargon

Economic cycle. Economies do not rise and fall at a consistent rate. They experience a regular trade or business cycle, where the rate of growth of production, incomes and spending fluctuates over time.

Exam question (25 minutes)   answer: page 132–3

(a) Assess the case for Britain joining the euro.

(b) Examine the policy options open to countries such as Germany when dealing with rising unemployment.

(c) Examine the likely impact of rising budget deficits on the value of the euro.

International institutions

International economics are increasingly dominated by international organisations. The effects of these organisations on trade and investment flows are increasing.

Checkpoint 1

How does the WTO differ from GATT?

Checkpoint 2

How does the role of the World Bank differ from that of the IMF?

Watch out!

Critics of the IMF claim that IMF policy-makers deliberately supported capitalist military dictatorships friendly to US and European business. They also suggest that the IMF has been hostile to the views of democracy, human-rights groups and trade unionists. These criticisms helped to promote the anti-globalisation movement.

World Trade Organization

The World Trade Organization (WTO) is the successor to the General Agreement on Tariffs and Trade (GATT). The WTO has 134 members who make decisions on the basis of unanimity. No single country has the power of veto. Members have four broad aims:

→ To extend free-trade concessions to all members.
→ To establish freer global trade with reduced barriers.
→ To make trade more predictable by establishing rules.
→ To remove subsidies in order to make trade more competitive.

The key functions of the WTO are shown in the diagram below.

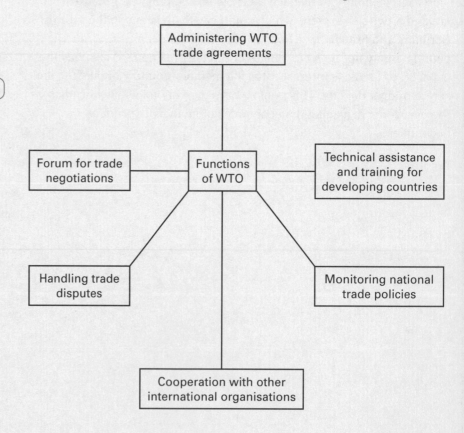

International Monetary Fund

The International Monetary Fund (IMF) works to promote economic stability and prevent crises. The IMF will offer assistance to help resolve crises and to promote growth and alleviate poverty.

The IMF engages in three core activities: surveillance, technical assistance and lending.

→ **Lending** is offered to member countries to correct balance of payments problems.
→ **Technical assistance** (training) is offered in several areas: fiscal policy, monetary and exchange rate policy, banking and financial supervision and statistics.
→ The IMF conducts **appraisals** of each member country's economic situation and discusses policies that are conducive to stable exchange rates and economic development.

World Bank

The mission of the World Bank is to fight poverty and raise living standards of the developing world.

The World Bank provides policy advice, technical assistance and finance for development projects that will improve the infrastructure of low- and middle-income countries. Interest is payable on loans, and so projects must be commercially viable.

The projects supported by the World Bank are wide-ranging and include:

→ Education projects
→ AIDS programmes
→ Water and electricity projects
→ Transport projects

The World Bank Group is made up of five distinct organisations: the International Bank of Reconstruction and Development, the International Development Association, the International Finance Corporation and the Multinational Investment Guarantee Agency.

Check the net

All the major international organisations have their own websites for further research:
WTO: www.wto.org
IMF: www.imf.org
Worldbank: www.worldbank.org

Checkpoint 3

What effect do subsidies have on international trade?

Check the net

For a critical view of the IMF, visit www.essentialaction.org and www.globalissues.org.

Watch out!

The World Bank has been criticised for undermining the governments of developing countries through structural adjustment programmes.
The World Bank has been criticised for acting under the influence of major Western countries, to the detriment of the development of local economies and the people living in developing countries. It has been suggested that the World Bank should intervene in order to rescue irresponsible loans from private institutions to developing-world governments.

The jargon

Structural adjustment programmes (SAP). Loans offered on condition that countries adopt policies aimed at market liberalisation, such as privatisation, ending subsidies and currency devaluation.

Exam question (30 minutes)   answer: page 133

(a) Assess the impact of structural adjustment policies on developing countries.

(b) Assess the impact of the World Bank on developing countries.

Answers
Macroeconomic issues and policies

Micro, macro, the circular flow of income

Checkpoints

1 One factor is inheritance: the easiest way to be wealthy is to belong to a wealthy family and receive a legacy. If you are lucky and clever enough, this wealth can then be used to generate income, e.g. inherited land can be used for agriculture, housebuilding or other income-generating businesses.

2

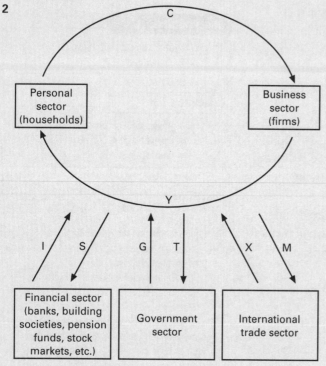

This diagram shows all the money flows. Corresponding real flows include factor services (land, labour, capital, enterprise) from households to firms, in exchange for income; output of goods and services from firms to households, in exchange for consumption expenditure; financial services, from banks and other institutions to their customers in return for their savings; public services from government to citizens; and goods and services exported by domestic firms to overseas customers in return for their spending on internationally traded items.

Exam question

(a) See the discussion of GDP, AD and AS on page 82.

(b) If planned injections = planned withdrawals, then the circular flow of income is in **equilibrium**, meaning that there is no reason for national income to increase or decrease. If planned injections > planned withdrawals, then we can predict that national income will rise. If planned injections < planned withdrawals, then we can predict that national income will fall. Note that although planned injections can be different from planned withdrawals, at the end of any time period actual injections must equal actual withdrawals. Logically, the amount spent by consumers must equal the amount received by producers. But equally logically, there is no reason why their consuming and producing plans should be equal in advance.

Macroeconomic indicators

Checkpoints

1 Two constants well-known to mathematicians and physicists are:
- π (pi), the ratio between the circumference and diameter of a circle, approximately 22/7.
- g, the gravitational constant, the acceleration of any object falling freely to earth: 980 cm per second per second.

According to Einstein, the only true constant in the universe is c, the speed of light, which is approximately 300 million metres per second. Unlike Einstein, economists deal with the behaviour of human beings rather than natural phenomena and are unlikely to discover any real constants, as people are unpredictable and can react against predictions. The monetarists thought that there was a constant relationship between the money supply and inflation, but this idea proved worthless in practice, as people were able to use plastic alternatives to cash. The more that governments tried to directly limit the supply of money, the more the growth of money supply became uncontrollable. This is related to **Goodhart's law**, which suggests that if a variable is targeted because it is a symptom of a problem, then the problem will not be cured. Instead, the indicator merely becomes unreliable as an indicator. This could apply, for instance, to waiting lists as an indicator of the efficiency of hospitals.

2 A higher interest rate in the UK is likely to attract foreign currencies into UK banks. This increases the demand for pounds and raises the exchange rate of the pound against other currencies. This will make imports appear cheaper to UK consumers, and UK exports appear dearer to foreign consumers and, depending on the PED of exports and imports, adversely affect the balance of payments.

Exam question

(a) This is the best answer, as Britain has a high tendency to import. Any increase in spending power is likely to encourage people to buy goods and services. Many services are home-produced, but a glance around any shopping centre will reveal that these days many goods are manufactured overseas. Therefore, imports rise.

(b) Unemployment is likely to fall due to higher demand, provided at least some of the demand is directed at home-produced goods and services.

(c) Household savings are either unaffected or likely to fall as savers become borrowers.

(d) Unlikely to be directly affected.

Traditional aims of macroeconomic policy

Checkpoints

1 See the discussion of stagflation on page 106. It was inflationary in that industrial costs and, hence, prices were pushed upwards. It was deflationary in that jobs were lost as industry tried to reduce costs and the increased unemployment depressed demand.

2 Britain has long had a high tendency to import, or, to use the jargon, a **high marginal propensity to import** (MPM). Britain has always needed to import things that it cannot produce itself, such as pineapples and bananas. But since UK manufacturing has virtually collapsed, Britain now imports many things that it has more or less given up producing, e.g. electrical goods, clothing, motorcycles. The formal definition of MPM is 'the fraction of any increase in income spent on imported products'. If a country's MPM is high, then it follows that higher incomes at home can lead to balance-of-payments difficulties.

Exam question

This question can be answered from the point of view of possible conflict between policies: a high rate of economic growth will support the objective of full employment but might conflict with the objectives of low inflation and balance-of-payments equilibrium (see page 72). It can also be answered from an environmental perspective: rapid growth might lead to unacceptable levels of pollution, resource depletion and other negative externalities, such as noise, stress and urban overcrowding (see the discussion of environmental policy on page 154).

Supply side: microenvironment of macro-policy

Checkpoints

1 The idea of flexible labour markets dates back to the Thatcherite supply-side policies of the 1980s. These policies are essentially anti-trade union and involved giving management the right to hire and fire. They result in the casualisation of the workforce and the uncertainty of short-term contracts and part-time work. They are modelled on US labour laws. Flexible working practices, on the other hand, involve a more European style of supply-side policy, used most successfully in Norway and the Netherlands. They involve partnerships between employers, trade unions and other stakeholders, and they involve such things as multiskilling, removing demarcation lines for more flexible working, and a focus on education and training.

2 First, there has been a shift away from heavy industry and manufacturing into services, where work tends to be sedentary rather than physical. Second, the nature of work has become more uncertain, as part of the flexible labour

market philosophy. It is quite possible that uncertainty at work contributes to stress levels.

3 **Production** is the process of turning inputs into an output (a flow concept, measuring a variable such as output per hour from a production plant). **Productivity** is the efficiency of the production process (a ratio concept, measuring a variable such as output per person-hour).

Exam question

To answer this question, you need to outline the differences between the two and give some examples of each type of policy. The assumption contained in the question can be questioned, as modern thinking is not that it is a case of 'either/or' but that there is a role for each, complementing each other, with demand management fine-tuning the economy in the short run in order to achieve inflation targets, and supply-side policy working in the long run to improve productivity and competitiveness. Also see the discussion of relationships in macro theory on page 80.

Rules-based budgetary policy

Checkpoints

1 It would presumably be the duty of the MPC to increase interest rates in order to reduce aggregate demand to avoid inflationary pressure from the budget boost.

2 'Boom' refers to a period of expansion and a higher level of economic activity. 'Bust' refers to an economic slowdown. 'Boom and bust' suggests a cyclical pattern of economic activity and has also been referred to as the 'stop–go cycle'.

Exam question

(a) Governments spend for three reasons:
- **Allocation** – in order to allocate resources in a way that differs from that which market forces would dictate, e.g. for the NHS, defence or education.
- **Distribution** – in order to reduce inequalities in society.
- **Stabilisation** – in order to improve economic performance. As argued above, this is more likely these days to be aimed at the supply side rather than the demand side of the economy.

(b) Before the advent of rules-based budgetary policy, it was assumed that a budget surplus was deflationary, because it withdrew money from the circular flow, while a budget deficit was reflationary in terms of spending and output, because it represented an overall injection into the circular flow, but could also be inflationary if the government was tempted to finance its deficit through excessive borrowing, which was later repaid through the printing of money rather than through extra real output. It should be noted that a balanced budget is not necessarily neutral in terms of overall aggregate demand. There is the possibility of a balanced budget multiplier, because some of the money taken out of the circular flow and then spent by the government might not have been spent by the private sector – it might have been saved instead. Under the modern regime of inflation targeting and interest-rate policy (see page 78), it is the duty of the independent central bank, if it considers that a budget is not neutral, to adjust the interest rate so that in effect it neutralises the budget's influence on inflation.

Examiner's secrets

Candidates tend to appear very weak when answering questions like 'Why do governments spend?' or 'Why do governments impose taxes?', which in effect are almost the same question. They will write at length on items in the government budget, such as health and education, and will give the impression of general knowledge rather than a systematic piece of economic analysis. Use the words 'allocation', 'distribution' and 'stabilisation' as a basis for discussion, and your answer is likely to be much more impressive as a piece of economic writing.

A balanced budget is neutral in its effect on aggregate demand in the short run. Its effect on the economy in the long run depends on the purposes to which the budget is put. It could be spent on wars, Millennium Domes or other purposes with doubtful economic returns. Or it could be spent on priorities such as transport, education and health, all of which have direct effects on productivity and competitiveness. So it could be argued that the uses to which tax revenues are put are more important than balancing revenues with expenditure.

Inflation targeting, interest-rate policy, output gaps

Checkpoints

1 This is a recognition of the Keynesian idea of a tradeoff between inflation and employment. The lower band implies that inflation can fall too low, so that demand slumps and unemployment rises to unacceptably high levels. In recent years, for example, Japan has had negative inflation (falling prices). This has had two important consequences: interest rates have been near or at zero, so that adjustments in monetary policy have little or no effect on the economy; and spending has slowed right down: why buy a big-ticket item like a TV or a car this month when it might be cheaper next month? This slowdown has badly affected Japanese employment levels.

2 Demand is affected in three main ways. Suppose interest rates are increased: (1) saving becomes more attractive, thus reducing spending; (2) consumption is decreased, especially on big-ticket items like cars and household appliances, which are often bought on credit; (3) investment is reduced, as firms often use borrowed money in order to finance the purchase of new capital equipment.

Exam question

Uninterrupted growth, persistently low inflation and falling unemployment all indicate a stable economy. Here, you should explain what is meant by 'stability', in terms of achieving macroeconomic objectives. When discussing balance, you could distinguish between external and internal balance. The UK economy has been externally unbalanced in recent years, with a near-collapse of exporting and record balance-of-payments deficits. It has also been internally unbalanced, with the housing market experiencing inflation at a tremendously greater rate than the rest of the economy, and retailing and services booming while manufacturing declines. There are also persistent disparities in living standards between and within regions.

Relationships in macro-theory

Checkpoints

1 • **Output gap:** planned growth is greater than trend growth (there is overused capacity).
   • **Negative output gap:** planned growth is below trend growth (there is spare capacity).

2 The vertical axis of the SRAS graph shows price level, while SRPC shows inflation, which is the change in the price level over time. These two axes therefore measure very similar things. The horizontal axis of SRAS measures output, while SRPC measures unemployment. These two variables are opposites, in that an increase in output can be expected to reduce unemployment. It follows that as the SRAS curves upwards, so the SRPC curves downwards as a mirror image.

Exam question

Be careful with this. In textbooks and in exams, it is not unusual to see a PPF diagram where point a is described as 'unattainable' in the short run. This could well be the correct answer in a multiple-choice exam, and you need to be aware of this. However, for discussion purposes in a written answer, you should also be aware that point a is 'unattainable' only in the sense that it lies outside normal productive capacity in the short run. In the long run, of course, it is attainable given the success of supply-side policy. However, in some circumstances, normal productive capacity could be exceeded in the short run. At a time of national emergency, such as all-out war, factories could work day and night, people could work 12- or 16-hour shifts, machinery could be speeded up, and so on. Point a could possibly be attained, but only at a price (overtime payments, higher maintenance costs, more machinery breakdowns, greater fuel and energy costs), and so it would be an inflationary position. So, in this sense, a might be attainable but arguably not sustainable.

GDP, AD and AS in the UK

Checkpoints

1 Suppose a new car is produced at a factor cost of £10 000, but during the production process there is

wear and tear on car-making machinery of £1. We could add £10 000 to measured national income in gross terms. However, if we allow for depreciation (or capital consumption), the true additional to national income (net national product) is £9999. It is important that a country should be aware of depreciation. If steps are not taken to replenish worn-out capital (replacement investment), then productivity and competitiveness will certainly decrease over time.

2   It depends. In developed countries such as the USA, the UK and other large EU members, GNP tends to be larger than GDP. This is because the UK, for example, benefits from inward investment (overseas companies locating plant on UK territory) but also from outward investment (UK companies locating plant on overseas territory). This means that flows of profits from overseas assets both leave and enter the UK; in this case, inflows exceed outflows, so that GNP exceeds GDP. In less developed countries, where inward investment is far more likely than outward investment, the opposite is likely to be the case, unless, as sometimes happens, large numbers of migrant workers leave the country and remit part of their earnings to family back home (increasing GNP). On the other hand, debt repayments to banks or governments in other countries will reduce GNP.

3   'Market price' (in the sense of the price on a sales ticket in the shop) can be increased by raising expenditure taxes. This does not necessarily represent any increase in the real output of the product. Similarly, a subsidy can reduce the ticket price, and reduce the amount spent on each unit of the product, but does not necessarily represent actual output. Factor cost measures the value of resources used to make a product, and is therefore likely to be very closely related to real output, as opposed to the retail prices attached to that output.

Exam question

When the car was first built and sold as new, £10 000 was added to the measured national income for that year. This was the value added by car manufacturers at that time. My selling the car second-hand to the garage adds nothing to the national income. The sale represents a change of ownership of assets, rather than the creation of a new asset. Previously I had the car and the garage had £3000; now the garage has the car and I have £3000. In doing up the car and selling it on for £3500, the garage has added value of £500, and so this amount should be added to measured national income for this year.

Uses and limitations of GDP league tables

Checkpoints

1   Social capital is a stock concept (see page 70) and is the accumulation of past flows of investment in physical capital (houses, offices, shops, factories, other buildings, machines, transport systems, other infrastructure), human

capital (skills, qualifications, health) and institutions (schools, universities, hospitals, emergency services, legal systems).

2   The money to pay for social capital comes out of national income. A country that is willing to save and invest for the future is likely to build up capital more effectively than a country that spends on items for immediate consumption. Wise investment in social capital makes a country more efficient and, hence, better able to create national income in the future.

Exam question

The quick answer is 'no'. The key to a full answer is to show an awareness of what it is that GDP measures and then to focus on what GDP does not measure.

> **Examiner's secret**
>
> Although it might be worded in different ways, this fundamental question is very common in some shape or form in economics examinations. A knowledge of the main uses and limitations of GDP league tables can, therefore, pay large dividends.

Underlying concepts: saving, investment, multiplier

Checkpoints

1   Capital goods are assets that are purchased not for their own sake but because they can be used in the production of goods and services. Examples include factories, machines, shops, offices (business capital); houses, schools, hospitals, transport systems (social capital). Some assets can be both consumer goods and capital goods; for example, a car owned by a taxi driver can be regarded as a consumer good when used for social, domestic and pleasure purposes, but as a capital good when it is working as a taxi, and thus providing a business service.

2   **Cause:** in the UK, the state of the housing market is a major cause of personal debt. The peculiar phrase 'affordable housing' implies that most houses are unaffordable and people buying houses are having to borrow heavily. In recent years, credit-card companies have made borrowing easier; critics would say that it is far too easy.

Effect: in the short run, debt can increase economic activity by creating consumer demand. In the long run, however, debts have to be repaid; if the borrowing has been used for unproductive purposes, then this can have a depressing effect on the economy. It can also cause social problems such as family stress and bankruptcy. Ideally, debt should be used to finance investment rather than consumption, so that repayments can be made out of higher production in the future.

Exam question

Governments often refer indirectly to the multiplier principle by quoting what is in effect a payroll multiplier. For example, it might be claimed that having the Olympics in London will create x direct jobs and y indirect or spinoff jobs. Usually, these claims are made without supporting evidence and could well be exaggerated. The business sector also often makes claims for a multiplier; representatives of the tourist industry, for example, claim that tourists create direct and indirect employment in the areas that they visit, but it is rarely mentioned that some tourist developments, such as airports and cheap flights, might reduce domestic tourism and export jobs to other countries.

A more precise knowledge of multiplier coefficients would be useful in, for example, predicting the effect of investment in a new motorway or railway line, the important point being that in order to create income of, say, £1 million, extra spending need only be a fraction of £1 million. Multiplier effects can come from any injection, and many politicians and economists believe that export-led growth is an effective policy for encouraging economic development.

A knowledge of multipliers is useful in predicting economic trends and the effects of positive and negative output gaps (see page 78). It is important to realise that as well as upward multipliers resulting from injections and creating income, output and employment, there can also be downward multipliers creating recession and unemployment.

Some critics of government involvement in the multiplier process argue that public spending can result in crowding out – instead of creating new investment, it simply replaces private sector investment. If this is true, then it might be a good thing or a bad thing, depending on priorities. Suppose government expenditure on a new industrial estate crowds out private-sector investment in a shopping mall, or government expenditure on a leisure centre crowds out private-sector investment in a gambling casino. Whether these crowdings out are viewed as desirable depends on people's priorities and the type of society in which they wish to live.

Economic growth and sustainability

Checkpoints

1 China, India, Ireland.
2 Leisure and non-marketed activities have been growing at a slower rate than the output of goods and services, while the output of 'bads' and 'regrettables' has been growing faster.
3 Educational qualifications differ greatly from country to country, as do things such as school-leaving age and, indeed, starting age. Adult literacy rates can be measured in a standardised way across countries and cultures and can, therefore, serve as an indicator of educational standards. One drawback is that illiteracy tends to be underrecorded in developed countries, where the ability to read and write at a basic level is invariably reported to be around 99% of the population. This reduces the

sensitivity of this part of the HDI comparison between advanced economies. Adults in countries such as the UK are reluctant to admit that they have literacy problems and often go through life using avoidance strategies, e.g. asking friends and relatives to fill in official documents for them rather than tackling the problem itself.

Exam question

You will already know (see the circular flow of income and the multiplier on pages 68 and 86) that the first three of these factors can contribute to economic growth, in the sense of capacity utilisation (actual growth), while public spending can contribute to the growth of productive capacity itself (potential growth). Public spending is also important for the supply side of the economy. At times of high levels of growth in the UK economy, there have been both high levels of demand and high levels of supply (output). In considering development as opposed to growth, it is important to consider the composition of these variables as well as their levels. Public spending, for example, can contribute to growth without contributing to development. The government of a dictatorship might spend huge amounts of money on manufacturing armaments, which are then used against their own population. Economic growth might well be high, but expenditure on health and education provision would do far more for development.

Definitions and measures of inflation

Checkpoints

1 One disadvantage is that it takes time to collect and analyse the data. The data are, therefore, always historic. This is a recurring difficulty for the government when it is trying to manage the economy. The analogy has been made that managing the economy is like trying to drive a car forward while looking in your rear-view mirror for direction. A second limitation is that over time, the basket of goods will change, raising questions of comparability over time.
2 The principal benefit of the CPI is it allows UK performance in controlling inflation to be measured against the performance of other European countries. The way that the RPI is calculated means that it is not possible to make comparisons.
3 Inflation is a general and sustained rise in prices.

Exam question

(a) A sharp fall in inflation might be expected to have a positive effect on consumer confidence. It is also likely to be reflected in lower borrowing costs, leading to an increase in consumer expenditure.

House-price inflation may also encourage people to look at house purchase as a speculation, buying houses to live in and also for later resale in the hope of achieving a capital gain. Householders may also use increasing equity to support increased consumption. This is known as equity withdrawal and would increase aggregate demand.

(b) One aspect of house-price inflation is that people on low incomes may be priced out of the market. The government may have to intervene into the market in order to provide low-cost housing. House-price inflation would have a significant impact upon the RPI.

Consequences (costs) of inflation

Checkpoints

1 Borrowers are likely to benefit from inflation as the real cost of borrowing falls. Losers are likely to be those on fixed incomes, such as pensioners, as their income lags behind the rate of inflation, and savers, who will see the real rate of return on their investments fall.
2 The Internet may reduce shoe-leather costs, making it easier to compare the prices of goods on the Internet. However, not all firms advertise on the Internet, and searching the Internet still involves labour costs, as it takes time to compare prices.
3 Menu costs are likely to be affected as inflation is likely to affect exchange rates in the long term. Firms may be expected to adjust price lists in order to reflect adjustments in nominal prices and exchange rates.

Exam question

One strategy the government might adopt is to increase the supply of labour where there are particular skills shortages. This can be achieved by increasing training provision or by offering incentives to trainees. This process may take time to have an effect.

The government might encourage foreign workers with essential skills to move to the UK. European enlargement has stimulated an increase in the number of economic migrants and has helped to fill some skills gaps. This policy has been adopted by other European countries, including Germany.

Demand pull and cost push inflation

Checkpoints

1 The terms 'cost push inflation' and 'demand pull inflation' are associated with Keynesian economics. Inflation can arise as a result of a decrease in aggregate supply. The two main sources of decrease in aggregate supply are an increase in wage rates and an increase in the prices of raw materials. A decrease in aggregate supply may lead to an increase in costs. The resulting increase in prices (inflation) is called cost push inflation. Other things being equal, the higher the cost of production, the less will be produced. At a given price level, increasing wage rates or rising prices of raw materials such as energy lead firms to decrease the quantity of labour employed and to cut back on production.

Inflation due to an increase in aggregate demand is called demand pull inflation. This type of inflation may occur due to increases in the money supply, increases in government purchases and increases in the price level in the rest of the world.

2 Monetarists take the view that there is a close relationship between money and aggregate demand. They believe that the economy is either at or close to full employment. An increase in aggregate demand will lead to inflation. Monetarists believe that inflation is always and everywhere a monetary phenomenon.

Keynesians argue that inflation occurs due to changes in real variables. Keynesians offer two explanations as to the cause of inflation. The first is demand pull inflation (inflation occurs when there is too much money chasing too few goods). The second cause of inflation identified by Keynesian economists is cost push inflation (inflation is caused by increases in the costs of production).

3 The impact on living standards will depend upon whether income manages to keep pace with or outstrip the rate of inflation. If it does, then living standards may increase, particularly for homeowners, who may see the cost of borrowing fall. Government employees may fare less well. Government tends to encourage public-sector-pay settlements that are below the rate of inflation. This means that public-sector workers may see their real incomes fall, which will have a negative impact on incomes.

Exam question

(a) Policy options for controlling the rate of inflation include fiscal policies (reducing government expenditure or increasing direct or indirect taxation), monetary policies (using interest rates to curb spending) and exchange-rate and supply-side policies. Answers should offer an analysis of how alternative approaches might work and include an assessment of the implications and likely effectiveness of each policy.
(b) Wages and salaries represent around 70% of UK national income. Given this proportion, increases in wages are one of the most significant causes of increases in production costs. There is a strong correlation between wage push inflation and cost push inflation as a result.

Measures of unemployment

Checkpoints

1 The number of people in employment rose by 334 000 (September 2005) while the numbers unemployed also rose by 41 000 because more people entered the labour market. This resulted in a simultaneous rise in the numbers employed and a rise in the numbers seeking work.
2 It would lower the economic activity rate.
3 Of the three survey methods, the economic activity rate is likely to give the highest measure of unemployment.

Exam question

Gathering data is useful because the data provide the government with an indicator against which it can measure its economic performance. It also enables the government to identify trends in unemployment and allocate resources towards benefits or training provision as needed.

Causes of unemployment

Checkpoints

1 Frictional unemployment could be reduced by improving information on vacancies and retraining.
2 Cyclical unemployment.
3 The natural rate of unemployment is the rate below which it is impossible to reduce unemployment in the long term. In the short term it may be possible to reduce unemployment below the natural rate by increasing aggregate demand. In the long term this reduction cannot be sustained.

Exam question

(a) An economic downturn may be expected to have a number of effects on the labour market. Unskilled workers with no transferable skills are likely to be the most affected. Increasing the pool of labour may lead to a reduction in wage rates. Firms are likely to layoff workers in an attempt to control costs. The impact of a downturn will be felt unevenly. For example the building trade is likely to be affected quite early on, whilst employment in food retail.

(b) A range of possible policies might be identified. These might include supply side policies and reflationary policies.

The use of supply side policies may improve the workings of the supply side of the policy. Measures may include reduction of income tax, increased expenditure on education and training and a reform of the benefit system. These measures may take time to have an effect and may disadvantage some groups, particularly those on benefits.

Reflationary policies to boost the level of economic activity might include:

- Increasing the level of government expenditure
- Cutting taxation (either direct or indirect) to encourage spending
- Cutting interest rates to discourage saving and encourage spending
- Allowing some money supply growth

The downside with this type of policy is that it may have wider implications for the economy beyond those intended. Reflating the economy may stimulate demand, leading to inflationary policies. One consequence may be a cycle of stop–go growth.

Consequences (costs) of unemployment

Checkpoints

1 During the 1970s the Conservative government sought to reduce the pool of labour by raising the school leaving age. This reduced the number of unskilled 16 year olds entering the labour market. Later governments have introduced training schemes which delay the entry of younger workers into the labour market. Successive governments have also sought to remove older workers from the pool of labour by removing the need for older workers to 'sign on'. Reclassifying workers as being unable to work (paying them a higher level of benefit) may also help to reduce the pool of labour.

2 One of the major impediments to relocation is housing costs. Areas of high unemployment tend to have lower house prices. Areas of high employment tend to have higher house prices. Relocating from one area to another in search of work may be made harder by a shortage of affordable housing.

3 The loss of revenue from income tax, National insurance contributions and VAT and, Increased government expenditure on finding jobs for the unemployed, retraining schemes and possibly redundancy payments in the public sector.

Exam question

(a) Assuming that the economy is initially in equilibrium, an increase in investment will have a multiplier effect on national output and employment. If we assume that there are unemployed resources in the economy, then firms will respond to the increase in demand by increasing output. In an effort to increase output, additional workers will be drawn into employment and will receive incomes. These workers can be expected to spend at least part of their incomes. This will have a multiplier effect as planned spending exceeds planned income.

(b) This statement applies the principles of supply and demand, which state that less of a product or service will be demanded as the price rises. The demand for labour is derived and is dependent upon the demand for goods and services produced. An increase in wages is likely to lead to an increase in the price of the product that the labour is used to produce. A rise in the price of a product is likely to lead to a reduced demand for that product and less demand for labour. The marginal productivity theory can be used to explain the demand for labour.

The impact of a rise in the cost of labour on employment levels will depend on the price elasticity of demand for the product.

The existence of trade unions may ensure that wage levels increase while employment levels are maintained. It will very much depend, however, on the level of pay increase and the bargaining power of the trade union.

Stop–go policies

Checkpoints

1 If higher costs push up the prices of UK manufactures, then they may become relatively more expensive, and this may reduce demand for sterling.

2 The government does not have to intervene in order to correct a balance-of-payments deficit. It could allow adjustments in exchange rates to correct an imbalance. The real issue is how long it will take for an exchange-rate adjustment to occur and influence the balance of payments.

Exam question

(a) Rising levels of employment may lead to an increase in aggregate demand. This may occur as incomes rise and aggregate demand increases as a result. Increasing investment may result in a rise in employment. This would also lead to a rise in aggregate demand.

(b) Labour shortages may force firms to increase wages in order to recruit and retain staff. This will increase the costs of firms. If a firm decides to pass on the cost to its customers rather than absorb the increased cost itself, its prices may become less competitive.

The simple Phillips curve tradeoff

Checkpoints

1 An increase in interest rates could help to control demand pull inflation. Higher borrowing costs are likely to reduce consumer demand for goods bought using credit.
2 Increases in consumption, investment, government spending or exports may all lead to an increase in aggregate demand.
3 A fall in the inflation rate could increase the competitiveness of UK goods. If the UK inflation rate was below the rate of the UK's trading partners, then the demand for exports may increase. The reduction in unemployment will depend upon the original level of unemployment, the cost of labour versus technology, and how much output increases.
4 Phillips recognised that there are always likely to be some people temporarily out of work, between jobs or unemployable.

Exam question

(a) The Phillips curve illustrates a tradeoff between inflation and unemployment rates. The lower the rate of unemployment, the higher the rate of inflation, and vice versa. The data that the Phillips curve was originally based upon suggested that it was possible to manage the economy in order to achieve relatively low inflation and unemployment. Economic data from the 1960s onwards saw the Phillips curve shift outwards. The tradeoff between unemployment and inflation occurred at higher rates of inflation and unemployment. Recent economic experience suggests that the Phillips relationship has shifted inwards. The control of inflation is affected by public perception. During the 1960s and 1970s, there was an expectation of inflation, and this affected wage demands and economic behaviour. The challenge of achieving a high level of employment while controlling inflation is potentially harder to achieve, since it requires aggregate demand to increase without creating inflationary pressure.

(b) A reduction in aggregate demand may be expected to lead to an increase in stock levels. Firms may seek to improve cashflow by disposing of stock and reducing output. As output is cut back, firms may place workers on short-term contracts or make redundancies, increasing unemployment. Expansion plans may be put on hold, and this may affect investment in capital projects, affecting the construction sector and capital goods suppliers. Reduced demand and the desire to dispose of stock may lead to discounting and reduced prices, reducing inflationary pressure. Unemployment may also have an effect on disposable income, reducing consumption.

Expectations-augmented Phillips curve

Checkpoints

1 The tradeoff referred is to is between the rate of unemployment and the rate of inflation. The relationship between inflation and unemployment was argued to be inverse. That is to say that if employment levels rise, then rate of inflation may be expected to rise. Conversely, as the inflation rate falls, so the number of jobless may be expected to rise.
2 Slumpflation.
3 Money illusion is the tendency of people to be confused by changes in prices or wages when in reality no real change has occurred, e.g. if wages and prices double, some individuals may still feel they are better off because their salaries have increased from £20 000 to £40 000.

Exam question

(a) The term 'natural rate of unemployment' was first used by Milton Friedman, when introducing the expectations-augmented Phillips curve. The theory of a natural rate on unemployment is based on the belief that a competitive market economy will be self-adjusting and that it will reach an equilibrium level of unemployment comprised of frictional and structural unemployment. The natural rate of unemployment is the level of unemployment that exists at the equilibrium real-wage rate, equating the aggregate demand for labour with the aggregate supply, clearing the labour market.

(b) Monetarists believe that it is not possible to expand aggregate demand in order to reduce unemployment levels. Monetarists believe that the only effective strategy to reduce unemployment is to adopt free-market supply-side policies. This view is challenged by Keynesians, who argue that government intervention using supply-side policies and demand management can be effective.

The nature and importance of international trade

Checkpoints

1 A current-account deficit occurs when the money value of total imports exceeds the money value of total exports.
2 • A greater choice of goods.
   • A larger market for producers.
   • Access to goods that a country cannot produce itself.
   • Trade can provide access to new technology.
   • International specialisation raises output.

3 One factor might be a deterioration in the quality of UK manufactures and a lack of innovation.

  A second factor might be the contraction of the UK manufacturing base.

4 Specialisation may be expected to lead to improved quality of goods and may lead to lower-costs good as producers are able to exploit economies of scale.

5

	Flat-screen television	DVD players
Country A either	2	6
Country B either	3	30

Country B (opportunity cost ratios): flat-screen televisions 10/1 compared with 3/1; DVD players 1/10 compared with 1/3.

Exam question

(a) A discussion of policies that the government might adopt in order to improve a deficit in the balance of payments includes import controls, deflation and supply-side policies. When answering a question such as this, it is necessary to explain how the policies may influence a balance-of-payments deficit. For example, imposing import controls may reduce the quantity of imports entering the country. The downside of this strategy is that other countries may retaliate and impose restrictions on UK exports. Whether the imposition of exports controls leads to an improvement in the balance of payments will depend very much on the particular circumstances.

  The policies selected may well be influenced by consumer purchasing preferences, the availability of domestically produced substitutes, and the cause, size and duration of a balance-of-payments deficit.

  There are opportunities to demonstrate evaluative skills when answering this question. Will the proposed strategy have the desired effect? Will there be a time lag between introducing the policy and its effects emerging? What are the potential tradeoffs of a adopting a particular policy?

(b) Membership of the EU might encourage inward investment because membership of the EU ensures the free flow of goods between member states. This means that a Japanese firm manufacturing in the UK can export its goods to other countries in the EU without restriction. Honda, Nissan and Toyota and a host of other Japanese companies have located in the UK to take advantage of this rule.

Free trade versus protection

Checkpoints

1 The UK shoe industry has declined because it has found it difficult to compete with inexpensive foreign imports from countries such as Indonesia, Italy, Spain, Portugal and China. There has also been a lack of investment in UK shoe manufacturing, and producers are trying to compete using outdated equipment. A change in tastes and preferences as consumers have switched to wearing trainers more than smart shoes has also affected sales of shoes.

2 Some critics of trade liberalisation want the opening-up of markets to be conditional on developing countries accepting minimum labour standards. They argue that goods manufactured using child, slave or prison labour should be banned. The aim is to improve the lot of poor workers in the developing world and prevent manufacturers exploiting poor working conditions in order to gain an unfair trade advantage. The downside to this approach is that children could be driven out of employment and into begging, prostitution or starvation.

3 Trade creation occurs when joining a customs union results in an increase in trade between member countries as the gains from trade develop. Trade diversion occurs when access to cheaper goods produced outside the union is restricted. This will result in less trade with countries outside the union.

4 A number of possible costs of international trade can be identified:
  • Declining industries (sunset industries) may find that their decline is accelerated, causing an increase in unemployment.
  • Foreign producers may dump excess production, distorting markets.
  • Countries could be affected adversely by war or political unrest, which may cut off essential supplies. This was a problem for Britain in both world wars.
  • Infant industries (sunrise industries) may struggle to compete and establish in the market if faced with competition from imports.
  • Overspecialisation can cause problems (diseconomies of scale and susceptibility to sudden shifts in demand).

Exam question

(a) Trade liberalisation, together with structural adjustments and privatisation, increased the speed of globalisation. This has profound implications for developing countries. It creates new opportunities – wider markets for trade, an increasing range of goods traded between countries, increased capital flows between countries and increased access to technology for developing countries. Economists at the World Bank have argued that trade liberalisation is central to improving the economic prospects of developing countries. Trade liberalisation, resulting in the reduction of import and export barriers to trade, coupled with a reduced role of the state, creates conditions that are conducive to inward investment by Trans National Corporations (TNCs). A response focusing on the advantages and disadvantages of trade liberalisation will be expected to rehearse the argument for and against protectionism, e.g. impact on employment, infant industry argument and the export promotion/import substitution argument.

(b) A balance argument is required in order to answer this question. One view is that trade liberalisation will encourage specialisation and encourage producers to be technically efficient. A contrasting argument is that international trade does not occur on a level playing field and the poorest economies risk exploitation. The 'banana wars' highlight the problems of economies facing structural change as a result of trade liberalisation.

(c) It is apparent that with the growth in global trade and the growing trend towards sourcing manufactured goods from countries with low labour costs, there is a need for British firms to focus on improving competitiveness. This may mean focusing on innovation, reputation, relationships with customers and identifying new ways of adding value to the goods and services offered.

Fixed and floating exchange rates

Checkpoints

1 Just because sterling depreciates against one currency does not mean that other currencies will not depreciate against that currency. For example, sterling and the US dollar may depreciate against the euro. Consumers in the eurozone may have a choice of products from the USA and UK that are now relatively cheaper. Retailers in Europe do not have to pass the benefits of depreciation on to their customers. Furthermore, demand for exports may be relatively inelastic.

2

Quantity of pounds traded on the foreign exchange market

If the demand for exports increases, then the demand for pounds will increase, shifting the demand curve to the right and resulting in an appreciation of sterling.

3 A strengthening in the value of the pound will have a positive effect on manufacturers that import materials from abroad. The relative cost of these materials might be expected to fall. On the other hand, exporters may find it harder to sell their goods abroad, depending on the price elasticity of demand for their products.

Exam question

(a) A strong pound will create winners and losers. Winners are likely to be those firms that import goods and services. The relative cost of imports might be expected to be lower. Tour operators will benefit from relatively cheaper hotels, and fuel costs may be lower (if the pound has strengthened against the dollar, since oil is traded in dollars). Firms that lose out as a result of sterling appreciation are likely to be exporters, which will find that

the relative cost of their goods has increased. The extent to which firms find their sales are affected will depend upon the price elasticity of demand for their goods. Those firms with a low PED will find their sales relatively unaffected. Those with a high PED will be affected more significantly. Firms may use hedging accounts in order to minimise the impact of exchange-rate movements.

(b) A depreciation in sterling relative to other currencies lowers the price of exports in terms of foreign currencies. For example, if the exchange rate was £1 = $2, a then UK good priced at £6 would sell for $12 in the USA. If the value of sterling were to fall to £1 = $1.5, then the same good would sell for $9. The lower price of the good abroad should ensure additional sales. If the demand for the product is elastic, then the percentage rise in quantity demanded should exceed the percentage fall in price.

(c) European sugar-beet farmers receive around 1.7 billion euros a year from the European Commission. The EU price for sugar is almost three times the world market price. CAP encourages overproduction and provides export subsidies in order to keep the excess off the European market and keep the prices high. The EU also imposes high import tariffs on most countries wanting to sell their own sugar in the EU. The system of subsidies has cut incomes of developing countries and has cost jobs. Under pressure, the EU has agreed to cut the subsidised price of white sugar by 40%.

EU issues

Checkpoints

1 UK, France, Germany, the Netherlands, Luxembourg, Belgium, Italy, Spain, Denmark, Austria, Greece, Sweden, Finland, Ireland and Portugal.

Exam question

(a) Economic migration between member states has been a source of concern for some member states. Unions have been concerned that migrant workers will be used to depress wages and reduce employment opportunities for domestic workers. There is evidence that construction firms from countries of the former Soviet Union have tendered for construction contracts in Sweden using labour from Latvia, at Latvian rather than Swedish wage rates. Similar concerns have been raised in Ireland, where migrant labour has been used in its booming construction industry.

The counter-argument is that migrant workers will help to fill skills shortages and will allow the economic potential of countries to be fulfilled. Migrant labourers will pay taxes and national insurance and may help to solve the demographic problems facing Italy and other EU economies.

(b) New members have opted to join for a number of reasons. Membership of an enlarged Europe would give members greater political influence. Membership is also seen as a catalyst of growth, drawing EU grants and subsidies and encouraging inwards investment.

Potential costs and benefits of UK membership of the euro

Checkpoints

1 Austria, Belgium, Finland, France, Germany, Portugal, Greece, Ireland, Italy, Luxembourg, the Netherlands and Spain.
2 Companies that rely upon automated vending would be affected adversely. Machines would have to be modified or replaced, adding to the companies' costs significantly. Firms running gambling machines and games machines would be affected similarly. Exporters to the EU might see significant benefits because of a single currency due to lower transaction costs.
3 A single currency may make it easier to compare prices across borders, but the geographic distance may ensure that price discrimination persists between countries

Exam question

(a) The benefits of joining the euro may be greater exchange-rate stability and the removal of transactions associated with cross-border trade. Advocates of the euro argue that prices across the eurozone are likely to converge. Joining the euro may lead to additional inward investment and job creation in the UK. The European Central Bank will control the macroeconomy and reduce susceptibility to external shocks.

   The potential downsides of joining the euro include the loss of business for financial markets in the City of London. Business cycles may not be synchronised between the UK and other members of the euro. The difficulties that this may cause are already being demonstrated by the Italian economy. Joining the euro will place the UK government in an economic straitjacket with limited power to control its own macroeconomic policy. The value of the currency cannot be determined independently once the UK joins the euro. This means that it cannot devalue its currency in order to increase the short-term competitiveness of UK exports.

For	Against
Living standards in the eurozone may rise	UK citizens may be reluctant to abandon the pound
£1 billion a year could be saved on transaction costs	It is unlikely that one interest rate will suit all countries
Trade with other members of the euro may increase	The UK will lose control of exchange rate policy
Downward pressure on prices	European Central Bank may raise interest rates, causing an economic slowdown and higher unemployment in all member states
Long-term stability and low interest rates	

(b) The inability of Germany, France and Greece to comply with the Growth and Stability Pact could cause economic problems for other members. The European Central Bank has the power to raise interest rates, and this could result in economic slowdown and higher unemployment, as aggregate demand is reduced due to higher borrowing costs.

The eurozone's Growth and Stability Pact

1 Creative accounting by Greece could cause difficulty for other member countries if the ECB decides to address inflationary pressures caused by deficit spending. The problems Greece experienced have been compounded by its hosting of the 2004 Olympics, which resulted in a massive increase in public expenditure in order to ensure that the games were ready on time. If interest rates are increased, every country in the eurozone will be affected.
2 One implication of falling productivity and rising unemployment is that Italy's international competitiveness is being eroded. Deficit spending might be used, but public finances are already a cause for concern. The Italian government is no longer able to control interest rates or exchange rates, so that to some extent the economy is in a economic straitjacket. Some political parties have urged the abandonment of the euro and the reintroduction of the lira. The economic and political costs of such a move are enormous.
3 Giving Germany and France special consideration by not imposing sanctions on them for breaching the Growth and Stability Pact could have damaging long-term implications. It is questionable whether other countries will be shown the same degree of tolerance. This could be a source of future tension. Other countries, such as Greece and Italy, may resent the imposition of sanctions upon them for breaching the Growth and Stability Pact. Failure to impose sanctions devalues the measures intended to instil fiscal discipline to member countries. It may also lead to the ECB imposing interest-rate increases in order to ensure economic stability.

Exam question

(a) The case for joining the euro is likely to focus on points such as a reduction in exchange rate volatility, which may enhance trade, and specialisation within member countries. This may enable producers to exploit further economies of scale. Transaction costs would be eliminated when trading within the eurozone, and menu costs would also be reduced as price lists would need to be printed only once. Monetary union and the Growth and Stability Pact would encourage economic discipline. The reduction in inflation and the reduced trade risks may lead to lower real interest rates, encouraging investment and innovation.

   The downsides of joining the monetary union focus on the loss of independence and the inability to manage the UK as national circumstances change. The USA remains the UK's largest trading partner. Joining the euro will not reduce the transaction cost between the USA and the UK. The biggest argument for not joining the euro is that all the major indicators suggest that the UK has outperformed other countries within the eurozone.

(b) The policy options open to Germany when dealing with rising unemployment are limited. Increasing the budget deficit in order to stimulate aggregate demand is not an option, since the government is already in breach of the Growth and Stability Pact. Interest rates are determined by the ECB and are already low. There is some scope to engage in market reforms and improve labour-market flexibility, but such a move may be politically unpopular.

(c) The impact of budget deficits on the value of the euro may depend upon the action taken by the ECB. If the financial markets become sufficiently concerned about breaches of the Growth and Stability Pact, then they may reduce investments in the eurozone and sell euros.

International institutions

Checkpoints

1 The WTO, set up in 1995, is an international body whose purpose is to promote free trade by persuading countries to abolish import tariffs and other barriers. The WTO is the only international agency overseeing the rules of international trade. It polices free-trade agreements, settles trade disputes between governments, and organises trade negotiations. WTO decisions are absolute, and every member must abide by its rulings.

GATT stands for the General Agreement on Tariffs and Trade. GATT centred on rounds of negotiations between countries to agree on trade liberalisation. In all, there were eight rounds of talks between 1947 and 1993.

The WTO has a much broader scope than GATT. Whereas GATT regulated trade in merchandise goods, the WTO also covers trade in services, such as telecommunications and banking.

2 The main role of the IMF is to monitor economic performance of countries, provide advice and guidance to those countries experiencing difficulties, and offer loans to help countries deal with balance-of-payments problems. The role of the World Bank is to promote development and growth by offering advice, finance and technical support to developing countries.

3 Subsidies may increase trade for some countries if goods and services are subsidised but can reduce trade for those countries that do not subsidise. The overall effect of subsidies can be to destabilise markets and create excess supply. A good example of the devastating impact of subsidies on international markets are the US payments to cotton farmers and rice growers.

Exam question

(a) Countries approaching the IMF for financial assistance are likely to be experiencing economic difficulties that are creating exchange-rate difficulties and having an adverse impact upon economic activity. In order to assist countries, the IMF may agree loans, but in return it expects countries to agree to economic adjustment policies that will return the external payments position to health and establish conditions for sustainable economic growth.

The IMF will identify policies that countries should address, and lending will be conditional on the agreement of specific targets. These policies typically will require government spending to be cut, privatisation of public corporations and the liberalisation of markets. Critics argue that these policies have increased poverty. Cuts in public spending typically affect people on the lowest incomes, reducing access to healthcare and education. Privatisation often leads to job losses and reductions in pay. Export promotion has led to the displacement of subsistence farmers in order to allow the development of agribusiness. The reduction in tariff barriers may cost jobs, while high interest rates may discourage investment. SAPs seem to work on the basis of short-run pain for long-run gain.

(b) The World Bank's aim is to combat poverty and raise the living standards of people in developing countries. It provides loans, advice and technical assistance to low- and middle-income countries. On the plus side, it provides funding for education and HIV/AIDS projects and has assisted projects to provide safe drinking water, electricity and transport to poor people.

Critics argue that the World Bank has helped to increase the debt burden of the poorest countries. Programmes of debt relief have had limited impact, while the imposition of structural adjustment reforms has caused hardship. A 2002 report by non-governmental organisations (NGOs) suggested that reforms have not reduced poverty and have damaged the environment.

It is evident that export promotion policies in Vietnam have helped to destabilise commodity prices and have caused hardship for farmers in Latin America and India.

Revision checklist
Macroeconomic issues and policies

1	Distinguish between macroeconomic stocks, flows and ratios.	Confident	Not confident. **Revise** pages 68–9
2	Distinguish between leading and lagging economic indicators.	Confident	Not confident. **Revise** pages 70–71
3	Identify the main components of the circular flow of income.	Confident	Not confident. **Revise** pages 68–9
4	Define gross domestic product. Evaluate its uses for single-country and international comparisons.	Confident	Not confident. **Revise** pages 82–5
5	Explain the multiplier process.	Confident	Not confident. **Revise** pages 86–7
6	Define inflation. Explain how inflation is measured.	Confident	Not confident. **Revise** pages 90–91
7	Discuss the consequences of inflation. Highlight the costs (disadvantages).	Confident	Not confident. **Revise** pages 92–3
8	Explain possible causes of inflation. Distinguish between demand pull and cost push inflation.	Confident	Not confident. **Revise** pages 94–5
9	Explain and critically discuss the policy of targeting inflation, estimating output gaps, and using interest rates to influence demand.	Confident	Not confident. **Revise** pages 78–81
10	Define unemployment. Explain how unemployment is measured.	Confident	Not confident. **Revise** pages 96–7
11	Discuss the consequences of unemployment. Highlight the costs (disadvantages).	Confident	Not confident. **Revise** pages 100–101
12	Explain possible causes of unemployment. Distinguish between types of unemployment.	Confident	Not confident. **Revise** pages 98–9
13	Explain what is meant by the natural rate of unemployment.	Confident	Not confident. **Revise** pages 98–9
14	Make a list of supply-side policies. Explain how they might help to reduce unemployment, and stimulate growth.	Confident	Not confident. **Revise** pages 74–5, 80–81 and 88–9
15	Discuss the effectiveness of supply-side versus demand-management policies.	Confident	Not confident. **Revise** pages 74–5
16	List the main objectives of macro-policy. Distinguish between monetary and fiscal (budgetary) policy.	Confident	Not confident. **Revise** pages 72–7
17	Explain how macro-objectives are affected by expansive/restrictive monetary policy and reflationary/deflationary fiscal (budgetary) policy.	Confident	Not confident. **Revise** pages 72–3
18	Explain why policies might conflict: → Explain why full employment at home might cause balance-of-payments difficulties (stop–go policies). → Use a simple Phillips curve to show conflict between full employment and low inflation in the short run. → Explain why expectations of future inflation might defeat anti-inflation policy in the long run.	Confident	Not confident. **Revise** pages 102–103, 104–105 and 106–107
19	Discuss the importance of international trade.	Confident	Not confident. **Revise** pages 108–111 and 120–121
20	Discuss the opportunities arising from the enlargement of the EU.	Confident	Not confident. **Revise** pages 114–15
21	Evaluate the eurozone's Stability and Growth Pact.	Confident	Not confident. **Revise** pages 118–19
22	Explain the differences between fixed and floating exchange rates.	Confident	Not confident. **Revise** pages 112–13
23	Discuss the potential costs and benefits of UK membership of the euro.	Confident	Not confident. **Revise** pages 116–17

Here we consider topics that have both microeconomic and macroeconomic aspects. This chapter focuses on applying economic concepts and theories to real-world contexts. It is important to have a clear understanding of how government policies may affect individuals and societies. There is a degree of overlap between the exam themes. For example, globalisation has implications for economic development and transport policy has an impact upon the environment.

Exam themes

→ Causes and effects of globalisation

→ European response to globalisation

→ Challenges facing countries seeking economic development

→ Difficulties facing transitional economies, and opportunities facing emerging economies

→ Challenges facing the government in developing a transport policy

→ The debate regarding public/private healthcare and the challenges facing the government

→ Factors affecting the housing market

→ The sport and leisure sector

→ Causes and consequences of poverty and social inequality

→ Environmental issues and economic policies

Topic checklist

AS ○ A2 ●	Edexcel	AQA	OCR	WJEC	CCEA
Globalisation	●	●	●	●	●
The single European market	●	●	●	●	●
Economic development	●	●	●	●	●
Emerging and transitional economies	●	●	●	●	●
Transport		○	●		
Health	○	○			
Housing		○			
Sport and leisure		○	●		
Welfare economics, income distribution, poverty	○●	○●	○●		●
The environment, environmental policy	○	○●			●

Globalisation

Globalisation has become extremely topical. The idea underpinning globalisation is that we have become a part of one large global village. National borders now have less significance. Trade and communications are the driving force in the move towards a global community. One consequence of globalisation is increasing interdependence. Investment decisions made by Sony in Japan can lead to unemployment in Bridgend in the UK.

Checkpoint 1

What factors have led to the expansion of globalisation?

Checkpoint 2

How might pressure groups limit the activities of TNCs?

The jargon

The term 'globalisation' is used to describe the economic and social changes as a result of increased international trade and cultural exchange. The term is a reference to the increase of trade and investing due to the reduction of barriers and increasing interdependence of countries.

Globalisation: good or bad?

Globalisation refers to the creation of a single world market rather than a series of separate markets. Globalisation has profound implications for both developed and developing countries. There are a number of factors that have led to the increasing pace of globalisation. These include the reduction in obstacles to trade and improvements in communications systems. The topic of globalisation creates polarised opinions. There are those who see globalisation as the mechanism for reducing inequality, narrowing the divide between the richest and the poorest countries, and there are those who see globalisation as an opportunity for transnational corporations (TNCs) to exploit less developed countries and widen the divide between north and south.

Critics of globalisation describe it as a worldwide drive towards the creation of a globalised economic system dominated by supranational corporate trade and banking institutions that operate across national borders and are not accountable to democratic processes or national governments.

The World Development Movement (WDM), an NGO that gave evidence to a Parliamentary investigation into globalisation, described economic globalisation as 'the removal of barriers to business activity across international borders and within societies'. It noted that this development had also led to the global spread of harmful activities, such as trafficking in women and children for sex and slavery, illegal trading and money laundering.

Supporters of the process of globalisation would argue that globalisation is a process of increasing international interactions and accelerating international trade, capital and information flows. In addition, it has a political and social dimension, promoting free-market capitalism and influencing the culture of the global community.

Forces of globalisation

The driving force of globalisation has been in part the reduction of barriers to trade and technological innovations, which have done so much to improve communication.

Technological changes

Advances in transport and communications technology are a distinctive feature of globalisation.

Technological advances have affected the structure of transnational corporations and the location of production. The change in trade patterns since the Second World War, with the growth of trade in manufactured goods and intermediate goods, reflects a global reorganisation of production by companies. This has been made possible by information and communication technologies and also declining transport costs enabling companies to operate in different locations in cost-effective ways.

Trade liberalisation

In 1947, the General Agreement on Tariffs and Trade (GATT) was negotiated, providing a framework for a policy of trade liberalisation. In 1995, GATT was replaced by the World Trade Organization (WTO) to promote trade liberalisation through negotiated agreements and by resolving trade disputes.

Capital market liberalisation

Capital market liberalisation is a distinctive feature of globalisation. Technological developments have enabled instantaneous financial transactions. The liberalisation of financial markets has resulted in what the Director of the Royal Institute of International Affairs described as a 'qualitative leap in the scale of liberalisation'. Liberalisation has been promoted by the International Monetary Fund, the World Bank and the Bank for International Settlements, as one of the key dimensions of globalisation.

Checkpoint 3

Identify two adverse consequences of economic globalisation.

Check the net

http://pilger.carlton.com/globalisation
www.jusbiz.org
www.tuc.org.uk/theme/index.cfm?theme
=globalisation
www.worldbank.org/oed

Examiner's secrets

When examining the impact of globalisation, consideration should be given to the following issues:
→ Increase in international trade.
→ Increase in international flow of capital.
→ Loss of national sovereignty.
→ Development of global financial systems.
→ Increasing importance of multinational corporations.
→ Increase of economic practices such as outsourcing by multinational corporations.
→ Increased role of international organisations such as the WTO, WIPO and IMF.

Exam question (30 minutes)   answer: page 156

(a) Examine the likely impact of World Trade Organization-endorsed sanctions on European exports.

(b) Examine the implication of sourcing products in developing countries for a company such as Nike.

(c) Examine the links between international trade and economic growth.

The single European market

The single European market (SEM) has some macro-economic purposes, since it is aimed at increasing output, trade and employment in the EU. However, it is also based on microeconomic principles, mainly economies of scale, specialisation, productivity and efficiency.

What is the SEM? ●●●

One way of thinking about the EU is to see it as a reaction to globalisation. From this angle, it is a counterbalance to the dominating economic influence of the USA. The SEM officially came into existence on 1 January 1993. Since 1 May 2004, it now has 28 member countries: 25 EU countries plus the three members of the European Economic Area (EEA) agreement (Iceland, Norway, Liechtenstein).

In principle, the SEM allows free movement throughout the EEA of:

→ Goods and services
→ Capital
→ Labour.

Watch out!

Examination candidates invariably mention the free movement of goods in connection with the SEM, but they often forget about services, capital and labour.

In practice, there is still some way to go in creating a true single market. For instance, there is still not complete agreement on how to sell services across Europe, and there are still some restrictions on labour mobility, especially with respect to the new members (accession countries). Unlike any other single market, the SEM does not have a single currency, although 12 members belong to the euro.

Why was the SEM created? ●●●

Checkpoint 1

Why might tourists only receive a partial view of the cost of living in the USA?

Checkpoint 2

What reasons other than economies of scale might there be for cheaper consumer prices in the USA?

When Europeans visit the USA, they notice that the prices of many consumer goods and services – petrol, fresh food, restaurant meals, CDs and DVDs, for example – are much cheaper than at home. One reason for this is that US producers have a huge single market: they can operate their production processes at optimum output levels by selling across an entire continent and thus benefit from economies of scale.

In the late 1980s, the **Cecchini Report** identified the barriers (or impediments) that prevented the free movement of goods, services, capital and labour. These included:

→ Different national practices
→ Testing procedures
→ Bureaucratic obstructions
→ Frontier formalities
→ Failure to agree on Europe-wide product standards.

Check the net

The report was entitled *1992: The European Challenge* and can be accessed via www.eu.int.

The report was based on a survey of 11 000 business people. It claimed that these impediments were costing the EU some 5% of its GDP per year and that their removal would deliver non-inflationary growth of 7% in the medium term, with five million new jobs.

Economies of scale and specialisation in the SEM

Without the single market, it would be necessary for a firm producing cosmetics, for example, to have factories located in more than one country and producing more than one product. With the single market, the firm can, for instance, produce all of its toothpaste in the UK, shampoos in Spain, perfume in France and skin creams in Italy. And then it can sell these products across the entire continent. Similarly, a car manufacturer can make its engines in the UK, transmission systems in Germany, and other components in Poland, and then assemble the cars in Spain, instead of having to replicate all of these activities on a smaller scale in several countries. This specialisation is crucial in bringing down prices.

Examiner's secrets

Remember that specialisation increases efficiency and goes hand in hand with economies of scale. This point is nearly always overlooked by candidates discussing the SEM.

Exam question (30 minutes)   answer: pages 156–7

Apart from the free movement of goods and services, what other aspects of the single European market affect UK citizens on a daily basis?

Economic development

Checkpoint 1

Is import substitution through protectionism likely to encourage multinational investment in a country?

The jargon

LDCs. Lesser developed countries.
LEDCs. Less economically developed countries.
MEDCs. More economically developed countries.

Watch out!

There are a number of economic models that seek to explain how economic growth might be achieved. In each case, there are three central building blocks:
→ Production function
→ Saving function
→ Labour supply function (related to population growth).

Development means 'improvement in a country's economic and social conditions'. More specifically, it refers to improvements in ways of managing an area's natural and human resources in order to create wealth and improve people's lives.

Making comparisons

Economists compare levels of development between different countries or regions and the people who live in them – referring to more economically developed countries (MEDCs) and less economically-developed countries (LEDCs). Development can be considered in terms of either economic or human development.

Development economics looks at the economic, social, political and institutional changes needed to bring about large-scale rapid improvements in human wellbeing, especially for poor people in developing countries.

Development is measured by outcomes. Development occurs when key indicators of human wellbeing improve. The reduction of poverty, inequality and unemployment and the achievement of economic growth within a growing economy are indicators of economic development.

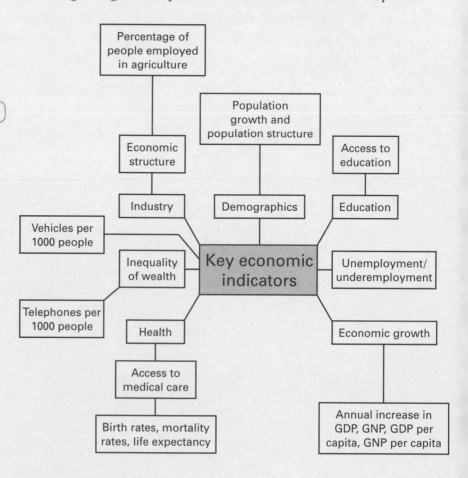

Strategies for boosting growth ●●●

A range of strategies have been employed in order to achieve economic growth in developing countries. Some countries have sought to develop their economies by import substitution, erecting barriers to imports and encouraging domestic producers to produce goods. The use of tariffs and the adoption of protectionist policies is an inward-looking development strategy.

An alternative approach is to engage in export promotion. This is an outward-looking development strategy. Producers are expected to improve efficiency and exploit comparative advantage. Export promotion has proved successful for the Asian tiger economies of Hong Kong, Taiwan, Singapore and South Korea. These countries have been able to move away from exporting commodity products that have been subject to price fluctuations and falling real prices. Instead, they have developed a manufacturing base, producing added-value products. The 47 least developed countries remain heavily dependent upon the export of primary commodity products.

Tourism has brought benefits to some developing countries, providing a source of foreign exchange and leading to an increase in invisible exports. The downsides to the development of tourism are that the growth of all-inclusive holidays means that tourism spending does not benefit local communities. Many holiday developments are foreign-owned and profits do not remain in the country. In some cases, local inhabitants may be displaced without compensation in order to allow tourism development. Tourism may also create environmental externalities. In Goa in India, for example, pollution has damaged the marine ecosystem and has created water shortages, which have affected farmers.

Attracting transnational corporations (TNCs) has been seen as a route to economic development for some LDCs. TNCs have provided significant employment opportunities in countries such as Vietnam and Indonesia, although much of the work is low-paid and low-status. Critics of TNCs have pointed to human rights abuses, the use of child labour and breaches of minimum-wage legislation in developing countries as evidence of exploitation. Sports-shoe manufacturers have faced particular criticism for being footloose – locating in one country and then relocating to another when labour costs rise.

Examiner's secrets

If you are asked to explain possible strategies for growth, then you will be expected to provide a reasoned and developed answer examining the possible implications of your proposed strategies.

Check the net

http://en.wikipedia.org/wiki/economic_
development
www.tutor2u.net/economics/content/
topics/development/development_models
_balanced_growth.htm
www.tutor2u.net/economics/content/
topics/development/development_models
_dependency.htm
www.tutor2u.net/economics/content/
topics/development/development_models
_introduction.htm

Checkpoint 2

Is import substitution through protectionism likely to encourage multinational investment in a country?

Exam question (30 minutes)   answer: page 157

(a) Explain why high birth rates might cause economic problems for a developing country.

(b) Discuss the economic advantages that should result from increased flows of foreign direct investment into a country such as Mozambique.

(c) Assess the impact of production contracts for multinational corporations on developing countries.

Emerging and transitional economies

The jargon

Emerging or developing market economy (EME). Economy with low to middle per capita income. Approximately 80% of the world's population lives in EMEs.

Transitional economy. Used to describe countries that are in the process of moving from a centrally planned economy towards free-market principles.

Emerging economies are those countries that are beginning to participate globally as a result of implementing reform programmes and undergoing economic improvement. The rapid growth of emerging economies, in particular China, is shifting the global balance of economic activity. By 2015, China could account for around 20% of world output in real terms. This level of development presents challenges for emerging and developed economies and is likely to bring about changing patterns of trade.

The collapse of the Berlin Wall led to economic upheaval. Former Communist countries have had to manage the transition from command economy to free-market economy.

Checkpoint 1

What are the short-term consequences of market reform in command economies?

Emerging economies: China

China, because of its scale, provides a unique case study of an emerging economy. China's strong economic growth has transformed the global economy. Undertaking market liberalisation, in order to gain membership of the World Trade Organization, is estimated to have cost 30 million jobs. The jobs were lost as state subsidies were ended and the Chinese government increased opportunities for private enterprise. Since joining the World Trade Organization in late 2001, exports have increased sharply. China makes 90% of the world's toys, half the world's cameras and a quarter of the world's washing machines. The EU is so concerned about Chinese textiles flooding the global market that it has urged China to restrict its textile exports to avoid flooding the global market and damaging producers.

China's economic growth is putting pressure on the world's resources. Oil prices have risen sharply, fuelled by China's rising demand. China consumed more than one million barrels a day in 2003. In the first quarter of 2005, China consumed about six million barrels a day. Demand for oil is driven by a 75% increase in car-ownership.

High levels of economic growth have placed pressure on infrastructure, resulting in energy blackouts in Shanghai, and energy rationing. Economic growth is also placing pressure on the country's natural resources. Air and water pollution is a serious problem. More than three-quarters of the water flowing through China's cities is unsuitable for drinking because of pollution from industrial waste. Scores of rivers have dried up and water tables are getting ever lower.

The benefits of economic development have not been distributed evenly. The growth of the past decade has been restricted largely to the eastern seaboard, leaving the possibility of serious social and economic unrest in the developing world western interior, where there are more than 150 million unemployed workers.

China, like many other emerging countries, has proved attractive for manufacturing firms. TNCs have been attracted by low labour costs (manufacturing workers earn 4% of what their British counterparts are paid). There is also a recognition of the enormous potential of China's

Watch out!

Typical characteristics of a transitional economy are:
→ Low incomes and high employment.
→ High degree of income inequality.
→ Falling productivity.
→ Centralisation of income and growth in urban areas and service sectors.
→ Excessive bureaucracy .
→ A seller's market.
→ Shortages.
→ High inflation.
→ Import restrictions.
→ Limited competition.

expanding domestic market. More than 1.3 billion people live in China, and living standards are rising. Firms such as B&Q and Tesco are looking to exploit opportunities for growth in China.

Transitional economies

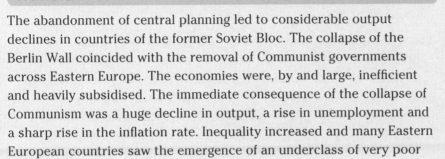

The abandonment of central planning led to considerable output declines in countries of the former Soviet Bloc. The collapse of the Berlin Wall coincided with the removal of Communist governments across Eastern Europe. The economies were, by and large, inefficient and heavily subsidised. The immediate consequence of the collapse of Communism was a huge decline in output, a rise in unemployment and a sharp rise in the inflation rate. Inequality increased and many Eastern European countries saw the emergence of an underclass of very poor people.

As part of the process of economic reform, large inefficient state-run industries were privatised. Typically, these industries were undercapitalised and overstaffed. The end of subsidies and the loss of protected Eastern European markets resulted in the contraction or collapse of many state-run firms.

The Czech Republic, Hungary, Poland and Estonia have been the most successful in bringing about market reform. These countries have allowed property rights and undertaken labour market reforms. Independent trade unions are allowed and wage regulation has been abandoned. The governments in these countries have continued to regulate telecommunications, energy generation and passenger transport. In all of these countries, financial markets are being developed.

East Germany has benefited significantly from the process of reunification with West Germany. Nonetheless, living standards in the east lag behind those in the west. Since reunification, more than 1.2 million people have migrated from East Germany. Unemployment in East Germany is more than twice the national average, despite government spending of more than €1.3 trillion on improving communications and attracting investment into the region.

Checkpoint 2

Why have some emerging economies chosen to focus on export promotion?

Checkpoint 3

Examine the benefits of attracting investment from Western companies for transitional economies.

Watch out!

Economic dislocation is a characteristic of many transitional economies – upheaval in the 1990s caused considerable instability in many Eastern European countries. Previously subsidised industries were left struggling to survive. Political instability had an adverse impact on investment and economic growth.

Exam question (20 minutes)   answer: page 157

(a) Examine the problems that population migration may cause for transitional economies.

(b) Assess strategies that the German government might introduce in order to address the economic problems of East Germany.

Transport

Transport is essential for both business and individual citizens. Increasingly, government is seeking to involve itself in the provision of transport and to develop an integrated transport policy.

Check the net

Follow the links for alternative views on the benefits of congestion charging:
www.no-congestion-charge.com
www.cfit.gov.uk/congestioncharging

Checkpoint 1

How might a sustainable transport policy reduce environmental problems?

Checkpoint 2

Why is it necessary for the government to use cost–benefit analysis when assessing new road schemes?

Road transport ○○○

The government has sought to introduce a number of measures to control the environmental impact of private vehicles. A large toll road has been opened around Birmingham, and road pricing is being considered. The government is committed to examining ways of introducing road pricing in the next decade. Meanwhile, the London congestion charging scheme has surpassed all expectations and is now the world's largest traffic-management scheme, delivering real improvements to journey times in the city centre and improved quality of life for the majority who do not access central London by car. Duty on petrol has been increased. Originally tax increases were sold to the public as an environmental measure, but increasingly they have become an important source of revenue for the government. Car users in the UK are among the most heavily taxed in Europe.

Congestion charging has been introduced in the City of London, reducing journey times in central London and improving the quality of life for local residents. It has not generated the revenues anticipated and the charges are likely to increase. Critics have suggested that congestion charging is being used as a way of raising revenue rather than as a way of influencing commuters' travel arrangements.

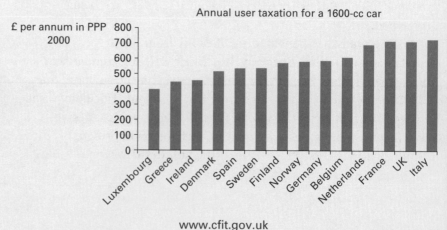

£ per annum in PPP 2000 — Annual user taxation for a 1600-cc car

www.cfit.gov.uk

Rail transport ○○○

Rail privatisation has had mixed results. The promised improvements in rail transport have not been achieved. Rail accidents have highlighted the need for massive investment in maintenance. Train-operating companies criticise the short-term franchises they were initially awarded as a disincentive for investment. The rail regulator permitted price increases ahead of inflation as a way of curbing demand on intercity routes. Given that demand on many of the commuter routes is inelastic, this is unlikely to reduce overcrowding.

Improvements are now being seen in rail transport, due largely to a massive injection of funds into rail maintenance and the renegotiation of rail franchises. Rail travellers made more than 1.05 billion journeys by train in 2004, the highest number for 45 years. If further improvements in service and punctuality are to be achieved, then continued investments is required. The relatively high cost of rail travel means that there is an incentive for car owners to continue to use their vehicles. Environmental pressure groups have suggested that rail tickets should be priced at the point where marginal social costs intersect with marginal social benefit.

Air travel

Exogenous shocks have transformed the airline industry. The aftermath of 11 September 2001 saw many national airlines forced into liquidation. Those that remained had to cut costs and reduce their route networks.

The budget airlines prospered. Ryanair, easyJet and bmibaby cut prices and marketed aggressively. Their passenger numbers soared. They recognised that cutting frills, flying to obscure destinations and keeping aircraft in the air and making money was a viable business model if the price was right.

The government is faced with some tough decisions on the long-term future of air transport. While recognising the need to safeguard the long-term economic prosperity of the aviation industry, there is also a desire to minimise the impact of aviation on the environment. Environmental pressure groups would like to see taxes imposed on aviation fuel.

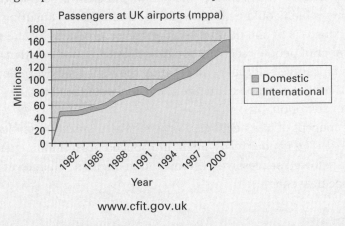

Passengers at UK airports (mppa)

www.cfit.gov.uk

Canals are the future

The government is working with British Waterways to expand the use of barges in and around London. Under the scheme, barges could be used to transport rubbish, recycling material and building materials. One scheme could take 100 000 lorry journeys off the road. Canals provide an environmentally attractive alternative to road transport.

Exam question (40 minutes)   answer: page 158

(a) What type of transport business might actually benefit from an increase in fuel taxes?

(b) How might increasing environmental taxes on fuel affect international competitiveness?

(c) Explain why it is necessary for the government to use cost–benefit analysis when assessing new road schemes.

(d) What are the economic implications of increased traffic congestion for transport operators and other firms in the UK?

Watch out!

The air transport industry is growing at rates above the average growth of the economy of the European Union. The community must try to reconcile pressing environmental needs with the development of an industry that is an important element in ensuring the competitiveness of the economy and for job creation.

The jargon

Exogenous shocks. Events that occur outside the economy but that have an impact on the economy. Examples include terrorist attacks, natural disasters and a decision by OPEC to restrict oil production.

Checkpoint 3

Why should economists be concerned with increasing car ownership?

Checkpoint 4

Identify one group that may be affected by a large rise in fuel prices.

145

Health

The concept of the welfare state refers to the government provision of measures to ensure achieve basic living standards and alleviate need across society. The Beveridge Report (1942) laid out the framework for a welfare state that would relieve poverty, reduce inequality and achieve greater social integration.

The Beveridge Report developed the idea of social insurance and led to the creation of a national health service (1945), paid for by a system of national insurance and assistance.

Public health as a merit good

After the Second World War, the UK government came to the conclusion that a market-led healthcare system did not meet the needs of society and was inequitable. Charging for healthcare meant that the poorest people in society were denied access to healthcare. The creation of the NHS recognised that healthcare was a merit good. Charging for treatment would lead to underconsumption, while providing free healthcare for all would benefit the whole of society. The spread of communicable disease could be controlled and individuals could be encouraged to participate fully in society.

The provision of healthcare was one way of ensuring a redistribution of income, which could be both equitable and efficient. Ensuring that the workforce is fit and healthy could increase productivity and reduce the number of people receiving social assistance. Good health can be seen as a positive externality. In creating the NHS, the government recognised that private healthcare provision would lead to underconsumption.

The concept of free healthcare provision was quickly amended as costs rose. The Labour government introduced prescription charges. This has allowed successive governments to increase charges and introduce new charges.

Rationing

The supply of healthcare services is fixed at any given moment. There is a limit to the number of operations and treatments that can be carried out. This means that healthcare provision must be rationed. Treatments must be prioritised and patients must be placed on waiting lists.

Checkpoint 1

What is the opportunity cost of providing healthcare?

Checkpoint 2

Why is healthcare a merit good?

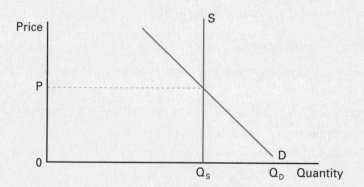

The inelastic supply curve highlights the need to ration healthcare, either by price or by prioritising need. Both strategies have serious drawbacks and challenge the underlying premise of the NHS. Free health would result in undersupply. Charging (P) would achieve equilibrium but would have a political cost.

Private provision ●●●

Other countries have opted for public or private healthcare insurance schemes. In the USA, some large firms have offered private healthcare as part of their employees' pay packages. This type of benefit is becoming less common as costs rise. Employees who are made redundant lose the healthcare insurance, which can be a problem.

There are a number of drawbacks to private healthcare insurance. First, illness is linked to income and lifestyle. Those people most in need of medical treatment are likely to be those least able to afford it. Second, when applying for insurance, there is an incentive to provide false information or to delay treatment where there are concerns in order to avoid having to disclose a pre-existing condition (e.g. AIDS). Third, medical practitioners may be tempted to prescribe unnecessary drugs or treatments because they know that the insurance company rather than the patient is paying.

Health reforms ●●●

During the 1990s, the UK Conservative government sought to introduce market reforms to the NHS. General practitioners (GPs) were given greater freedom. Budgets were devolved and GPs could buy services for their patients. Hospitals were given greater independence. The effect of these reforms was to create internal markets. The perceived benefits were slow to arrive, and the scheme resulted in additional administration costs.

Recent initiatives include private-finance initiatives to build hospitals and the contracting out of services to private healthcare providers, which are being encouraged to specialise in routine procedures, helping to cut waiting lists. NHS 24 was introduced in order to reduce pressure on GPs but has been subject to criticism regarding staffing and service levels.

NHS provision of dental care is under particular strain, with large numbers of dentists opting to go private and requiring patients to take out private dental insurance. New NHS dentists are being swamped with new patients, who travel long distances to attend for appointments.

The Office for National Statistics reports that although NHS spending increased by 39% between 1995 and 2003, productivity fell by 8%. Meanwhile, the government chooses to focus on other indicators.

Checkpoint 3

Why is healthcare unable to meet the demands placed on it?

The jargon

Merit good. A good that is underconsumed because individuals may consider how the good may benefit them as individuals rather than the benefits that consumption may offer society. This is because the positive externalities good are not internalised by consumers. A further factor may be cost. High cost may exclude many in society from consuming the good, particularly people on low incomes.

Checkpoint 4

Are prescription charges regressive?

Exam question (15 minutes) answer: pages 158–9

(a) Examine the arguments regarding public/private provision of healthcare.

(b) Assess the arguments for rationing healthcare.

Housing

The housing market covers owner-occupied accommodation, private rented housing, housing-association provision and local-authority housing. Here we give candidates an opportunity to apply knowledge they have gained in order to demonstrate understanding of how the housing market operates.

Importance of the housing market

The construction sector is often seen as a leading indicator of the state of the UK economy. It is often one of the first sectors to be affected by an economic downturn and the first to show signs of recovery when there is an economic recovery.

When the housing sector is booming, consumer confidence is likely to be high and consumer spending is likely to increase. Rising house prices boost equity and encourage homeowners to increase borrowing and stimulate spending on consumer goods. Buying and selling houses creates income from furniture removals, soft furnishings, furniture and decorating materials.

Demand for housing

Demand for property to buy will depend upon a number of factors.

Price

The demand curve for homes to buy is downward sloping and is based on the ability and willingness to buy. If house prices rise, the willingness to buy a house will reduce. If house prices fall, there will be more potential buyers.

Cost of substitutes

The cost of alternative accommodation is likely to influence demand for housing. If the cost of rented accommodation rises, then it becomes more attractive to buy your own home.

Cost of borrowing

Interest rates have a direct effect on demand for housing, although the impact of interest rate rises is often lagged. Mortgage lenders have helped to stimulate demand by relaxing lending rules and letting people borrow more money relative to their incomes.

Income

Evidence suggests that demand is income-elastic and that as income rises, people will seek to join or move up the housing ladder, buying bigger properties.

Social trends

Increasing divorce rates and marriage occurring later in life has led to an increase in single-occupancy households. Increasing social mobility has led to a greater demand for larger homes with higher specifications.

Government policy

Government policy can influence the availability of loans. Stamp duty (tax on house purchases) may also have an impact on demand.

The government has put forward proposals to extend state-sponsored shared-ownership schemes to assist first-time buyers. Under this scheme, housebuyers will buy part of the property and the remainder will be bought by the government and lender.

Interest-rate policy now rests with the monetary policy committee and is not in discretion of the government.

Supply

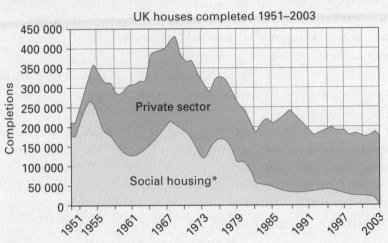

UK houses completed 1951–2003

* Includes local authorities and housing associations

Source: ODPM

The supply of housing will be influenced by house prices and the rents that landlords are able to charge. A significant constraint on housebuilding is the supply of suitable land. Rising land, labour and material costs have all combined to raise house prices. Market analysts working for the government have concluded that the huge gap between housing supply and demand is behind runaway house-price inflation. They believe that if more homes are made available, then house-price inflation will be lower. The move could also help key workers buy homes.

Exam question (20 minutes)   answer: page 159

(a) How might a fall in house prices affect the demand for rented accommodation?

(b) Explain why houses in London may be more expensive than comparable houses in Newcastle.

(c) Evaluate the impact of shared ownership schemes.

Sport and leisure

The sport and leisure sector is a fast-growing sector of the UK economy. The growth of the sector has increased employment opportunities and created opportunities for economic regeneration.

Within the sport and leisure sector, there is a high degree of interdependence.

Leisure activities

The most popular leisure activities in the UK today are watching television, listening to the radio and reading. The proliferation of TV channels has made the television market increasingly fragmented, increasing the cost of advertising. Sky has achieved significant growth in its market share by securing exclusive live rights to showing Premiership football, rugby union and test cricket. Televised sport remains central to its continuing growth.

Other popular activities include listening to music, DIY and gardening. Participation in these activities varies according to gender, age and socioeconomic grouping.

The number of people watching sporting events exceeds the number of people playing sport. Spectator numbers at sporting events have risen in recent years, due partly to increased amounts of leisure time and partly to rising disposable incomes.

Checkpoint 1

Why have a number of brewers exited the brewing market?

Economic regeneration

The government has recognised the importance of sporting and leisure events as a mechanism for urban regeneration. During the 1990s, garden festivals were held in Liverpool, Stoke and Ebbw Vale. The festivals were located on brownfield sites, which were cleared and redeveloped. Infrastructure was put in place at an early stage so that the sites could be developed for commercial purposes at the end of the festival. Tourism promotion also helped to promote the locations to firms interested in relocating.

The Millennium Dome project, although not a commercial success, ensured that the contaminated land surrounding it was cleared and that the infrastructure was put in place for further development. In Cardiff, the Millennium Stadium has been a more obvious success, bringing tourists into the city centre and generating additional income for hotels, bars and shops. The negative externalities associated with holding a sporting or musical event are litter and noise pollution.

Checkpoint 2

Why do satellite television companies offer promotional discounts to new customers?

Spectator sports

The main spectator sport in the UK is football. The Premiership generates annual profits of £124 million and the average turnover of a Premiership club is £65 million. In the 2002–03 season, Premiership match attendances averaged 35 000. This contrasts with average attendance at Coca Cola League matches of 10 600. The difference in average attendance highlights the fact that the product is not homogeneous. Supporters of football clubs have a significant degree of brand loyalty. This means that watching a particular club is not easily substitutable. The cost of forming a club and the rules regarding entry into the league means that there are significant barriers to entry.

Successful clubs such as Manchester United and Chelsea have monopoly power. They are able to exploit this power by charging higher prices for tickets. Manchester United has excess demand for tickets. The supply of tickets for home matches is inelastic. The same problem applies to major matches. Fans want tickets, but there are not enough tickets to go round at the market price. Ticket touts may sell tickets at a higher price.

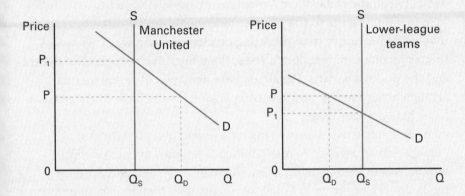

Lower-league teams may find that they have excess supply and need to reduce prices in order to achieve market clearance. Ticket pricing for sporting events also provides evidence of price discrimination. Pensioners and children are offered discounted tickets. Tickets also vary in price according to the location of the seats in the ground.

Check the net

www.bized.ac.uk/current/leisure
www.bized.ac.uk/current/argument/
arg20-5.htm

Watch out!

The UK leisure industry, covering a range of diverse businesses such as tour operators and football clubs, earns around £1.7 billion a week. Analysts have linked high leisure spending to rises in levels of disposable income and comparatively long working hours, which may lead people to spend more heavily in the little leisure time available to them. The leisure-sector boom has also grown as a result of the development of technology-driven products and items such as compact discs, DVDs, video games and cable TV. The sector is subject to exogenous shocks. 11 September 2001 is estimated to have cost hotels, guest houses and tourist attractions in the UK £2 billion in lost revenues.

Exam question (10 minutes)   answer: page 159

(a) Live 8 gave away tickets for a live concert. Ticketholders tried to resell them. Why?

(b) Examine the impact of Glastonbury Festival on the local area.

Welfare economics, income distribution, poverty

There is no single cause and no single consequence of poverty and social inequality in the UK. The causes of poverty vary from marital status to literacy levels. The consequences of poverty can be seen in poor-quality housing and poor educational attainment.

Causes of poverty

Employment in the manufacturing sector has declined, and this has contributed to a slowdown in the growth of real wages. Unskilled workers in the service sector are the worst paid. Meanwhile, wages in the financial services and ICT sectors have risen, widening the gap between the richest and the poorest people in society.

Benefit payments to the poorest individuals are adjusted to reflect inflation rates rather than reflecting changes in earnings. This means that as incomes outstrip price rises, the differential between the richest and the poorest widens. Pensioners are affected adversely by this arrangement; Age Concern has campaigned for the basic state pension to be linked to earnings.

A clear link exists between unemployment and poverty. As unemployment levels rise, the number of people living in poverty also increases. Rising levels of employment have helped to reduce the incidence of poverty. Nonetheless, the government is committed to reducing benefit dependency and forcing people out of the poverty trap.

Government policy

The government's recent strategy to address income inequality has included the introduction of a national minimum wage and a switch towards means-tested benefits. The CBI was initially critical of the minimum wage, arguing that it would lead to a loss of international competitiveness, job losses and fuel inflation. None of these predictions has come true.

Working Families Tax Credit and Children's Tax Credit have been introduced, and Child Benefit has been increased in real terms to benefit families. Pensioners have been targeted by the introduction of the Minimum Income Guarantee for Pensioners.

Long-term unemployed people have been targeted with the Expanded New Deal Programme. Critics have argued that this scheme is expensive and has produced limited benefits.

More affluent families have seen their incomes reduced by the ending of mortgage-interest tax relief for homeowners and an increase in National Insurance contributions for higher-income earners.

The way forward

The key to reducing relative poverty in the long run is for the UK economy to create sufficient jobs offering a decent rate of pay in order to raise the living standards of the poorest people in society. Rising employment can stimulate a rise in average incomes. In the long term,

Checkpoint 1

Is inequality a problem?

Checkpoint 2

What does a Gini coefficient measure?

Checkpoint 3

Identify two measures that Labour have introduced in order to reduce inequality.

there is a need to improve the stock of human capital, giving those who are outside the formal labour market the skills they need to enhance their employability.

Tax reforms could provide an incentive for people to take up work rather than remain in the poverty trap. Means-tested benefits are also a way of targeting poverty. Recent schemes have shown that they are difficult to administer, however, leading to significant overpayments.

It is an inescapable fact that the incomes of the lowest paid people in society must rise faster than the incomes of the wealthiest people in society if relative poverty is to be reduced. There is little sign of this happening at the moment.

Regional variations ●●●

A report conducted by the Joseph Rowntree Foundation identified a number of consequences of poverty. These included low-birth-weight babies, homelessness, obesity, criminal activity, teen drug abuse and reduced access to social services.

The charity Child Poverty Action Group highlighted that only Mexico has worse regional inequality than the UK. Wales is poorer than the rest of the UK, and annual incomes in the north-east of England are £4000 a year less than in the rest of the UK. In Scotland, Glasgow has some of the worst unemployment blackspots in the country.

Gender and race ●●●

Inequality extends to race and gender. People of ethnic background are more likely to experience unemployment. Black graduates are seven times more likely to be unemployed than their white counterparts. Meanwhile, women in the workplace are likely to receive lower rates of pay than men.

It is clear that inequality continues to thrive in the UK.

Checkpoint 4

What evidence is there of wealth inequality in the UK?

Examiner's secrets

When writing extended answers, try to offer a balanced examination of the issues. Look at both sides of the argument. Answers are seldom black and white. Try to remember that you have two hands: 'On the one hand . . . and on the other hand.' If you remember this and apply it in the exam, you are likely to improve the quality of your analysis and evaluation, the higher-order skills that carry the greatest reward.

Exam question (30 minutes) answer: page 160

(a) Assess the impact of the shift from direct taxation to indirect taxation on poverty.

(b) Evaluate the success of Labour's strategies to reduce inequality.

(c) Examine the causes of poverty.

The environment, environmental policy

The focus of this topic is the role of economics in understanding environmental issues and how economic policies can be used to influence decisions affecting the environment. The challenge for candidates is to apply knowledge of economic and business concepts in a range of contexts.

The jargon

There has been much discussion of international measures to restrict global carbon emissions in order to moderate global warming. There is widespread agreement that the most economically efficient mechanism would be some system of tradeable emission permits.

The environment and growth ○○○

Successive governments in both the developed and the developing world have targeted long-term economic growth as a key priority of their economic policy. The challenge facing government is to achieve continuing economic growth, satisfying the pressure for ever higher living standards, while at the same time conserving scarce resources.

The challenge for developing countries is much greater. Living standards in developing countries are much lower, and the pressure to raise GDP is greater. This means that the social and environmental costs of economic growth are ignored. China, for example, has three cities in the top-ten list of the world's most polluted cities.

The tradeoffs between growth and the environment are difficult for some countries to balance. The USA, for example, has 4% of the world's population but produces 20% of the world's greenhouse gases. Introducing regulation and taxation to curb emissions would be politically unpopular.

Watch out!

Cambridge Econometrics, in a report published July 2005, suggests that the government will not meet its target to reduce domestic carbon emissions by a fifth by 2010. Even to achieve a 12.75% reduction it would be necessary to increase the price of tradeable permits in order to cut emissions from coal-fired power plants. This would have implications for energy prices and inflation. The European Union's greenhouse-gas-emissions trading scheme issues industries with tradeable permits for the carbon dioxide they are allowed to produce. Efficient producers may sell on their unused allocation to other producers. This gives producers an incentive to reduce emissions.

International measures ○○○

The United Nations Conference on the Environment in June 1992 raised the profile of environmental issues and led to the adoption of Agenda 21, which sets objectives for countries committed to sustainable development. The Kyoto Protocol agreed in 2001 set targets for the reduction in emissions of six greenhouse gases. The USA has refused to adopt the Kyoto agreement and challenges the scientific evidence of global warming. The impact of the Kyoto agreement on countries is mixed. It is estimated that complying with the Kyoto agreement could reduce the EU's GDP by 0.06% (at 2010). Japan in contrast may see its GDP increase by 0.9%. The USA, by remaining outside the Kyoto agreement, may gain a competitive advantage by avoiding the costs of compliance.

Government policy ○○○

Increasingly, the UK government and the EU have sought to make firms internalise the full cost of their activities. A number of environmental measures have been introduced in order to encourage firms to reduce waste and to ensure that the polluter pays.

The government has introduced a Landfill Tax Credit, which charges polluters for every tonne of rubbish they bury in the ground. This has encouraged firms to look for alternative uses for waste.

Tax differentials have been introduced for smaller, less polluting cars. The aim is to encourage motorists to purchase cars that are less

Checkpoint 1

Illustrate how a subsidy paid to environmental energy providers might encourage the consumption of renewable energy.

environmentally damaging. Environmentalists have criticised the reduction in road tax as being too small to have a significant impact on motorists' purchasing decisions.

The European Union directive on Waste Electronic and Electrical Equipment (WEE) is expected to be introduced in the UK in early 2006. This directive requires producers of consumer electronics (everything from hairdryers to musical cards) to recycle and dispose of waste electrical goods.

Emissions trading has been introduced. It is intended to reduce the amounts of carbon released into the atmosphere by factories, power plants and commercial office blocks.

Companies will be given an allowance of carbon that they can emit. Companies exceeding their pollution quotas will face a fine. Those firms that produce less carbon can sell on the remainder of their allowance to other firms.

The government's aim is to control – and gradually reduce – total industrial emissions. Plans to cut emissions by 20% by 2010 will be difficult to meet (emissions rose in 2005). Government plans have been criticised by the CBI, which suggests that the government risks 'sacrificing UK jobs on the altar of green credentials'.

Checkpoint 2

What might be the benefits of using environmental taxes to improve the quality of the environment?

Checkpoint 3

State the arguments for and against the use of fines as a means of reducing environmental pollution.

Check the net

http://europa.eu.int/pol/env/index_en.htm
www.foe.co.uk
www.greenpeace.org

Exam question (30 minutes)   answer: page 161

(a) Identify the short-term effects of the new energy tax on small to medium-sized manufacturers.

(b) Evaluate the case for the imposition of environmental standards.

(c) Assess two strategies that the government could adopt in order to reduce the environmental impact of increasing car use.

Answers
Cross-cutting themes

Globalisation

Checkpoints

1 A number of factors have led to the increasing pace of globalisation. These include the reduction in obstacles to trade and improvements in communications systems. It is a process in which geographic distance is less important in the establishment and maintenance of cross-border economic, political and sociocultural relations.

   Critics of globalisation define the term quite differently, describing globalisation as a worldwide drive towards a globalised economic system dominated by supranational corporate trade and banking institutions that are not accountable to national governments.

2 Pressure groups might seek to highlight unfair trading practices, human rights abuses and the externalities caused by a particular firm's trading, manufacturing or mining activities. Alternatively, pressure groups might pressure national governments to regulate the activities of TNCs. A number of large TNCs have modified their activities, putting in place voluntary codes in response to consumer boycotts of their products.

3 One adverse consequence of globalisation is that producers have chosen to relocate some manufacturing activities abroad in the search of cost advantages. This has created structural decline in developed countries and led to unemployment blackspots. Developing countries have not always benefited. Footloose companies have switched production between countries in order to exploit exchange-rate movements and wage differentials. Critics of globalisation suggests that it has created a race to the bottom between the poorest countries.

   A second disadvantage is the erosion of cultures. The French government in particular has sought to counter the Americanisation of French culture with legislation. Some Muslim countries have sought to produce local products in direct competition with those produced by US corporations.

Exam question

(a) The imposition of sanctions is likely to hit producers not related directly to the dispute. The increase in tariffs is designed to ensure enforcement. They are intended to compensate a country for the loss of trade that it suffers as a result of unfair trading practices. Where sanctions have been used in the past, they have been punitive, doubling the rate of duty levied on a particular product. This makes it difficult for those to compete. For example, the US government almost doubled prices of Scottish cashmere imported into the USA as part of the sanctions introduced to penalise EU countries for discriminating against 'dollar bananas'. The resulting loss of markets may cause downsizing or failure of firms unable to find alternative markets.

(b) There are potential costs and benefits to this strategy. The benefits may include locating near to developing markets, cheap labour, lower costs, transfer pricing, tax

advantages and looser government control. Costs may include adverse publicity because of low pay and poor working conditions, pressure groups targeting the company, and consumer boycotts.

(c) An examination of the economic performance of developing countries that have adopted protectionist policies and those countries that have engaged in export promotion seems to indicate a positive relationship between international trade and economic growth. The Asian tiger economies have achieved impressive growth levels by adopting an export-led growth strategy. Such an approach may stimulate inward investment and skills transfer.

The single European market

Checkpoints

1 Tourists tend to notice consumer prices but, unless they are very unfortunate, are not exposed to the cost of items such as hospital treatment. Neither do they participate in the education system or have to seek employment or permanent housing.

2 Another possibility is the tougher competition and anti-monopoly regime in the USA (see page 54).

Exam question

Points that could be raised include the following:

- **Price transparency.** Companies find it more difficult to hide behind the smokescreen of tariffs and customs barriers. Consumer groups have become more vocal about what is called 'rip-off Britain', with car manufacturers being accused of charging higher prices in the UK than other European customers would tolerate. This trend would, of course, be boosted by UK membership of the euro.

- **Competition policy.** The EU has toughened up its policy on anti-competitive practices and monopoly (see the discussion of competition policy on page 54). It has also become a major player, like the USA, in trade negotiations on a world scale.

- **Job opportunities.** Sections of the UK media take a very negative view of the SEM. The accession of Poland, for example, was presented as a threat rather than an opportunity, and the tabloid papers predicted a flood of immigrants swamping the UK labour market. It says something about British attitudes and entrepreneurship that Poland was regarded as a source of cheap labour rather than 30 million potential new customers for British businesses. It also forgets that it is the SEM that allows British people to live and work anywhere in Europe if they so wish. Many UK senior citizens take advantage of this opportunity with their retirement homes in Spain. Perhaps more young Britons could seek opportunities of their own if the British education system were to invest in European-style standards of modern language teaching.

- **Regional policy.** After the common agricultural policy (CAP), the second largest item in the EU budget is spending on regional development. Often, this has meant subsidising the poorer areas of Europe and, in effect, compensating for their lack of facilities compared with the more prosperous regions. The SEM has encouraged Europe-wide infrastructure projects, such as new and improved transport networks, which if successful will improve access to and from peripheral areas and enable regions to benefit from trade rather than aid.

Economic development

Checkpoints

1 The short answer is yes. Multinationals engaging in inward investment would benefit from those same protectionist policies when locating in that country. The downside is that if the companies want to export, they may face retaliatory policies from countries that have been denied the opportunity to export to that country.

2 The short answer is yes. If a multinational sets up in a developing country that has protected its market, then it will also be protected by the barriers to imports. The downside to this situation is that if it tries to export products from the developing country, then it may face retaliatory protection.

Exam question

(a) High birth rates are likely to affect savings ratios and investment levels. A large number of dependents can be a drain on household incomes, affecting living standards, access to education and quality of life. Birth rates are an indicator of economic development. High birth rates will reduce GDP per head. High birth rates and cultural attitudes may also remove women from the workforce, reducing the productive potential of the economy.

(b) FDI can help to promote economic growth in less developed countries such as Mozambique. The benefits of major foreign investment into the country can be measured by rise in GDP and export earnings. In the case of Mozambique, FDI into an aluminium-smelting plant helped double Mozambique's exports, created 1000 jobs and helped raise economic growth. Tax revenues have also risen sharply.

   The downside of FDI in Mozambique is that the benefits of FDI have not been felt throughout society. The trickle-down effect has been limited.

(c) Production contracts with suppliers in developing countries can increase the flexibility of multinationals. They can play suppliers off against each other in order to secure lower production costs. Lower production costs in this scenario invariably are achieved by forcing down labour costs.

Emerging and transitional economies

Checkpoints

1 The short-term consequences of market reform in command economies are likely to be a rise in unemployment as firms are exposed to international competition and subsidies are ended. Inefficient firms will contract and, in some cases, close. In many cases, market reform leads to a contraction of the economy. Those industries with potential may be privatised, attracting foreign investors.

2 Some countries have accepted the view that export-led growth will encourage domestic producers to become more efficient and improve the quality of their products in order to be competitive. Resources will be allocated to those sectors where the country is most efficient and that will be most able to compete in international markets. Producers will benefit from comparative advantage and specialisation.

3 The benefits of attracting investment from Western companies is that it provides investment that is in short supply in transitional economies. More importantly, investment by Western companies may provide technical expertise and a work culture not found in companies that previously had operated in a command economy.

Exam question

(a) Migrant workers tend to be the youngest, most dynamic and most well-qualified members of the workforce. Population migration represents a loss of productive potential from the economy. The balancing argument is that in the long term, these individuals may return with enhanced skills and may be able to offer a greater contribution to the economy. Migrant workers may also stimulate economic activity in their own country by sending money home to relatives.

(b) The problems facing East Germany include the decline of traditional industries, high levels of unemployment and population migration. Subsidising inefficient producers is not an option. Encouraging investment and rationalisation by market-oriented firms is. Supply-side policies need to be introduced in order to incentivise workers and business. Retraining programmes need to be put in place in order to improve employability. Surplus housing needs to be cleared in order to reduce wasted provision and improve the environment. Improvements in infrastructure would also be desirable.

Transport

Checkpoints

1 A sustainable transport policy would seek to minimise the external costs of road transport such as noise pollution, vehicle emissions and congestion. This may involve a system of subsidies and disincentives. Incentives are likely to include subsidies to public transport or shared-vehicle schemes, so that the marginal social cost equals the marginal social benefit. Encouraging the use of bicycles through the provision of cycle routes may also contribute to a reduction of environmental problems. It is not likely to be a panacea, however. Disincentives would discourage use of private transport.

2 The assessment of new road schemes necessitates the government considering the private costs of development as well as the wider social impact of such a development. Social costs such as the loss of amenity, damage to sites of special scientific interest and disruption to local communities need to be weighed against reduced travelling times and improved accessibility.

3 Increasing car ownership gives rise to increasing externalities. The impact of these externalities needs to be considered, and strategies need to be implemented in order to minimise the impact of car ownership. Increasing car ownership places increasing pressure upon infrastructure, and the government needs to assess the impact of increasing traffic congestion and ways of easing traffic congestion in a cost-effective way. Economists can guide the government in selecting ways to encourage motorists to internalise social costs of motoring (through taxation) and provide evidence to support the development of public transport.

4 • Transport companies will be affected by rising fuel prices.
  • People living in rural areas who have limited access to public transport.
  • Holidaymakers who may face a fuel charge on their package holiday.

Exam question

(a) Public transport companies may benefit if fuel taxes encourage commuters off the road and on to public transport. Rail companies and canal barges may also benefit if it becomes cost-effective to take freight off the road.

(b) Companies engaged in the development of technologies aimed at reducing the environmental impact will benefit from environmental taxes and may be able to export the technology developed. Producers in the short term may see their costs rise. Whether their product is substitutable will determine whether they can pass the environmental tax on to their customers and whether their international competitiveness will be affected. The imposition of environmental policies on international competitiveness will be reduced if they are imposed in other countries.

(c) In answering this type of question, it is appropriate to begin with a definition of cost–benefit analysis and develop your explanation of how it might be used to assess new road schemes using the COBA model (a cost benefit analysis package used by the Department for Transport). You should then expand your explanation to demonstrate that new roads are a quasi public good and that it is appropriate to have some assessment of the impact of new roads given that the current system for charging is based on fuel charges and road tax. CBA would allow the government to judge how far public expenditure on road schemes reflects the needs of road users and the priorities of the government.

(d) This question requires an understanding of how economists calculate the costs of traffic congestion. Important elements of any response will be the valuation

of travel time and a recognition that being delayed by traffic congestion has opportunity costs. These may include increased fuel costs and the underutilisation of transport capacity (trucks caught up in traffic jams are not being used efficiently). Firms may need to increase stock levels in order to compensate for delays in deliveries. Maintenance costs and depreciation of vehicles may increase for transport operators. Increased transport costs may have an effect on overall business costs and consumer prices. Firms may re-evaluate their business location in order to minimise costs. Higher transport costs may contribute to an erosion of international competitiveness.

Health

Checkpoints

1 The opportunity cost of providing healthcare is the alternative use that the money spent on healthcare could have been put to.

2 Healthcare is a merit good because it raises the wellbeing of society and reduces the risk of contagious disease.

3 Healthcare is unable to meet demand for a number of reasons:
  • The population is ageing, increasing demand for healthcare services.
  • Improvements in healthcare mean that more people can be treated.
  • Obesity is creating health problems.
  • Smoking kills people and generates demand for treatments to deal with the consequences of smoking.

4 The answer is not clear cut. Those on benefits do not have to pay for prescription charges. Those on low incomes may have to pay prescription charges. They are also one of the groups most in need of healthcare. For this group prescription charges may be regressive.

Exam question

(a) Private healthcare can satisfy the needs of many people. Private healthcare schemes require contributions to be made by patients. Those who can afford treatment can gain access to it. The problem is that many people on low incomes will not be able to gain access to healthcare. The loss of productive workers and the increased risk of epidemics is a social cost.

(b) Rationing healthcare has become an emotive issue. The reality is that improvements in medical care have meant that doctors are increasingly able to intervene and save lives or improve the quality of life. As a result of medical improvements, costs have risen. Spending on healthcare means that money must be diverted from elsewhere in the economy. This may mean that the government reduces investment in education, research and development, or elsewhere. The other alternative is that the government may have to increase taxation in order to meet healthcare expenditure, thus reducing disposable income.

The argument for rationing is that it ensures that treatments give the greatest benefit. The difficulty of the process is placing a monetary value on the life or quality of life of a patient.

Housing

Checkpoints

1. Price

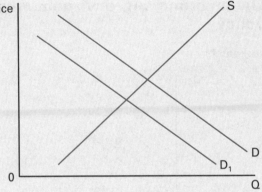

There are a number of possible explanations why house prices fell during the first quarter of 2003. A typical response may show the demand curve shifting to the left, leading to a new, lower equilibrium price. An explanation for this might be the economic slowdown in the UK economy, leading to potential buyers being more cautious to committing themselves to a major purchase.

2. Falling house prices may reduce the number of houses being put on the market and may make homeowners more cautious about borrowing against the value of their homes. If the fall in house prices is particularly sharp, then homeowners may find themselves in a position of negative equity.

Exam question

(a) A fall in house prices might lead to an increase in demand for houses and a reduction in demand for rented accommodation. Homeownership and renting are substitutes. The cross-elasticity of demand is positive. The impact of lower house prices may not be immediate. The cost of purchasing a house is significant, legal costs will have to be paid and a deposit may be required. As a result, demand may not increase quickly.

(b) The difference in house prices may be due to a number of supply and demand factors. Employment levels and income levels tend to be higher in London. This means that London buyers are able to afford larger mortgages and pay higher prices for property. London has a much greater proportion of jobs in the IT and financial services sector, which will boost average incomes. In the Newcastle area, a much greater proportion of the workforce was once employed in the manufacturing sector, which has been in decline in recent years. This will have implications for effective demand.

Population migration away from the north-east and towards London and the south-east will also influence demand for housing.

Planning restrictions will have implications for the supply of housing. Supply may be inelastic, leading to market disequilibrium in London. In the north-east, restriction on supply may not be so restrictive.

(c) Shared-ownership schemes may help first-time buyers and people on low incomes to get on to the housing ladder. It may also help to fuel house price inflation if the supply of houses is not increased.

Sport and leisure

Checkpoints

1. A number of brewers have exited the brewing industry because the economics of brewing mean that the profit margins on brewing are so small. Firms such as Vaux and Bass have left the brewing sector and sought to focus on the hotel sector, where profit margins are higher.

2. Satellite companies offer initial discounts to attract customers. They recognise that if they can get customers to subscribe to their service initially, then they may be able to retain those customers in the longer term because of customer inertia.

Exam question

(a) This is a matter of supply and demand. The tickets had a value to some people in excess of their face value. They were prepared to pay the £200 or £300 being asked for the tickets. The individuals placed a higher value on attending the concert than the people who had originally acquired the tickets.

Glastonbury Festival brings revenue to the area and can help to regenerate the area. Employment will be created for those involved with staging the event, catering and providing security. The event may well raise the profile of the area and encourage people to visit the area at other times of the year.

The downside of the event is that it may have an environmental impact, with increased noise and litter. Strategies to deal with the problems may create new opportunities. One solution to control noise pollution is to provide late-night dancers with headphones so that they can dance to the music of their choice. It's quiet and very funny to watch!

Welfare economics, income distribution, poverty

Checkpoints

1. Inequality is inevitable in a market economy, where the demand for skills and labour is variable. Inequality becomes a problem when there is no equality of opportunity, and this can lead to social and racial tensions, as was seen in areas of social deprivation during the 1980s and 1990s. The task facing governments is not to eliminate inequality but to address barriers preventing individuals participating in society and to address the problems of those experiencing relative poverty.

2 The Gini coefficient is a measure of the degree of inequality in a given distribution of income, expressed as a percentage: 0% represents perfect equality and 100% represents perfect inequality.
3 Measures that might be identified include:
   - A national minimum wage.
   - Greater use of means-tested benefits.
   - The Working Families Tax Credit.
   - Increases in the value of Child Benefit and a new Children's Tax Credit.
   - Introduction of the Minimum Income Guarantee for pensioners.
   - New Deal Programme for long-term unemployed people.
4 The wealthiest 10% control more than 50% of the UK's wealth. One in three families in the UK have no savings.

Exam question

(a) The shift in emphasis from direct to indirect taxation has contributed to an increase in relative poverty. Successive governments have reduced the marginal rate of taxation over the past 20 years. This has enabled people to keep a higher proportion of the income they earn. The benefits of lower rates of taxation have been shared disproportionately. Those on above-average incomes have gained the most.

Those on low incomes tend to spend a higher proportion of the disposable incomes. Increasing direct taxation on items such as tobacco, alcohol, fast food and fuel have a regressive effect.

(b) Labour has ended mortgage-interest tax relief and increased National Insurance contributions. At the same time, a range of benefits have been introduced, including the Working Families Tax Credit, increases in the value of Child Benefit and a new Children's Tax Credit. The New Deal has been introduced in order to give long-term unemployed people the skills needed to re-enter the workforce.

Improvements in the economy have led to more jobs being created and a rise in wage rates. Tax reforms have taken people out of the poverty trap. What is evident is that the number of children living in poverty has fallen, although the government has not achieved its target. The poorest families have seen their net incomes rise. Means-tested benefits have been targeted towards pensioners and families on the lowest incomes. Overall, inequality as measured by the Gini coefficient, has increased.

Poverty does not have a single cause. Poverty is caused by a number of economic and social factors. Differences in wages and earnings have given rise to poverty. For example, pay levels in the financial services and IT sectors have increased faster than those in the food-processing sector. Pay for unskilled workers has tended to lag behind those of skilled workers. Some sectors of the economy, such as the manufacturing sector, have contracted, creating long-term unemployed people. People on benefits have seen benefits fail to keep pace with earnings, increasing relative poverty. Pensioners on state pensions have been particularly affected by this.

Unemployment is one of the principal causes of poverty. There is a correlation between rising unemployment rates and increases in relative poverty. This is exacerbated when no one in a household is in paid employment.

The environment, environmental policy

Checkpoints

1

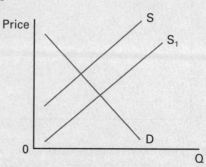

A subsidy is a sum of money by government to producers, so that the price to the customer will be less than it might have been. A subsidy will reduce the market price paid by consumers, although the factor cost will be higher. Subsidies may be paid for social reasons or, as in this case, to stimulate demand for goods that have a wider social benefit but where technology costs may initially make pricing uncompetitive.

2 Such an approach draws upon the principle that the polluter pays. Ensuring that polluters pay to improve the quality of the environment is equitable.

3 Fines can be an appropriate way of internalising the cost of pollution and may encourage firms to clean up their acts. Fines may not have the desired effect if the fines imposed are less than the savings achieved by allowing the pollutants into the environment. Advantages of using environmental taxes to improve the quality of the environment are:
   - They raise finance for the government.
   - They may reduce consumption of environmentally damaging products.
   - Taxation can encourage firms to develop technologies and may reduce the need for regulation of the industry.
   - Firms could be encouraged to achieve the optimal level of production if tax is set at the right level.

The downsides of this policy may be:
   - Environmental taxes could have a redistributional income effect, hitting those on low incomes the most.
   - There are obvious difficulties in setting the tax levels at the right level to ensure optimum consumption.
   - Where demand for a product or service is inelastic, the use of environmental taxes may do little to reduce consumption, e.g. petrol taxes.
   - Environmental tax may have an inflationary effect, pushing up prices.

Exam question

(a) The short-term impact is likely to be an increase in costs as firms have to absorb the cost increase. The most energy-efficient firms may gain a competitive advantage. The least efficient may not be able to survive in the market, depending on the elasticity of demand for their product.

(b) Environmental standards set benchmarks against which firms can be measured. Financial penalties can be imposed on those firms that fail to comply. The downside is that environmental standards are effective only if they are challenging and are monitored and enforced.

(c) The government used tax differentials on leaded and unleaded petrol. This proved effective, encouraging motorists to switch to unleaded petrol. Congestion charging has proved effective in London, reducing road congestion in Central London. It has, however, failed to raise the anticipated revenue needed to improve public transport. In this respect, the success of the strategy has been mixed.

Revision checklist
Cross-cutting themes

By the end of this chapter you should be able to:

1	Understand the implications of globalisation for less developed and more developed countries.	Confident	Not confident. **Revise** pages 137–40
2	Understand the challenges facing countries seeking economic development.	Confident	Not confident. **Revise** pages 140–41
3	Recognise the difficulties facing transitional economies and the opportunities facing emerging economies.	Confident	Not confident. **Revise** pages 142–3
4	Appreciate the challenges facing the government in developing a transport policy.	Confident	Not confident. **Revise** pages 144–5
5	Understand the debate regarding public/private healthcare and the challenges facing the government.	Confident	Not confident. **Revise** pages 146–7
6	Apply appropriate theory to the housing market.	Confident	Not confident. **Revise** pages 148–9
7	Use theory to examine the sport and leisure sector.	Confident	Not confident. **Revise** pages 150–51
8	Assess the causes and consequences of poverty and social inequality.	Confident	Not confident. **Revise** pages 152–3
9	Discuss the role that economics has in understanding environmental issues and how economic policies can be used to influence decisions.	Confident	Not confident. **Revise** pages 154–5

Resources

This chapter offers some final information and advice for exam preparation for AS and A2 exams. The first part identifies the most common command words used by examiners. Students are often unaware of what these words actually require them to do. Knowing what the examiner requires you to do and what skills you must demonstrate is advantageous. There is also an explanation of levels of response marking. Questions worth, say, eight or more marks are often marked according to performance levels. If you wish to progress through the mark ranges, you must ensure that your answer complies with these criteria.

Exam boards

It is useful to have a copy of your exam specification. You can obtain one from the board's publication department or by downloading the specification from the board's website. The boards will also supply copies of past papers.

Edexcel
One90 High Holborn, London WC1V 7BH – www.edexcel.org.uk

AQA (Assessment and Qualifications Alliance)
Publications Department, Stag Hill House, Guildford, Surrey GU2 5XJ – www.aqa.org.uk

OCR (Oxford, Cambridge and Royal Society of Arts)
1 Hills Road, Cambridge CB1 2EU – www.ocr.org.uk

WJEC (Welsh Joint Education Committee)
245 Western Avenue, Cardiff CF5 2YX – www.wjec.co.uk

CCEA (Council for the Curriculum Examinations and Assessment)
29 Clarendon Road, Clarendon Dock, Belfast BT1 3BG – www.ccea.org.uk

Command words

Candidates risk losing marks because they fail to understand the command words that examiners use. It is important that you read and understand the command words and do what is asked of you.

Command words provide students with guidance on the skills that examiners want students to demonstrate.

Questions carrying eight or more marks will be marked using a level mark scheme. Marks will be allocated according to the candidate's ability to meet four assessment objectives. Candidates will need to demonstrate knowledge, application, analysis and evaluation.

Examiner's secrets

Examiners are looking for an opportunity to award candidates for their use of economic terms and theories and the appropriate use of diagrams. Some candidates manage to write answers to an entire exam paper without using any terms, theories or diagrams.

Examiner's secrets

The command words used by an examiner will guide you as to the type of answer required. Make sure that you do what is required.

Examiner's secrets

Make certain that you answer every part of the question. Not all exam questions are written well. Reading a question quickly may mean that you misread the question and don't give the answer the examiner wants. Some questions ask you to look at two issues. For example, 'Examine the implications of a rise in interest rates for unemployment and the rate of inflation.' In order to get full marks, you must consider the impact of a rise in interest rates on both inflation and unemployment rates.

Command words

If you can understand the skills that an examiner wants you to demonstrate, you can provide a more focused response. Time is a constraint in exams, and candidates need to ensure that they understand what a question requires them to do and tailor their responses accordingly. For example, the use of the word 'explain' requires candidates to give reasons for taking a particular decision or action. There are a range of possible command words, but the most frequently used are described below.

Analyse	Requires candidates to identify cause and effect and how factors may be linked, e.g. unemployment and inflation.
Assess	Candidates will be expected to make informed judgement.
Define	Explain what you understand by a term. This command is usually used to test knowledge.
Evaluate/ critically assess	Judgements are required. There will be an expectation that candidates will apply knowledge of appropriate economic concepts and theories when analysing a context. Reasoned comment will be required.
Examine	A higher order command word, requiring candidates to demonstrate knowledge in relevant contexts, and offer analysis. Judgements will be required to reach the top of the mark range. Evaluative comment may also be required. Candidates should seek to develop points which they raise. Superficial statements will gain limited reward.
Explain	Demonstrate understanding of why something has occurred. Candidates will be required to apply knowledge.
Illustrate	Use diagrams and/or appropriate examples to explain what is happening or might happen.
Outline	Requires a brief explanation or summary description.

Remember that in order to evaluate, you must show balance. Look at both sides of an argument and highlight advantages and disadvantages. Some candidates find it helpful to remember that they have two hands, e.g. **On the one hand**, a reduction in interest rates may be beneficial, as it may stimulate borrowing, increase aggregate demand and lead to a reduction in the level of unemployment. **On the other hand**, a reduction in interest rates may lead to the economy overheating as it nears full capacity and result in demand pull inflation.

Don't forget: command words tell you what skills the examiner wants you to demonstrate:

→ **Define:** demonstrate knowledge.
→ **Examine:** demonstrate knowledge and apply relevant ideas and concepts in context.
→ **Analyse:** demonstrate knowledge; apply ideas and concepts and identify cause and effect.
→ **Evaluate:** demonstrate knowledge; apply ideas and concepts; offer analysis and build balanced judgements.

Level of response marking

Level responses

In order to achieve the highest grades (A/B), candidates will need to consistently achieve marks in the level 3 and level 4 mark ranges. It is a good idea to write practice answers and then compare them with the level descriptors below in order to check whether your answers are meeting the target standard.

It is not sufficient to produce a list of facts. Answers should develop responses coherently. Only answers that are in context can progress beyond level 1.

Level	Typical descriptor
4	The response demonstrates detailed, accurate and wide-ranging knowledge that is relevant to the question. The answer brings together appropriate concepts, theories and methods in order to draw informed conclusions. Ideas should be expressed clearly and should use appropriate economic terms.
3	The response should demonstrate a grasp of relevant areas of knowledge, selecting and applying knowledge appropriate to the response. Answers should demonstrate the use of economic concepts, theories and methods. Economic terms should be used. Candidates will be expected to communicate arguments, explanations and develop informed conclusions.
2	The response demonstrates some knowledge in a generalised way. The answer may not be linked to the question stem. The answer may demonstrate knowledge of concepts and theories, but conclusions may be based on unsubstantiated assertions. Economic terms may be used. Candidates will communicate ideas in a straightforward way.
1	The response will develop some knowledge and understanding. The answer will use a limited range of concepts, theories and methods in a simple way. Candidates will communicate simple arguments and explanations and offer simple conclusions.

An example of a level response mark scheme is shown below:

Q. *Examine the likely consequences of a strong pound for British manufacturing firms.*

Knowledge 2 marks, application 3 marks, analysis 3 marks, evaluation 2 marks.

This question is intended to provide candidates with the opportunity to demonstrate a broad understanding of the significance of a strong pound for manufacturing firms, both importers and exporters. Candidates would be expected to demonstrate an understanding that importers will benefit from a relatively strong pound while exporters may be hampered by a strong pound. There may also be an awareness that some firms may be unaffected by the relative strength of the pound due to the price elasticity of demand for their goods.

Level 4

Candidates will make at least three sound points regarding the likely consequences of a strong pound for firms. Candidates will be expected to differentiate between the positive consequences of a strong pound and the negative effects of a strong pound for importers.

Level 3

Sound points are made but answers may lack the full development needed to progress to level 4. The significance of the strong pound may not be appreciated fully. Responses should demonstrate a grasp of relevant areas of knowledge, selecting and applying knowledge appropriate to the response.

Level 2

Expect two valid points made regarding the significance of a strong pound. Candidates will demonstrate some relevant knowledge of exchange rates.

Level 1

Responses indicate some relevant knowledge. Answers provide insights without development.

Revision

When discussion turns to revision, the old truism often gets used: 'Students who fail to prepare, prepare to fail.' Time spent revising is not wasted. For some students, revision can provide a comfort blanket; for others, it is something to be endured. The reality is that an A grade achieved after thorough revision is better than a D or E grade achieved after weeks of socialising and extra money earned from the part-time job. As with all things, the decision to forgo revision has an opportunity cost: that could well be exam success.

Plan

Well before the exam, you need to plan out how you will revise – and you need to stick to it. Divide up the topics for revision into manageable blocks. Prepare a timetable. Build in treats, such as nights out and trips to the cinema, but remember that a hangover and revision don't go together.

Environment

Find somewhere quiet to revise, away from distractions. You won't revise effectively in a noisy, crowded room. Try to stay away from windows – they are a distraction, and you will spend your time staring out of them.

Prioritise

Prepare a checklist of what you know and what you don't. If you know it, you don't need to revise it. If you don't know it, then you need to spend time learning it. Try writing lists of important information and post them round your room. Looking at these lists while dressing is a good way of absorbing information.

Examiner's secrets

Synoptic questions are designed so that they contain material from as many modules as is possible. This is done not in a random and disconnected way but by exploiting the links that occur naturally within the subject. These links are fairly easy to generate, and so you cannot identify possible questions in a way that might have been possible in premodular days.

Examiner's secrets

Don't read the questions casually! Find out as much as you can about how much you have to do for every part. There is little to be gained from a question that you start well but, because you didn't read and analyse to the end, loses focus. Make sure that you attempt every part of a question. A common weakness is that candidates start a question because it involves a simple calculation for three marks but then find that they cannot answer the second part of the question, which requires detailed analysis and comment that they cannot do.

Practise

Time spent in exam practice is never wasted. Get as many past papers as possible and answer them. Most important of all is to plan your answers and develop links between theories in order to reach conclusions. Learning answers by rote in the hope that the relevant questions may appear in the exam is risky. It is far better to draw mind maps that highlight interrelationships and tradeoffs. Ask for feedback from your teachers. Learn from your mistakes. It is OK to slip up on practice papers as long as you learn from your mistakes. Completing practice papers is an important part of the learning process.

Developing evaluation skills

Time

Spending hours at a time revising the same topic is counterproductive and the law of diminishing returns comes into play. If you revise for too long, you become tired and you don't absorb information. After about 40 minutes, your concentration span will dip. Have a break. Go for a walk around the house or the garden and get the blood circulating. Give yourself a reward for the work you have done, but preferably not a biscuit every time otherwise you will pile on the calories. Make sure that you have plenty to drink. Being properly hydrated helps improve concentration, as does moving around, which will get the blood flowing to your brain.

Be an active learner

Don't sit with a book or your notes in front of you and read all the time. Summarise your notes and try to draw flow diagrams and spider diagrams, which will help you learn.

Learn from past mistakes

Take the time to look at past marking schemes and examiners' reports. Find out what examiners were looking for in an exam answer and then read the examiners' report to find out what candidates actually did. You should find some useful tips.

Developing evaluative skills is important for candidates aspiring to obtain higher grades. Candidates who don't demonstrate consistent performance at level 3 and level 4 will not gain an A grade.

Building an answer

There are no magic techniques that will guarantee you exam success, but there are strategies that you can employ to increase the likelihood of exam success. Revision is an important first step and can ensure that you have the basic knowledge needed to answer a question. The second step is to apply knowledge to the context. In order to do this, read questions carefully and select theories and concepts that are relevant to the question. Every year, candidates manage to lose marks by misreading questions and not demonstrating the skills and knowledge needed to gain the marks available.

Having selected the appropriate knowledge, you need to apply it to the context. For example, demonstrating an understanding of why oil prices have risen would require you to apply knowledge of supply and demand. Explaining whether increasing demand would lead to a sharp increase requires you to apply knowledge of elasticity of demand and elasticity of supply. The use of appropriate diagrams will support analysis. Don't be afraid to use them: they can be time-saving and demonstrate your ability to apply knowledge in appropriate contexts.

The hardest task for many students is to evaluate. Evaluation requires students to reach conclusions and make judgements. If we take the example of oil prices, then basic supply and demand theory suggests that if the price rises, supply might be expected to increase. An evaluative response might conclude:

> Higher prices might stimulate a marginal increase in supply but responsiveness of supply to an increase in price may be determined by a number of factors. These factors may include the ease with which oil can be extracted, the speed with which oil fields on the margins of production can be exploited, the availability of spare refinery capacity and the willingness of OPEC (a cartel) to increase supply. If there is a long lead time, then it may not be possible to increase oil production significantly in the short run.

Students who don't take the time to read their answers often offer contradictory conclusions. This detracts from the quality of the argument. A candidate asked to examine whether the travel market is contestable would gain few evaluative markets for saying the travel market had large barriers to entry and was not contestable before saying that the travel market was competitive because specialist firms could easily enter the market.

Look at the two answers below – which would you give the most marks for?

Candidate A

The holiday market may be regarded as contestable because it's easy to enter. Start-up costs for a travel agency are as little as £75 000. It is possible to use personal skills such as the ability to sell anything. On the other hand, there are many barriers to entry. I believe that it would be very difficult to join the travel industry because it would be difficult to compete with well-established brands. I believe that it would be worthwhile entering the market if firms were selling in a niche market. In this case, you could say the holiday market was contestable.

Candidate B

Contestable markets will have relatively weak barriers to entry. Existing firms will face a constant threat of increasing competition. The holiday market is oligopolistic, with a four-firm concentration ratio of 0.7. This represents a significant barrier to entry. Existing holiday firms may well pose a significant threat to new entrants. Existing firms such as TUI and My Travel are able to exploit a number of different economies of scale. These include managerial, financial, purchasing and advertising economies of scale. As vertical integrated companies, they are able to restrict availability of seats on charter airlines and restrict the distribution of brochures by refusing to stock them in their travel agents. They are also able to impose full-line forcing on independent travel agents wanting to sell their holidays. The start-up costs are variable, ranging from £75 000 to set up a travel agent and £15 million to set up a medium-sized tour operator. On balance, brand loyalty, costs of entry and efficiency gains of the leading firms will reduce contestability in the holiday market.

We hope that you would choose candidate B.

Examiner's secrets

Listen to what is in the news, even on the day of the exam. A topical example to support a point will be viewed positively.

Examiner's secrets

Check your answer. A good acid test is to consider whether it could have been written by a non-economist.

Examiner's secrets

Look at your answer and see how many economic terms you have included.

Examiner's secrets

Make sure that you answer the question set. Some questions may contain two parts – you must answer both parts.

Exam guidance 1

Here are some hints on achieving top marks when attempting different types of exam question.

Multiple choice

These are of two types:

→ **Simple answer:** you choose the best of four responses and indicate your choice on an optical-reader sheet. These tests are marked by computer.

→ **Justified answer:** as well as choosing the best response, you write some comments as to why you have chosen this option and rejected the others. These tests have to be marked by humans, as they involve some judgement.

Each multiple-choice item has a **stem**, which poses a problem or asks a question, followed by four **options** (A, B, C, D). One of these options is the **best answer**, or **key**. The other three answers are incorrect and are called the **distractors**. You get one mark for each key that you choose. You do *not* lose marks for wrong answers. It follows that you should *always* attempt *all* of these questions. Even if you have to guess, you have a one in four chance of guessing correctly.

Sometimes, you can use your economic knowledge to eliminate some wrong answers, giving yourself a one in three or one in two chance. Ideally, however, you should not need to guess at all. Before you enter your choice on the answer sheet, consider each option carefully, to convince yourself that you know why your chosen key is correct and each of your identified distractors is incorrect. In the justified-answer type of multiple choice test, you will have to explain your reasoning briefly and clearly.

Data-response questions and case studies

Here, questions are usually designed to have an incline of difficulty. The first part of the question will be relatively easy, earning a few marks. The last part of the question will have more marks available, and the question will be more challenging, with higher-order skills required to earn these marks.

→ If you have a choice of question, choose carefully, on the basis of the **whole question**. Don't be put off a question because a small part of it is difficult for you; don't be attracted to it if a small part appears easy. Remember that the final part carries the most marks.

→ Label sub-questions clearly in the margin: (a), (b), etc.

→ Use black ink preferably or, second best, blue. Do not use red, green or purple ink, and *never* use correction fluid (it sticks pages together and the examiner might miss part of your answer).

→ Draw diagrams with a pencil and ruler; write labels in ink.

→ Note mark allocations. Use them to guide your time allocations and the detail of your answers.

→ Avoid the weakest approach, which is to simply copy out chunks of data without comment.

Watch out!

Never hand in a multiple choice answer sheet with some questions unanswered. Remember that there is no penalty for a wrong answer and marks will not be deducted. It is always worth guessing as a very last resort.

- → Be aware of an incline of difficulty: as you move through the questions, you should be using higher-order skills.
- → Also be aware of levels of response: always try to evaluate in the longer answers.
- → Use the data wherever possible, and refer to the data where appropriate.
- → Use your knowledge of economic principles.
- → Use your pre-existing economic awareness. Improve this from newspapers, TV and radio.
- → Have some pre-existing knowledge of ballpark figures, e.g. be aware that the national product of the UK (in round numbers) is £1 trillion, that the average growth rate of the UK economy is just over 2%, that 4% would be regarded as an inflation rate that is too high. Use these to set the given data in context.
- → Analyse/make predictions from different standpoints, e.g. producers/consumers; employers/employees; exporters/importers; manufacturers/service providers; savers/investors/borrowers/taxpayers, etc.

Essays

When writing essays, do:

- → Write legibly in preferably black, or if not then blue, ink.
- → Use pencil for drawing diagrams and ink for labelling and writing.
- → React to command words.
- → Pay attention to time constraints.
- → If an essay question is subdivided, allocate time in proportion to the marks for each part.
- → Plan your essay: write an outline (but remember to cross this out if you do not want the examiner to read your plan).
- → Use diagrams where appropriate. Remember that for many economic principles, a picture speaks 1000 words.
- → Always accompany a diagram with a written commentary, explaining what it is that the diagram shows.

Do not:

- → Use red, green or purple ink (these all have special significance at the exam board).
- → Overabbreviate. Don't write 'govt' for government. Standard economic abbreviations (AD/AS/EU, etc.) are acceptable, but it is good practice to spell them out in full when introduced for the first time, e.g. the first time you mention the EU in an essay, write 'European Union (EU)' and use the abbreviation 'EU' from then on.
- → Abbreviate your answer into bullet-point form. Bullet points are used on this page, but this is not an exam. If you have a list of advantages and disadvantages, for example, it is far better to write them as short paragraphs, introduced by 'First, . . . Second, . . . etc.'.

Examiner's secrets

Essay questions are intended to assess your ability to:

- → Produce a creative response.
- → Use the language of economics.
- → Write systematically and logically.
- → Engage in extended writing – you should note that examiners are under instructions to award specific marks for the quality of written communication.
- → Demonstrate higher-order skills.
- → Produce logical arguments.
- → Come to reasoned conclusions.

Link

Refer back to the discussion of command words on page 164.

Exam guidance 2

Here are some further hints on achieving top marks when attempting different types of exam question.

Coursework

The key points with coursework are:

→ Choose a topic that is manageable. This is absolutely crucial. Consider micro-topics as well as macro-topics, and make sure that your topic area is focused, for example:
   → 'What determines the prices of fruit in local supermarkets?' is better than 'Globalisation of food production'.
   → 'How would membership of the euro affect our local employers?' is better than 'Fixed and floating exchange rates'.
→ A topic in the form of a specific research question is highly recommended. At some stage, you will find that you have collected a lot of information. The key test as to whether a piece of information is relevant can then be applied: 'Does this information help me answer my research question?'
→ Start early.
→ Plan carefully.
→ Do not rely too much on one source.
→ Make sure that your coursework contains plenty of evidence that you can see the relevance of economic theory when applied to your topic.
→ Use a variety of sources. Use traditional library sources. Be careful with the Internet: it is useful but not always reliable. Always supply a bibliography, but never one that contains only websites.
→ Always seek advice from your teachers when you feel it necessary.
→ Always follow your teachers' advice. Remember that for coursework, your teacher is also one of your examiners.

Diagram work

Regardless of whether it is required specifically within a question (and it often will be), the use of a simple diagram is a helpful tool in economics.

The following practice exercises each involve the use of a simple supply and demand diagram. You can practise your exam technique by:

→ Carefully drawing and labelling a suitable diagram.
→ Writing a paragraph to explain clearly what is happening in your diagram.

The housing market

Suppose the government wants affordable housing in the south-east region. Examine possible methods and consequences.

The environment/transport

Compare the effects of (a) road-building, (b) taxing petrol and (c) road pricing.

Economics of sport and leisure

After a big event such as the FA Cup Final, newspapers nearly always report spiv tickets selling on the streets for a price many times their face value. Use supply and demand analysis to explain why this happens.

Product markets/the EU

Explain why governments often intervene to stabilise agricultural prices, and evaluate the results of the Common Agricultural Policy of the EU.

Labour markets

Discuss the implications of a national minimum wage.

In each of these five cases, the basis of your diagram can be those discussed in the topics Minimum price controls and Maximum price controls on pages 18 and 20.

Using our topic grids

When revising for your exam, our topic grids are designed to help you plan your work. You should be aware, however, that syllabuses and specifications are, unfortunately, not always clear as to exactly what you need to cover. Usually the required topics are mentioned by name, but sometimes they are there by implication.

In our grids, we have identified with an open dot (O) topics that appear in units in the AS specifications of the different boards. Topics that appear in units of the A2 specifications are indicated with a closed dot (●). We have used both dots (O●) for those topics that are mentioned specifically in both AS and A2 units.

However, when you are revising for A2, you should be aware of the importance of **synopticity.**

At least one of the A2 papers that you sit will be designated by the exam board as its synoptic paper – you should find out which. Even those papers that are not officially synoptic often cover a very wide area of the syllabus, e.g. AQA's paper 4, whether taken as a case study or coursework.

Even if a particular paper is not officially synoptic, the nature of economics as a subject is essentially synoptic, in the sense that very often you will find that you must understand one topic before you can understand the next. An important point follows from this: you should ensure that you are confident with the theory contained in your AS syllabus before you revise your A2 work.

Final note ●●●

In order to do well in your exams, the one true key secret is that you must do some work.

Prepare yourself and practise, practise, practise!

The fact that you have bought this book and are using it proves that you have understood this crucial point.

The authors wish you good luck in your exams and future career.

The jargon

Synopticity can be of two kinds:

→ **Horizontal synopticity.** Questions in one assessment unit can draw on knowledge from another unit at the same level, e.g. there could be some microeconomics involved in a question on macroeconomics.

→ **Vertical synopticity.** Questions in one assessment unit can draw on knowledge gained for a previous unit, e.g. an A2 question might require some knowledge learned previously for AS.

Watch out!

Find out from your exam board's specifications which A2 paper(s) is or are designated as synoptic.

Glossary

Aggregate demand (AD)

The total demand for goods and services produced in the economy over a period of time $(AD = C + I + G + (X - M))$.

Aggregate supply (AS)

Measures the volume of goods and services produced within the economy at a given overall price level.

Average cost

Means just what it says, the average cost. The cost of making all of a firm's output divided by the number of units made. $\dfrac{FC + VC}{output} =$

Balance of payments

A record of a country's trade dealings with the rest of the world. Trade which results in money entering the country will create *credits*. Trade which leads to money leaving the country will create *debit*.

The balance of payments is split into two sections:

(i) the *current account*, dealing with international trade in goods and services, and

(ii) *transactions in assets and liabilities* dealing with overseas flows of money from international investments and loans

Barriers to entry

Circumstances particular to a given industry that create disadvantages for new competitors attempting to enter the market. The most prominent barriers to entry are market share, competition, strategic alliances and intellectual property protection.

Boom

The boom phase of the business cycle is characterised by increasing investment, firms expanding output and rising consumer demand. Prices may rise and inflationary pressures may build up in the economy.

Budgetary policy

Budgetary policy relates to government fiscal policy (spending and taxation) and decisions taken over the level of spending and borrowing and, the amount of taxation.

Collusion

Collusion takes place within an industry when rival companies cooperate for their mutual benefit. Collusion may take the form of sharing information, setting prices or allocating market share.

Comparative advantage

The theory of comparative advantage explains why it can be beneficial for two countries to trade, even though one of them may be able to produce every kind of item more cheaply than the other. Countries will gain from specialising in those goods that they are relatively better at producing and trading these goods.

Contestable markets

A contestable market requires barriers to entry to be low. Barriers to entry may include special licences, patents, copyrights, high fixed costs and marketing barriers.

Cost-benefit analysis

A widely used technique for deciding whether to make a change. Cost/benefit analysis seeks to place a financial value on the intangible costs and benefits of a project in order to measure the net gain/loss.

Demand

The relationship between price and quantity demanded for a particular good and service. The demand relationship indicates the quantity the buyers want to buy at a given price.

Demerit goods

Goods which are thought to be bad for you, e.g. cigarettes and addictive drugs. Government may tax or ban such goods. Their costs spill over from the prime user.

Economic cycle

National output does not grow at a uniform rate. The economy goes through a cycle (boom, recession, slump and recovery). This affects incomes, production levels and production levels.

Economic efficiency

Means that all goods or services are allocated to someone. When a market equilibrium is efficient, then it is not possible to reallocate the good or service without making someone worse off.

Economic growth

The increase in the value of goods and services produced by an economy. It is usually measured by the percentage change in real gross domestic product (GDP).

Economics

A social science studying the production, distribution, trade and consumption of goods and services. How people make the best use of scarce resources.

Economies of scale

Refers to the reduction in unit costs as output increases. The marginal cost of producing a good or service decreases as production increases.

Elasticity

Measures the responsiveness of demand and supply to a change in price.

Emerging and transitional economies

Considered to be in a transitional phase between developing and developed status. Examples of such economies include China, India and countries in Eastern Europe.

Envelope curve

An *envelope* is the enclosing boundary of a set of curves that is touched by every curve in the system. The Long Run Average Cost Curve (LRAC) is constructed by drawing a curve around the short run average total cost (SRAC) curves.

Equilibrium price

The price on a free market where planned quantity supplied equals planned quantity demanded. There is no reason for price to change.

Equilibrium level of income

The level of national income at which planned aggregate supply equals planned aggregate demand; or where planned injections equals planned withdrawals. There is no reason for national income to change.

Eurozone

The countries using the euro as their everyday currency. At the time of writing, there are 12 member countries, each sending a representative to the European Central Bank in Frankfurt.

Exchange rate

The 'price' at which one currency, e.g. the pound, exchanges for another, e.g. the dollar.

Externality

A cost (negative externality) or a benefit (positive externality) which affects the economic welfare of an economic agent other than the prime producer or consumer of a good or service.

Factors of production

Economic resources, classified as land, labour, capital and enterprise, which are used in producing any good or service.

Free market

A market where the forces of supply and demand determine prices, without any intervention from outside agencies, such as governments or monopolists.

Free trade

Trade that takes place internationally without any barriers such as tariffs or quotas.

Games theory

A model which is useful in analysing the behaviour of oligopolists, who must predict the reaction not only of their customers, but also their rival firms, when they change their prices.

(GDP) Gross Domestic Product

The total value of goods and services produced within the geographical boundaries of a country over a year.

Globalisation

The ability to make any product anywhere in the world, using resources from anywhere, sell the output anywhere, and place the profits anywhere.

Human Development Index

An index which is used by the United Nations Development programme and puts countries into league tables based upon a combination of an economic indicator (Gross Domestic Product per head), an indicator of educational attainment and life chances (adult literacy), and an indicator of health and welfare (life expectancy at birth).

Inflation

A process of persistently rising prices eroding the purchasing power of money.

Less economically developed country

A country with relatively low GDP per head.

Lorenz Curve

A graph used to measure such things as income equality. If 10% of the population earn 10% of a country's income, 20% earn 20%, and so on, then the Lorenz curve is a diagonal at 45°.

Macroeconomics

The branch of economics concerned with total or aggregate economic activity. It examines the workings of the economy as a whole, rather than sectors of the economy.

Marginal cost

The amount added to total cost by producing one extra unit of output.

Marginal revenue

The amount added to total revenue by selling one extra unit of output.

Market failure

When markets fail to achieve the best use of resources due to the existence of, for example, monopoly or externalities.

Market

A network of dealings, bringing people with a demand into contact with people able to supply.

Merit good

A good whose consumption benefits not only the prime consumer, but also creates a spill-over to benefit others in society.

Microeconomics

The part of economics concerned with the study of sectors and markets. It tends to focus on issues such as individual choice and business decisions.

Monetary policy

Traditionally, this affects the supply of money in the economy by influencing the amount of lending by banks and other institutions; these days it is almost entirely focused on interest rates.

Monopoly

In economics, where there is one dominant firm in the marketplace; in law, definitions vary from country to country.

Multiplier

The multiplier principle depends on the fact that money injected into the circular flow of income is spent more than once. For example, an investment will increase national income by more than the amount invested.

Oligopoly

Where there are only a few suppliers and the actions of one firm affect other producers.

Output gap

Where planned output differs from productive capacity. An important indicator used in setting interest rates.

Perfect competition

A situation where there are a large number of firms of equal size, homogeneous products and consumers have perfect knowledge.

Private good

A good whose costs and benefits of consumption or production are confined to the individual consumer or producer.

Product differentiation

Where an attempt is made for a product to be seen as different to another firm's offering through branding and persuasive advertising.

Production possibility frontier

A graph that shows how different factors of production can be combined to produce a certain level of output. It illustrates basic economic principles such as choice, opportunity cost, efficiency and equity.

Profit

The reward to the factor 'enterprise', measured by the difference between total revenue and total cost (TR–TC). Economic theory often assumes that firms aim to maximise profits.

Public good

Usually, strictly speaking, a 'service' rather than a good. A public good, such as street lighting, clean air, or a crime free town is non-diminishable (one person's use does not deprive another) and non excludable (provision at all means provision for all).

Recession

Where there is a downturn in economic activity. Indicators include constant falls in output, rising unemployment and falling income. Officially, more than two successive quarters (three month periods) of negative growth.

Scarcity

Part of the basic economic problem – resources are finite, or limited. Scarcity means that choices have opportunity costs.

Short run

A period of time where there is at least one fixed factor in terms of size or quantity.

Stages of production

The processes involved in converting a raw material into a final product and conveying the product to the consumer. Primary production: agriculture, extraction. Secondary production: manufacturing and construction. Tertiary production: the service sector.

Supply

The willingness and ability to produce a product at a price. According to the 'law of supply' the higher the price, the greater the quantity supplied.

Supply side

Policies aimed at improving the productivity and output of the economy.

Unemployment

Occurs when there are people who want to work at the going wage rate but are unable to find a job.

World Trade Organization

An international institution concerned with issues related to promoting international trade without barriers.

Yield management

Otherwise known as 'price discrimination', a technique used to maximise total revenue, by increasing prices where demand is price-inelastic, and reducing price where demand is price-elastic. Low cost airlines, for example, use this as part of their business model.

Index